KEYWORDS IN ASIAN STUDIES

KEYWORDS IN WRITING STUDIES

Edited by
PAUL HEILKER
PETER VANDENBERG

UTAH STATE UNIVERSITY PRESS
Logan

© 2015 by University Press of Colorado

Published by Utah State University Press
An imprint of University Press of Colorado
5589 Arapahoe Avenue, Suite 206C
Boulder, Colorado 80303

The University Press of Colorado is a proud member of
The Association of American University Presses.

The University Press of Colorado is a cooperative publishing enterprise supported, in part, by Adams State University, Colorado State University, Fort Lewis College, Metropolitan State University of Denver, Regis University, University of Colorado, University of Northern Colorado, Utah State University, and Western State Colorado University.

∞ This paper meets the requirements of the ANSI/NISO Z39.48–1992 (Permanence of Paper).

ISBN: 978-0-87421-973-9 (paper)
ISBN: 978-0-87421-974-6 (ebook)

Library of Congress Cataloging-in-Publication Data

Keywords in writing studies / Edited by Paul Heilker and Peter Vandenberg.
   pages cm.
  ISBN 978-0-87421-973-9 (pbk.) — ISBN 978-0-87421-974-6 (ebook)
1. English language—Rhetoric—Study and teaching—Terminology. 2. English language—Composition and exercises—Terminology. 3. English language—Composition and exercises—Terminology. 4. Report writing—Study and teaching—Terminology. I. Heilker, Paul, 1962- editor of compilation. II. Vandenberg, Peter, editor of compilation.
  PE1404.K498 2014
  808'.042071—dc23
                          2014003785

24   23   22   21   20   19   18   17   16   15   10   9   8   7   6   5   4   3   2   1

For Aileen Murphy
For Karen Christine Langan

CONTENTS

Introduction

Paul Heilker and Peter Vandenberg

When *Keywords in Composition Studies* (*KCS*) was published in 1996, we did not intend to revisit the project. Following in the footsteps of I. A. Richards (1942, 1955) and Raymond Williams (1983), and with the assistance of our many astute contributors, we felt we had successfully made our case that one of the great strengths of our field can be found in the contested, unsettled nature of its key terms; that the more central and necessary the term, the more ambiguous and divergent its meanings; that a close look at the meanings of any critical term speaks volumes about our shifting cultural and disciplinary values; and that the complex conflicts embodied and enacted within our vocabulary itself, the many layers of voices reverberating within a given term, are less a cause for concern than they are something to be embraced and celebrated—a tremendously useful resource for the making and remaking of ourselves, our commitments, and the objects of our attention. As we noted in our introduction, we wanted *KCS* to be suggestive rather than exhaustive, to serve as a model of a different and productive way of reading our professional discourse—rather than as a glossary, an introduction to major figures and works in the field, or a reference work monumentalizing some particular vision of the discipline—and we concluded by exhorting others to join in that effort: "A study of evolving vocabularies must be a fluid project, one carried out not within this book but with it as we continue composing composition studies" (7). We were delighted with the book's reception and the appearance of a new assignment genre in composition theory seminars across the country, "the *Keywords* essay."

But things change. Indeed, a great deal is different since *KCS* was published nineteen years ago. As Kathleen Yancey noted even in 2004, "Literacy today is in the midst of tectonic change. . . . Never before has the proliferation of writings outside the academy so counterpointed the compositions inside. Never before have the technologies of writing contributed so quickly to the creation of new genres" (Yancey 2004, 298).

Whether one sees these changes as evolutionary or revolutionary, paradigm shift, marked discontinuity, or chaos depends very much on where one stands, of course, but what we study and who "we" are has changed dramatically over the last two decades.

First, it is impossible to overstate the speed or the effects of the evolution in communication technology since 1996. When *KCS* was published, the Internet was in its infancy. Gunther Kress suggested a decade ago that "we are moving out of an era of relative stability of a very long duration" (Kress 2003, 83)—the era of the printing press—and, thus, in "the era of the screen and multimodality some fundamental changes are inevitable as far as forms, functions and uses of writing are concerned" (61). "On the screen," he notes, "the *textual entity* is treated as a *visual entity* in ways in which the page never was" (65), and "in these new environments, writing is likely to move in the direction of its image origins," fundamentally altering a user's disposition toward meaning-making (73). And this new disposition is omnipresent, as Yancey notes: "Our daily communicative, social, and intellectual practices are screen-permeated" (Yancey 2004, 305). In like manner, as Bill Cope and Mary Kalantzis point out, new communications media have led to the emergence of multiliteracies: "the increasing multiplicity and integration of significant modes of meaning-making, where the textual is also related to the visual, the audio, the spatial, the behavioural, and so on" (Cope and Kalantzis 2000, 5).

As a result of a wide variety of theoretical, educational, professional, and institutional developments, not least of which is the influence of digital media, the general *telos* of university-level writing instruction in the United States has fundamentally shifted since 1996 from academic contexts and discourses to public spheres and civic discourses. Even a cursory look at the terms included in *KCS* demonstrates a focus on the academic text, the writing student, and the classroom: *academic discourse, argument, basic writing/writers, coherence, collaboration, critical thinking, discourse community, error, essay, evaluation, form/structure, grammar, invention, logic, marginalized/marginalization, peer evaluation, portfolio, process, revision, students, teacher, voice,* and *writing center.* Shortly after the publication of *KCS,* though, the "social turn" of composition in the 1980s became its "public turn" in the late 1990s and 2000s as we realized what may seem obvious now, "that writing in universities is only a small slice of writing that goes on elsewhere in the world" (Bazerman 2002, 33). As early as 1997, researchers like David Russell (1997) were seeking to understand how students and teachers "use the discursive tools of classroom genres to interact (and not interact) with social practices beyond individuals classrooms—those of schools, families, peers, disciplines, professions, political movements, unions, corporations, and so on" (505). Moreover, as Yancey notes, "writers in the 21st century self-organize into what seem to be overlapping technologically driven writing circles, what we might call a series of newly imagined communities, communities that cross borders of all kinds—nation, state, class, gender, ethnicity" (Yancey 2004, 301).

One such newly imagined community may well be writing studies—an increasingly global construct of academics comprising a methodological diversity and linguistic orientations scarcely considered in the mid-1990s. As the English language itself has evolved into "a *lingua mundi*, a world language" (Cope and Kalantzis 2000), the disciplinary formation that grew up around the uniquely US educational practice of first-year college writing—what we called composition studies in 1996— is now self-consciously struggling with its provincial origins (Horner and Trimbur 2002). "Dealing with linguistic differences and cultural differences has now become central to the pragmatics of our working, civic, and private lives," Cope and Kalantzis (2000) write, a statement increasingly true for everyone, but especially for those who teach and study writing. The changing demographics of US classrooms have helped expand attention to instructional practices, writing teacher preparation, and research methodology in L2 contexts, and the historical boundary between L1 and L2 is being permeated from both directions (see, for example, Matsuda et al. 2011).

Methodological plurality in the study of writing practices is becoming influential in the United States as domestic and ethnocentric studies make room for polycentric or intercultural research (e.g., You 2010) and deeply interdisciplinary work produced outside US borders (e.g., Torrance et al. 2012). The remarkable explanatory power of discourse analysis and contemporary genre theory have introduced US writing specialists to the work of writing researchers from multiple continents (e.g., Coe, Lingard, and Teslenko 2002; Johns 2002). Professional organizations with historically domestic orientations, including the College Conference on Composition and Communication and the Council of Writing Program Administrators, have begun to remodel with an international perspective; meanwhile, work in rhetoric and composition, a field once thought to have relatively little influence outside its own sphere, is increasingly cited in the work of non-US writing researchers and integrated in internationalization projects—enabled via the affordances of digital technology outlined above—such as GXB: Genre Across Borders and *Asociación Latinoamericana de Retórica.*

These developments situate postsecondary US writing instruction amid a galaxy of considerations for writing specialists, wherever they are. In "The Case For Writing Studies as a Major Discipline," Charles Bazerman argues that the study of writing is the study of "how people come to take on the thought, practice, perspective, and orientation of various ways of life; how they integrate or keep distinct those perspectives in which they are practiced; and how we organize our modern way of life economically, intellectually, socially, interpersonally, managerially, and politically through the medium of texts" (Bazerman 2002, 35). Such expansive work involves researchers and scholars from a great many domains and disciplines beyond composition studies, including, as Bazerman notes, anthropology, psychology, sociology, cultural history, linguistics, education, classics, political science, cultural studies, and science studies (32–35). He writes, "In short, the study of writing is a major subset of the history of human consciousness, institutions, practice, and development over the last five millennia" (Bazerman 2002, 36).

Here we see at least three powerful trajectories of *writing studies* at work. First, writing studies is invoked as a massively interdisciplinary examination of nothing less than the human condition since the dawn of civilization, something much bigger than and far beyond the scope of composition studies as any of us could imagine it in 1996. Second, by means of a spatial metaphor, writing studies is portrayed as an extensive and extending field, with composition at its conceptual center. And third, writing studies—and composition studies by association—is represented as a serious intellectual discipline worthy of professional respect, power, and resources. Other constructions of *writing studies* are in circulation as well, of course. For instance, Downs and Wardle (2007) collapse *writing studies* and *composition studies*, using the former as an exact synonym for the latter without commenting on that change in any way. Writing in *College Composition and Communication,* they repeatedly refer to writing studies as "our field" or "our discipline" (553, 554, 574, 575, 577, 578), and they deploy the term in ways that make it serve as an unproblematic substitution for *composition studies.* They write, for instance, that "[t]he field of writing studies has made part of its business for the last forty years testing [common and misleading] assumptions and articulating more complex, realistic, and useful ways for thinking about writing" (555), a time frame and agenda most readers would likely ascribe to composition studies. In like manner, they suggest that "writing studies as a field has largely ignored the implications of this research and theory and continued to assure its publics (faculty, administrators, parents, industry) that FYC [first-year composition] can do what nonspecialists have always assumed it can" (554–55).

Using *writing studies* as a marker for the research, theory, and stake-holders of FYC suggests a much narrower purview for the term than the one Bazerman invokes. Oddly enough, though, Downs and Wardle (2007) seem to have similar motives to Bazerman for doing so—that is, they seek to improve the disciplinary status and professional respect for the work of writing teachers. They contend that in redirecting efforts from teaching students how to write to "teaching *about writing*," it can be demonstrated that "writing studies is a discipline with content knowledge to which students should be introduced" (553, emphasis in original). Acting upon such a premise, they suggest, should raise "writing studies' standing in the academy and what it teaches in the courses it accepts as its *raison d'etre*, first-year composition" (553–54). Displacing *composition studies* and deploying *writing studies* in this way has a variety of rhetorical effects, the term now serving metonymically as a reassertion of the importance of theory in teaching (554); a claim to "authority over [our] own courses" (557); an argument in support of undergraduate research initiatives (558); a locus of increased professional, pedagogical, and personal ethics (560); a call for increased specialized training for writing instructors (575); a defense of disciplinary colonization of undergraduates (577); a justification for academic program-building; and a recapitulation/new expression of our yearning for and intent to achieve "full disciplinarity" (578).

One way to gauge the extent to which the study of writing can be considered a serious intellectual endeavor with full disciplinarity might be to look at how *writing studies* is being used to name or rename university departments, programs, and research centers, to consider what kinds of work and workers the term is used to subsume. Such an examination seems to suggest that in practice, generally, we are somewhere between Downs and Wardle's narrow construction of *writing studies* and Bazerman's more expansive one, with the term being used to imagine, (re)configure, and perhaps integrate various aspects of faculty activity—research, teaching, and service—in diverse ways across the very local contexts of specific institutions.

The Department of Writing Studies at the University of Minnesota, for instance, describes writing studies as follows: "Drawing together scholarly methods from the humanities and social sciences, the field of writing studies seeks to understand and enrich the ways people use written texts to shape the world." And the faculty there describes themselves thusly: "[We seek] to understand the social, disciplinary, and rhetorical functions of written, visual, digital, scientific and technical communication practices. . . . We investigate the intersections of communication with culture, politics, science, technology, and ethics." Pedagogically, at UMN, *writing studies* connotes a constellation of faculty and courses providing instruction in FYC, technical communication, professional writing, rhetorical theory, digital communication, literacy studies, and second language studies. Finally, *writing studies* at UMN synthesizes student and faculty support services often atomized in other institutions into writing centers, WAC/WID programs, and faculty development initiatives through the department's Center for Writing.

A close look at any of our institutions or discourses would likely reveal additional, novel, and perhaps idiosyncratic ways that *writing studies* operates as a keyword to influence powerfully what we can imagine, perceive, and conceive about who we are, what we do, and why. But it is nonetheless evident that we are now in a very different place than we were when *KCS* was published in 1996, a landscape so fundamentally altered that an examination of other influential keywords now in high circulation seems once again critically important to undertake. The material in this volume is thus wholly new: the terms addressed in the previous book are a product of their time and point quite specifically at "composition studies" as the domain of inquiry rather than at the broader, more complex intersections we might mark as "writing studies." However, while the landscape and hence the keywords we include here have changed, our approach to the project remains the same. As with *KCS* in 1996, the terms we have chosen to include here are those located at broad intersections of meaning, each one of critical importance precisely because its shifting meanings are "bound up with the problems it [is] used to discuss" (Williams 1983, 15). Our goal in this volume is not to provide fixed, unitary meanings of a term or even to privilege some meanings above others, but rather to illuminate how many divergent and contesting significations reside within our field's central terms. Our argument, which is embodied and enacted in each entry, is that it is less productive, less appropriate, and less promising to define or confine a term's meanings than it is to listen openly, generously, and carefully to its many, layered voices, echoes, and overtones, especially the dissonant ones.

We remain painfully aware that our effort to render the fluid, actively conflicting meanings of the terms runs the risk, thereby, of containing and domesticating them, and that every meaning we include may become valorized—and every meaning we fail to include become concomitantly devalued—in ways that seem to contradict the very intent of the project. The selective nature of our roster of keywords, we believe, is more inevitability than failing; what else could have emerged from our particular histories and locations but a *partial* view? However, as before, we did assert two essential criteria for inclusion: each term is a part of our general disciplinary parlance (often masking its power by its ubiquity and seeming innocuousness), and each is highly contested, the focal point of significant debates about matters of power, identity, and values. Indeed, these keywords are frequently used to define each other, which both masks and foregrounds their shifting dispositions: to help emphasize this interlexical activity, we use boldface to mark the first appearance of other keywords in each entry. Since we will surely omit terms that you think should have been included, we conclude here with the same request and challenge we offered what now seems like a professional lifetime ago: to treat this volume not as a glossary, introduction to the field, or reference work, but as an invitation to join us in our evolving study of our evolving vocabulary as we continue writing writing studies.

Finally, while we recognize that every text results from the work of many, many minds and hands, we want to offer special thanks to the following people: to our mentor, Gary Tate, for guiding us to the *Keywords* path; to our editor, Michael Spooner, for his encouragement and support throughout this project; to our many contributors, for their willingness to write (and revise and revise) these little monsters known as "keyword entries"; and to our editorial assistant, Christine Scherer, for helping us bring it all together. This book would not exist without them.

References

Bazerman, Charles. 2002. "The Case For Writing Studies as a Major Discipline." In *The Intellectual Work of Composition*, ed. Gary Olson. Carbondale: Southern Illinois University Press.

Coe, Richard M., Lorelei Lingard, and Tatiana Teslenko, eds. 2002. *The Rhetoric and Ideology of Genre*. New York: Hampton Press.

Cope, Bill, and Mary Kalantzis. 2000. "Introduction: Multiliteracies: The Beginning of an Idea." In *Multiliteracies: Literacy Learning and the Design of Social Futures*, ed. Bill Cope and Mary Kalantzis, 1–8. London: Routledge.

Downs, Douglas, and Elizabeth Wardle. 2007. "Teaching about Writing, Righting Misconceptions: (Re)Envisioning 'First-Year Composition' as 'Introduction to Writing Studies.'" *College Composition and Communication* 58 (4): 552–584.

Heilker, Paul, and Peter Vandenberg. 1996. "Introduction." In *Keywords in Composition Studies*, 1–8. Portsmouth, NH: Heinemann.

Horner, Bruce, and John Trimbur. 2002. "English Only and US College Composition." *College Composition and Communication* 53 (4): 594–630. http://dx.doi.org/10.2307/1512118.

Johns, Ann M. 2002. *Genre in the Classroom: Multiple Perspectives.* Mahwah, NJ: Erlbaum.

Kress, Gunther. 2003. *Literacy in the New Media Age.* London: Routledge. http://dx.doi .org/10.4324/9780203164754.

Matsuda, Paul Kei, Michelle Cox, Jay Jordan, and Christina Ortmeier-Hooper, eds. 2011. *Second Language Writing in the Composition Classroom: A Critical Sourcebook.* Boston: Bedford/St. Martin's.

Richards, I. A. 1942. *How To Read a Page: A Course in Effective Reading, with an Introduction to a Hundred Great Words.* New York: W. W. Norton.

Richards, I. A. 1955. *Speculative Instruments.* London: Routledge & Kegan Paul.

Russell, David R. 1997. "Rethinking Genre in School and Society: An Activity Theory Analysis." *Written Communication* 14 (4): 504–54. http://dx.doi.org/10.1177/0741088 397014004004.

Torrence, Mark, Denis Alamargot, Montserrat Castello, Franck Ganier, and Otto Kruse, eds. (2012). *Learning to Write Effectively: Current Trends in European Research.* Bingley, UK: Emerald Group.

Williams, Raymond. 1983. *Keywords: A Vocabulary of Culture and Society.* Revised Edition. New York: Oxford University Press.

Yancey, Kathleen Blake. 2004. "Made Not Only in Words: Composition in a New Key." *College Composition and Communication* 56 (2): 297–328. http://dx.doi.org/10.2307 /4140651.

You, Xiaoye. 2010. *Writing in the Devil's Tongue: A History of English Composition in China.* Carbondale: Southern Illinois University Press.

KEYWORDS IN WRITING STUDIES

AGENCY

Steven Accardi

The term agency is embedded in many discussions in writing studies, and, depending upon how it is used, reveals particular theoretical orientations. As a commonplace, agency signifies the ability or capacity to act, such as in the sentence, "The president has the agency to veto the bill." In *Genre and the Invention of the Writer*, Anis Bawarshi argues that in writing studies, the subject is often conceived as having agency, or being the sole possessor of agency, and thereby having the responsibility, in some cases, to take action (Bawarshi 2003, 53–5).

This conceptualization, for example, is seen in *Agency in the Age of Peer-Production*. Quentin Vieregge et al. (2012) study the transformative effect of digital peer-production tools on communication, collaboration, and the agency of teachers. Their use of agency connotes a force or power that can be owned or managed. They write, "[Teachers] want to play along without being pushed along. They want to assert their own agency without completely delegitimizing the agency of their programs, departments and colleges" (Vieregge et al. 2012, 4). Here individuals as well as collectives own agency.

Agency is similarly seen in discussions about writing program administration. While discussing the role of WPAs in the distribution process of composition textbooks, Libby Miles states, "Regardless, the voice of the consultant is the loudest and strongest in the textbook **production** process, and those of us who can should make more of that position of agency for the benefit of all" (Miles 2000, 37). Agency here inflects a power attributed to WPAs. Kelly Ritter, in her article, "Extra-Institutional Agency and the Public Value of the WPA," builds upon this notion of power: "[W]hat follows is rooted in a story about my own developing agency as an administrator, resulting from my negotiations with our state offices over common system rubrics for basic writers and basic writing placement" (Ritter 2006, 47). The term agency here resembles authority as well as power. This dual definition is rearticulated toward the end of her piece: "Rather than resist our power to influence these

DOI: 10.7330/9780874219746.c001

discussions and shape public perception, I submit that we do seize it and use it to help system offices help us to define and thus provide institutional agency for basic writers in the FYC curriculum" (Ritter 2006, 57).

In second language writing, notions of power and possession follow suit, as A. Suresh Canagarajah argues: "The value of the debate between LI [linguistic imperialism] and LH [linguistic hybridity] schools is that it expands our awareness of the complexities in the negotiation of power, developing the possibilities for teachers to exert their agency for simple but significant changes" (Canagarajah 1999, 213). Sandra McKay and Sau-Ling Wong employ the term similarly: "As subjects with agency and a need to exercise it, the [second language] learners, while positioned in power relations and subject to the influence of **discourses**, also resist positioning, attempt repositioning, and deploy discourses and counter-discourses" (McKay and Wong 1996, 603).

In each of these cases, agency reflects an ability, power, or authority that can be possessed by a subject or subjects. This usage links with a humanist–modernist theoretical orientation, one that suggests a writer is a rational individual, capable of inventing ideas autonomously and pursuing an intention to engage or provoke an audience. In short, humanism implies that agency is something a writer can possess and use—as when Marilyn Cooper states that "agency is an emergent property of embodied individuals" (Cooper 2011, 421)—or something that can be taken away: "[T]hey realize that they are seen as native informants and that their agency is wrested from them" (Partnoy 2006, 1667). Sometimes scholars reveal this orientation by mentioning that agency is something "**personal**" or deriving from "personal experience," something coming from the self. Gail Hawisher et al. (2006, 633) state that the "theme of personal agency also played itself out in terms of **gender** expectations and **computer** use," while Alan France notes, "Composition studies . . . is skewed toward agency, toward the personal experience of the world, including the experience of any structure that might determine or even constrain that experience" (France 2000, 148). France states further, "And the purpose of rhetorical education has been since antiquity, after all, learning the practices of personal agency in their relevant social context" (149).

A posthumanist or poststructuralist orientation, on the **other** hand, does not locate agency with the subject. According to this lens, agency is found circulating in discourse and dispersed into an ever-shifting field of power relations (Herndl and Licona 2007, 141). In other words, agency cannot be possessed. Christian Lundberg and Joshua Gunn explain that this posthumanist orientation reverses possession, from a subject possessing agency to agency possessing the subject. The reversal

refocuses our attention on the ways that the subject is an effect of structures, forces, and modes of enjoyment that might precede or produce it.
This reversal of agent's relation to agency directs attention to quintessen-
tially rhetorical concerns: to the constitutive function of trope, to modes
of address, to the dialectics of identification and difference, and even to
the power of concealing exercises of techne under the veil of the natural.
(Lundberg and Gunn 2005, 97)

Helen Ewald and David Wallace inflect a posthumanist orientation when
they state, "Although taking such a look might imply that agency is an
attribute of classrooms rather than individuals and, as such, might seem
a counterintuitive move, it is also a move consistent with the postmodern
sense that the agent or subject is situationally constructed rather than
autonomously present" (Ewald and Wallace 1994, 359). Here the term
agency constitutes an attribute of the classroom rather than a possession
of the subject–writer. Cheryl Geisler states that "Agency does not lie in
the hands of any one person at the proposal writing table, but rather lies
in the interaction among them" (Geisler 2005, 112). Agency, then, is not
a possession but rather a construct of discourse.

These oppositional usages of the term can be conflated, as Carl
Herndl and Adela Licona suggest, because "agency is still hampered by
the vestiges of humanist models of action" (Herndl and Licona 2007,
139). A scholar writing from a posthumanist orientation might use a
humanist construction of possession for the term agency. For example,
Ewald and Wallace, who subscribe to and argue for a posthumanist theoretical lens, write, "Thus, within the parameters that [the instructor]
has set, his students have agency in that they initiate topics for discussion, respond directly to each other, and influence what gets counted
as knowledge in the discussion" (Ewald and Wallace 1994, 347). As
Herndl explains elsewhere, in writing studies "theorists typically struggle
with the dilemma of how to understand the postmodern subject's ability to take purposeful political action without merely recuperating the
humanist individual" (Herndl qtd. in Geisler 2004, 10). Dorothy Winsor,
in *Technical Communication Quarterly*, adds, "I confess that I have had
trouble writing about [agency] in this article because I have found it
very difficult to avoid language that reifies agency and treats it as something a person has rather than a situation of which the person takes
advantage" (Winsor 2006, 412).

The term *agency* is not only used to discuss power and authority and
to inflect a humanist or posthumanist orientation. It also is used in
writing studies as an analytical tool to study power and social change.
Jeffrey Grabill and Stacey Pigg, for example, undertake a project that

examines agency in an online discussion forum and find that **identity performances** create movement that enables agency to move conversations (Grabill and Pigg 2012, 114–15). They argue that "[w]hen rhetors do not have access to each others' prior reputations, or clear pictures of their cultures, motivations, purposes, and reasons for communicating, identity building can become an important part of developing agency within a conversation" (116). As Grabill and Pigg use the term, agency is something outside of the individual, neither owned or housed in the subject's mind nor rescued from postmodernity. It is located within the rhetorical performance of identity building and the discourse of an online discussion blog. Such uses of agency, again, signify a posthumanist orientation.

Barbara Biesecker (1989) suggests that a subject cannot be taken as an origin or understood to be a static entity. A subject is continuously engaged in a process of alteration. And language is just as unstable as subjects, continuously changing and shifting in usage and meaning. The term *agency* follows suit.

References

Bawarshi, Anis. 2003. *Genre and the Invention of the Writer: Reconsidering the Place of Invention in Composition*. Logan: Utah State University Press.

Biesecker, Barbara A. 1989. "Rethinking the Rhetorical Situation from Within the Thematic of Differánce." *Philosophy & Rhetoric* 22 (2): 110–30.

Canagarajah, A. Suresh. 1999. "On EFL Teachers, Awareness, and Agency." *English Language Teaching Journal* 53 (3): 207–14. http://dx.doi.org/10.1093/elt/53.3.207.

Cooper, Marilyn M. 2011. "Rhetorical Agency as Emergent and Enacted." *College Composition and Communication* 62 (3): 420–49.

Ewald, Helen Rothschild, and David L. Wallace. 1994. "Exploring Agency in Classroom Discourse, or, Should David Have Told His Story?" *College Composition and Communication* 45 (3): 342–68. http://dx.doi.org/10.2307/358815.

France, Alan W. 2000. "Dialectics of Self: Structure and Agency as the Subject of English." *College English* 63 (2): 145–65. http://dx.doi.org/10.2307/379038.

Geisler, Cheryl. 2004. "How Ought We to Understand the Concept of Rhetorical Agency? Report from the ARS." *Rhetoric Society Quarterly* 34 (3): 9–17. http://dx.doi.org/10.1080/02773940409391286.

Geisler, Cheryl. 2005. "Teaching the Post-Modern Rhetor: Continuing the Conversation on Rhetorical Agency." *Rhetoric Society Quarterly* 35 (4): 107–13. http://dx.doi.org/10.1080/02773940509391324.

Grabill, Jeffrey T., and Stacey Pigg. 2012. "Messy Rhetoric: Identity Performance as Rhetorical Agency in Online Public Forums." *Rhetoric Society Quarterly* 42 (2): 99–119. http://dx.doi.org/10.1080/02773945.2012.660369.

Hawisher, Gail E., Cynthia L. Selfe, Yi-Huey Guo, and Lu Liu. 2006. "Globalization and Agency: Designing and Redesigning the Literacies of Cyberspace." *College English* 68 (6): 619–36. http://dx.doi.org/10.2307/25472179.

Herndl, Carl G., and Adela C. Licona. 2007. "Shifting Agency: Agency, Kairos, and the Possibilities of Social Action." In *Communicative Practices in Workplaces and the*

Professions: Cultural Perspectives on the Regulation of Discourse and Organizations, ed. Mark Zachry and Charlotte Thralls, 133–54. Amityville: Baywood. http://dx.doi.org/10 .2190/CPIC7.

Lundberg, Christian, and Joshua Gunn. 2005. "'Ouija Board, Are There Any Communications?': Agency, Ontotheology, and the Death of the Humanist Subject or Continuing the ARS Conversation." *Rhetoric Society Quarterly* 35 (4): 83–105. http:// dx.doi.org/10.1080/02773940509391323.

McKay, Sandra Lee, and Sau-Ling Cynthia Wong. 1996. "Multiple Discourses, Multiple Identities: Investment and Agency in Second-Language Learning Among Chinese Adolescent Immigrant Students." *Harvard Educational Review* 66 (3): 577–608.

Miles, Libby. 2000. "Constructing Composition: Reproduction and WPA Agency in Textbook Publishing." *WPA: Writing Program Administration* 24 (1–2): 27–52.

Partnoy, Alicia. 2006. "Cuando Vienen Matando: On Prepositional Shifts and the Struggle of Testimonial Subjects for Agency." *Publications of the Modern Language Association* 121 (5): 1665–69. http://dx.doi.org/10.1632/pmla.2006.121.5.1665.

Ritter, Kelly. 2006. "Extra-Institutional Agency and the Public Value of the WPA." *WPA: Writing Program Administration* 29 (3): 45–64.

Vieregge, Quentin D., Kyle D. Stedman, Taylor Joy Mitchell, and Joseph M. Moxley. 2012. *Agency in the Age of Peer Production*. Urbana: NCTE.

Winsor, Dorothy. 2006. "Using Writing to Structure Agency: An Examination of Engineers' Practice." *Technical Communication Quarterly* 15 (4): 411–30. http://dx.doi .org/10.1207/s15427625tcq1504_1.

BODY

Lorin Shellenberger

The keyword *body* or its related term, *bodies*, incorporates biological, cultural, physical, organizational, political, and rhetorical meanings. The term's complexity is illustrated through Susan Wells' frustration: there is "no 'natural' way of talking about the body, since the body always comes to us through multiple layers of cultural mediation" (Wells 2010, 144). Indeed, physical bodies are "sexed, raced, **gendered**, abled or disabled, whole or fragmented, aged or young, fat, thin, or anorexic" (Crowley 1999, 361), "a biology of hungers and pleasures, energy and fatigue, metabolic routine, disruption and repair" (Swan 2002, 286). Bodies are contradictory and unstable, "sites of both pleasure and pain" (Wells 2010, 145), "neither docile nor passive" (Lu 2006, 187), "everything and nothing" (Grigely 2002, 79), "mute" (Swan 2002, 286), and yet inextricably tied to voice (Mairs 1998, 61). The body is visible—"it is the body, not the soul, that sees and is seen" (Plato 1993, 83d)—and yet *more than* visible: "the body is not just what you see, but more especially what is unseen but known" (Wells 2010, 156).

Bodies are social constructions, symbols, and signifiers (Grigely 2002, 62), acted upon by **other** agents, and yet their reality is "incontestable" (Scarry 1985, 130). They are "constructions mediated by a range of cultural practices" (Wells 2010, 135), and "they include images and **discourse**, the tangible and the ephemeral, the literal and the figurative" (Grigely 2002, 62). According to Elizabeth Grosz, bodies are "inscribed, marked, engraved, by social pressures external to them," and "historical, social, and cultural exigencies . . . actively produce the body as a determinate type" (Grosz 1994, x).

Writing has a special relationship with the body. Writing can be seen as "bodily **work** conducted by, through, and on **material** bodies" (Lu 2006, 183) and as "crafting a particular body" (Fleckenstein 2003, 48). Writing is "not only *about* the body but *of* and *from* the body too" (Swan 2002, 284, emphasis in original). Writing constrains "how students go about working their bodies" (Lu 2006, 184). But bodies also place limits

DOI: 10.7330/9780874219746.c002

on writing: texts must "merge with" the body (Casanave 1997, 198) and bodies "are not easily ousted" from **personal** and professional (writing) lives (Fleckenstein 2003, 46). According to Joseph Grigely, the textual products of writing can be themselves bodies and also "extensions of the bodies that create them" (Grigely 2002, 82), while those that work with texts are "creators of reconstituted bodies" (71). Tina Kazan contends the created texts represent "the embodiment of a writer's ideas" and also "the corporeal presence of the absent writer" (Kazan 2006, 260). According to Kazan, online writing allows an author to "re-code her culturally coded body" to "reveal chosen identities that the body does not" (257–58). Still, rather than creating a "disembodied user that can easily inhabit any position desired," new media scholars argue that "the body is not so easily left behind" (Consalvo 2006, 359).

For those on the margins, the body is particularly vexed. These bodies are "marked" (Crowley 1999, 361): there are "illiterate bodies" (Mortensen 1999, 143), "marginalized bodies," "a dominant body" (Fleckenstein 2003, 49), and bodies colored "with the 'dirt' of reproduction" or "working-**class** labor" (Hallet 2006, 85). Such divergent bodies are seen as "contaminants in the university classroom" (Hallet 2006, 86), the "direct record of oppression" (Wells 2010, 159), the "objectified domain of knowledge" (Wells 2010, 149), and "instruments used in an [*sic*] process of acculturation" (Cruz and McLaren 2002, 188). Bodies can even be "imposed" upon others: in order to produce "'good writing,'" students of marginalized backgrounds must take on the unwelcome bodies of "white, heterosexual, middle-class males" (Fleckenstein 2003, 49).

The intersections of **disability** studies and writing studies illuminate *body* in significant ways. According to Lennard Davis, we generally seek to neutralize bodies: "bodies and bodily practices had to be standardized, homogenized, and normalized" (Davis 2002, 101) so that bodies could be viewed as "interchangeable" and "conceptualized as identical" (105). The disabled body, then, is a "marker of rhetorical defect," and bodies that are different are "viewed as deficiencies, perversions, or deformities" (Dolmage and Lewiecki-Wilson 2010, 27–28). As a result, such bodies "can have only negative rhetorical value" (27). According to Peter Kuppers, "one's own body is the shifting place from which and with which one knows the world," and, therefore, for disabilities studies scholars, "a need to evade, play with, or subvert the meanings of bodies—whether gendered, disabled, racial, or class-based[—is] paramount" (Kuppers 2004, 8, 122).

Bodies, and particularly female bodies, are things that can be used up or restructured. Bodies are commodities (Cruz and McLaren 2002,

204): for example, the bodies of teachers are "extractors and bearers of the commodity of labor power" (Lu 2006, 187), and the bodies of women are "capable of being owned, as 'their' or 'our' bodies" (Wells 2010, 134). The female body is viewed in opposition to or as deviant from the male body, and feminist bodies can be "refigured" and "reclaimed" (Dolmage and Lewiecki-Wilson 2010, 23, 28), and yet also "consumed" by or "erased" from the rhetorical tradition (28).

Moreover, Wells (2010) insists the body can be described spatially— "divided into zones of noncompliance, points of divergence from an ideal of beauty and charm" (148), "a discontinuous series of boundaries" (145), and "a negative space" (162)—while Grosz suggests the body cannot be "confined" by its "anatomical 'container,' the skin," and "the limits or borders of the body image are not fixed by nature" (Grosz 1994, 73). Elaine Scarry argues the body is both structural and permeable: "the body encloses and protects the individual within. . . . [I]ts walls put boundaries around the self preventing undifferentiated contact with the world"; its senses "like windows or doors," the body "enables the self to move out into the world and allows that world to enter" (Scarry 1985, 38).

The body has positive and negative connotations all at once. The body is described positively for its identification as a site of knowledge **production**, representing the "presence of learned culture," one's political **identity**, and a site of memory production (Scarry 1985, 109). According to Debra Hawhee, "thought does not just happen within the body, it happens as the body," because knowledge making "cannot be extricated from the body" (Hawhee 2004, 58, 195). The body is thus both a sign of virtue associated with the "production of honor" (Hawhee 4, 13) and a judge of character (Aristotle 2007, 1128a13–15), and yet the body is also not to be trusted. It has the "capacity to slip past the categories and codes of social discourse or to infiltrate and transform them" (Swan 2002, 286). The body is a trickster, and one who is body-aware possesses the "capacity for bodily disguise" (Hawhee 2004, 50). Bodies are also a hindrance, a "site of epistemological limitation" (Shapiro and Shapiro 2002, 27), a constraint (Buckley 1997, 179), a distraction (185), a limiting factor that must be "banned" (Fleckenstein 2003, 46) or "overcome or transcended" (Shapiro and Shapiro 2002, 27). Indeed, writing bodies are potentially dangerous: "to write from the body, from lived experience, is a fearsome thing; it is a way of exposing oneself to knives" (Cubbison 1997).

Second language scholars recognize that the "signaling possibilities of bodies are endless" (Schewe 2002, 76), and in literacy studies the body can drastically influence meaning: "writing using any known letter forms on the human body elevates those signs and places them outside of the realm of everyday literacy" (Ray 2009, 64). And finally, in professional writing and organizational communication, "employee bodies are both the medium and the outcome of practice and knowledge" (Trethewey, Scott, and LeGreco 2006, 125). According to Angela Trethewey, Cliff Scott, and Marianne LeGreco, current organizational discourse "still treats the employee's working body as an entity that can be rationalized, disciplined, regulated, and tested" (125). Much like understandings of bodies in other areas of writing studies, "the professional body is not a fixed, stable entity" (126).

References

Aristotle. 2007. *On Rhetoric.* Trans. George A. Kennedy. New York: Oxford University Press.

Buckley, Joanne. 1997. "The Invisible Audience and the Disembodied Voice: Online Teaching and the Loss of Body Image." *Computers and Composition* 14 (2): 179–87. http://dx.doi.org/10.1016/S8755-4615(97)90019-0.

Casanave, Christine Pearson. 1997. "Body-Mergings: Searching for Connections with Academic Discourse." In *On Becoming a Language Educator: Personal Essays on Professional Development*, ed. Christine Pearson Casanave and Sandra R. Schecter, 187–200. Mahwah, NJ: Ablex.

Consalvo, Mia. 2006. "Gender and New Media." In *The Sage Handbook of Gender and Communication*, ed. Bonnie J. Dow and Julia T. Wood, 355–70. Thousand Oaks: Sage Publications. http://dx.doi.org/10.4135/9781412976053.n19.

Crowley, Sharon. 1999. "Afterword: The Material of Rhetoric." In *Rhetorical Bodies*, ed. Jack Selzer and Sharon Crowley, 357–366. Madison: University of Wisconsin Press.

Cruz, Cindy, and Peter McLaren. 2002. "Queer Bodies and Configurations: Toward a Critical Pedagogy of the Body." In *Body Movements: Pedagogy, Politics and Social Change*, ed. Sherry Shapiro and Svi Shapiro, 187–207. Cresskill, NJ: Hampton Press.

Cubbison, Laurie. 1997. "What Does It Mean to Write from the Body?" *Women & Language* 20 (1): 31–4.

Davis, Lennard J. 2002. "Bodies of Difference: Politics, Disability, and Representation." In *Disability Studies: Enabling the Humanities*, ed. Sharon L. Snyder, Brenda Jo Brueggemann, and Rosemarie Garland Thomson, 100–108. New York: Modern Language Association of America.

Dolmage, Jay, and Cynthia Lewiecki-Wilson. 2010. "Refiguring Rhetorica: Linking Feminist Rhetoric and Disability Studies." In *Rhetorica in Motion: Feminist Rhetorical Methods and Methodologies*, ed. Eileen E. Schell and Kelly Jacob Rawson, 23–38. Pittsburgh: University of Pittsburgh Press.

Fleckenstein, Kristie S. 2003. *Embodied Literacies: Imageword and a Poetics of Teaching.* Carbondale: Southern Illinois University Press.

Grigely, Joseph. 2002. "Editing Bodies." In *Reimagining Textuality: Textual Studies in the Late Age of Print*, ed. Elizabeth Bergmann Loizeaux and Neil Fraistat, 60–84. Madison, WI: University of Wisconsin Press.

Grosz, Elizabeth. 1994. *Volatile Bodies: Toward a Corporeal Feminism.* Bloomington, IN: Indiana University Press.

Hallet, Mary. 2006. "She Toiled for a Living: Writing Lives and Identities of Older Female Students." In *Identity Papers: Literacy and Power in Higher Education*, ed. Bronwyn T. Williams, 77–91. Logan, UT: Utah State University Press.

Hawhee, Debra. 2004. *Bodily Arts.* Austin: University of Texas Press.

Kazan, Tina S. 2006. "Braving the Body: Embodiment and (Cyber-)Texts." In *Brave New Classrooms: Democratic Classrooms and the Internet*, ed. Joe Lockard and Mark Pegrum, 251–69. New York: Peter Lang.

Kuppers, Peter. 2004. *Disability and Contemporary Performance: Bodies on Edge.* New York: Routledge.

Lu, Min-Zhan. 2006. "Working Bodies: Class Matters in College." In *Identity Papers: Literacy and Power in Higher Education*, ed. Bronwyn T. Williams, 182–91. Logan, UT: Utah State University Press.

Mairs, Nancy. 1998. "Carnal Acts." In *Staring Back: The Disability Experience from the Inside Out*, ed. Kenny Fries, 51–61. New York: Plume.

Mortensen, Peter. 1999. "Figuring Illiteracy: Rustic Bodies and Unlettered Minds in Rural America." In *Rhetorical Bodies*, ed. Jack Selzer and Sharon Crowley, 143–70. Madison: University of Wisconsin Press.

Plato. 1993. *Phaedo.* Trans. C. J. Rowe. New York: Cambridge University Press.

Ray, Sohini. 2009. "From Inscription to Incorporation: The Body in Literacy Studies, Introduction." *Anthropological Quarterly* 82 (1): 63–8.

Scarry, Elaine. 1985. *The Body in Pain.* New York: Oxford University Press.

Schewe, Manfred Lukas. 2002. "Teaching Foreign Language Literature: Tapping the Students' Bodily-Kinesthetic Intelligence." In *Body and Language: Intercultural Learning through Drama*, ed. Gerd Bräuer, 73–94. Westport, CT: Ablex Publishing.

Shapiro, Sherry, and Svi Shapiro. 2002. "Silent Voices, Bodies of Knowledge: Towards a Critical Pedagogy of the Body." In *Body Movements: Pedagogy, Politics and Social Change*, ed. Sherry Shapiro and Svi Shapiro, 25–43. Cresskill, NJ: Hampton Press.

Swan, Jim. 2002. "Disabilities, Bodies, Voices." In *Disability Studies: Enabling the Humanities*, ed. Sharon L. Snyder, Brenda Jo Brueggemann, and Rosemarie Garland Thomson, 283–95. New York: Modern Language Association of America.

Trethewey, Angela, Cliff Scott, and Marianne LeGreco. 2006. "Constructing Embodied Organizational Identities." In *The Sage Handbook of Gender and Communication*, ed. Bonnie J. Dow and Julia T. Wood, 123–43. Thousand Oaks: Sage Publications. http://dx.doi.org/10.4135/9781412976053.n7.

Wells, Susan. 2010. *Our Bodies, Ourselves and the Work of Writing.* Stanford, CA: Stanford University Press.

CITIZEN

Mark Garrett Longaker

In 1954, Richard Weaver, then director of the FYC program at the University of Chicago, discussed the role of education in the formation of citizenship, saying, "participation in a democratic society is an active process. . . . [I]t involves the ability to reason clearly and independently," skills central to good writing (Weaver 2000, 167).

In 1998, David Fleming, director of FYC at the University of Wisconsin–Madison and later at the University of Massachusetts Amherst, suggested that writing teachers imagine each student "as a future citizen in a **community** of free and equal citizens" (Fleming 1998, 178).

In 2006, David Coogan, while directing service learning and community outreach programs, explained that the writing teacher/scholar should endeavor "not just to make good citizens but to enable student-citizens to write for social change" (Coogan 2006, 667).

These three statements demonstrate a common and longstanding concern about citizenship and the good "citizen." After recently reviewing scholarship that invokes the term, Amy Wan has concluded that writing-studies scholars often invoke the term passionately, but define *citizenship* in "vague" and "at best . . . uninterrogated ways" (Wan 2011, 29). Citizenship is defined as a "goal" for students to achieve and as an activity—"participatory action through writing" (31)—but Wan insists we "reconsider what is behind the rote invocation of citizenship" (46). Weaver, Fleming, and Coogan might agree that the denizen simply resides and observes. The citizen joins and participates. Yet, along with contemporary writing studies scholars, they imagine **civic** membership and participation in different ways.

Michael Pennell, for instance, explains that labor-market intermediaries (such as union-sponsored worker reeducation programs) provide "large numbers of new citizens" living in "rust-belt regions" and suffering "a postindustrial downturn" with "functional literacy . . . as workers study for their GED or for improved **English** skills" (Pennell 2007, 353). According to Pennell, the citizen belongs to an economy and participates

DOI: 10.7330/9780874219746.c003

by **producing** value. Michele Simmons and Jeffrey Grabill explain that "citizens" address local issues of common concern by learning specialist knowledge (such as environmental regulations) and becoming proficient in digital applications (such as online databases). They **work** in "community organizations" that publicly address "technologically and scientifically complex" issues through "civic **discourse**," which requires "complex interfaces to access and make sense of information" (Simmons and Grabill 2007, 439–40). According to Simmons and Grabill, citizens live in troubled areas and participate through electronic media. Finally, Robert Brooke (2012) explains that rural US geographies need a "new kind of citizen" who can participate in national conversations but who also actively builds communal life by engaging in local conversations about issues that resonate with **other** rural citizens (161). "[P]lace-conscious" writing instruction can develop "active citizens" who reside in rural areas and connect to national interests (165).

Furthermore, as Susan Wells observes, the term *citizen* "becomes a heightened example of **public** virtues or vices, and also . . . a prop for identification" (Wells 1996, 330). We harbor different understandings of where the citizen lives, how the citizen participates, and what the "good citizen" looks like. Weaver adored conservative citizens who uphold tradition. Fleming adulated democratic citizens who promote liberal, inclusive debate. Coogan championed activist citizens who challenge injustice.

Definitions of *the good citizen* extend beyond the abstract. Patricia Roberts-Miller demonstrates that many pedagogies assume a vision of the good democratic "citizen." Paraphrasing the political theorist Ronald Beiner, Roberts-Miller explains, "the state cannot remain genuinely neutral to citizens' conceptions of the good life because democracy would collapse were enough people to pursue total hedonism" (Roberts-Miller 2003, 540). According to Roberts-Miller, not only the state but also the writing classroom has a stake in the formation of good citizens because both government and writing instructors engage a "variety of models for democratic discourse" (539). The debate about the "good citizen" infuses discussions about writing pedagogy.

For instance, in the mid-1990s at the Community Literacy Center (CLC) in Pittsburgh, Carnegie Mellon University faculty asked local Pittsburgh residents to "engage in a broader conversation about issues" and to produce written work (such as reports and policy proposals) under the guidance of a university-appointed, student writing mentor. One such writing tutor participated in a meeting at a local community center, where everyone heard teenagers rap about suspension rates at an area high school (Peck, Flower, and Higgins 1995). Though their explanation of the project did not include the term *citizen*, those working at the CLC assumed a Deweyan model of democracy, "a mode of associated living, of conjoint communicated experience" (Dewey 1916, 87). Communitarian citizens engaged one another and the broader community in discourse that builds communal ties and shares community concerns.

In contrast to the communitarian citizen assumed by the CLC, consider Rosa Eberly's effort to help students become "citizen-critics" who produce "discourses of common concerns from an ethos of citizens first and foremost" (Eberly 2000, 10), or Christian Weisser's promotion of "public writing" so that students can better engage their "civic spaces" (Weisser 2002, 50–60). Both Eberly and Weisser, in different registers, assume that good democratic citizens debate public issues before seeking recourse through the state. The Westernized "public sphere" invites people to participate in democracy through deliberation (ideally in a rational and considerate manner). Susan Wells warns that this public sphere is no "pre-existing forum where citizens make decisions face to face" (Wells 1996, 326). The public sphere consists of "citizens' reports" filled out in police stations as well as healthcare debates mediated by newspapers and television **networks**.

The critical sociology leading to public-sphere theory (and to critiques of the twentieth-century public sphere) has led others toward a different understanding of citizenship as well as a different understanding of how the good citizen writes. The public sphere's rational, critical discourse may perpetuate the oppressive hegemony enjoyed by (white, male, heterosexual, traditionally educated, and typically wealthy) people who then exclude, dominate, marginalize, or colonize others. William Thelin, for instance, insists that writing teachers acknowledge "the democracy . . . [students] have experienced as citizens" and "prepare . . . [them] for active citizenship," even though "most students . . . do not feel that the trappings of democracy used by our government have given students much of a chance to participate" (Thelin 2005, 137–38). Ira Shor, a critical pedagogue like Thelin, attempts to empower radical democratic citizens by letting students set the course agenda, select common readings, and write the assignment descriptions (Shor 1992, 55–84). Thelin encourages students to investigate key concepts or cultural myths (such as "freedom") in critical analysis essays (Thelin 2005, 122).

In the three approaches (and their advocates) surveyed, we see three different visions of the good citizen—communitarian, publican, and critical—each underlying a specific writing pedagogy. Returning to Amy Wan's review of scholarship, however, we might conclude that the contested nature of the term *citizen* is not a problem for writing studies. Wan asks us to "consider the other multiple ways that habits of citizenship are encouraged through literacy learning" (Wan 2011, 45). People belong to various groups, societies, geographies, economies, and governments. They participate in numerous ways. And they imagine civic virtue in many forms. The challenge for the writing studies scholar and for the writing instructor, as Wan explains, is to clearly define *citizenship* in terms of belonging, participation, and virtue, and then to investigate how **literacy**, writing, digital acumen, and rhetorical skill all constitute the "citizen."

References

Brooke, Robert. 2012. "Voices of Young Citizens: Rural Citizenship, Schools, and Public Policy." In *Reclaiming the Rural: Essays on Literacy, Rhetoric, and Pedagogy*, ed. Kim Donehower, Charlotte Hogg, and Eileen Schell, 161–72. Carbondale: Southern Illinois University Press.

Coogan, David. 2006. "Service Learning and Social Change: The Case for Materialist Rhetoric." *College Composition and Communication* 57 (4): 667–93.

Dewey, John. 1916. *Democracy and Education.* New York: Free Press.

Eberly, Rosa. 2000. *Citizen Critics: Literary Public Spheres.* Champagne-Urbana: University of Illinois Press.

Fleming, David. 1998. "Rhetoric as a Course of Study." *College English* 61 (2): 169–91. http://dx.doi.org/10.2307/378878.

Peck, Wayne Campbell, Linda Flower, and Lorraine Higgins. 1995. "Community Literacy." *College Composition and Communication* 46 (2): 199–222. http://dx.doi.org/10.2307/358428.

Pennell, Michael. 2007. "'If Knowledge is Power, You're about to Become Very Powerful': Literacy and Labor Market Intermediaries in Postindustrial America." *College Composition and Communication* 58 (3): 345–84.

Roberts-Miller, Patricia. 2003. "Discursive Conflict in Communities and Classrooms." *College Composition and Communication* 54 (4): 536–57. http://dx.doi.org/10.2307/3594184.

Shor, Ira. 1992. *Empowering Education: Critical Teaching for Social Change.* Chicago: University of Chicago Press.

Simmons, Michele, and Jeffrey Grabill. 2007. "Toward a Civic Rhetoric for Technologically and Scientifically Complex Places: Invention, Performance, and Participation." *College Composition and Communication* 58 (3): 419–48.

Thelin, William. 2005. "Understanding Problems in Critical Classrooms." *College Composition and Communication* 57 (1): 114–41.

Wan, Amy. 2011. "In the Name of Citizenship: The Writing Classroom and the Promise of Citizenship." *College English* 74 (1): 28–49.

Weaver, Richard. 2000. "Education: Reflections on." In *In Defense of Tradition: Collected Shorter Writings of Richard M. Weaver, 1929–1963*, ed. Ted J. Smith, III, 167–75. Indianapolis: Liberty Fund.

Weisser, Christian. 2002. *Moving Beyond Academic Discourse: Composition Studies and the Public Sphere.* Carbondale: Southern Illinois University Press.

Wells, Susan. 1996. "Rogue Cops and Health Care: What Do We Want from Public Writing?" *College Composition and Communication* 47 (3): 325–41. http://dx.doi.org/10.2307/358292.

CIVIC/PUBLIC

Steve Parks

Current meanings of *civic* and *public* within writing studies trace their emergence as keywords to the post-World War II period, when the United States was formulating a Cold War strategy premised upon the belief of a consistent threat by the Soviet Union to democratic values. Within this context, the National Council of Teachers of English, when framing its civic mission in the late 1950s, stressed the strong relationship between writing, literature, and democracy, positioning **English** as central to the Cold War struggle as either math or science (NCTE 1958).

This mission was put under pressure as Civil Rights, Brown Rights, and LBGT movements began to press upon the meaning of *democracy*. As Nancy Fraser (1990) argues, the struggle to alter conceptions of "the public" are contingent on formerly private behaviors being transformed into public concerns. In writing studies, the activism of African-American and Latino teachers pushed for a definition of *public* in which their identities and speaking/writing patterns would be considered a valuable part of the norm (Blackmon, Kirklighter, and Parks 2011; Davis 1994). Using their collective subject positions, they articulated a new civic mission for writing studies, one based upon the ideal that the individual languages of students needed to be recognized and valued as public **discourses**.

In like manner, according to Blackmon, Kirklighter, and Parks (2011), scholars such as Geneva Smitherman (1977) and Carlotta Cardenas Dwyer (2011) began to make arguments about the historical exclusion (and oppression) of certain group identities within our field, demonstrating how language policies and textbook practices acted in tandem with larger, oppressive social forces. It is out of this context that CCCC initiated such policies as the Students' Right To Their Own Language and the National Language policy (Conference on College Composition and Communication 1974, 1988)

Nonetheless, as Edward Corbett (1969) argued, for instance, there was for some a sense that a rhetorical education could be called upon

DOI: 10.7330/9780874219746.c004

to better prepare students for their roles in civic life—the progressive and confrontational rhetoric of the 1960s representing to Corbett an inability to develop productive dialogue on important political issues. The claim that the study of rhetoric produces **citizens** able to speak virtuously on civic issues goes back to the **work** of Isocrates, Plato, and Aristotle (and later, of course, Quintilian). Despite their epistemological differences, each imagined they were teaching individuals to be public citizens, engaged in democratic processes across different elements of society—the courts, the assembly, and public ceremonies. Scholars such as Berlin (1987), however, argued that the resulting "civic" pedagogy was too static, dominated by a sense of normalcy that was not reflective of a heterogeneous teacher and student population, let alone the actual diversity of non-classroom space nationally. In response, some have sought to help students understand rhetoric as an intervention into a contingent moment with an ethical bias toward democratic debate. Such a rhetorical education can provide students with "the skills needed to create and sustain a public, as against a private, reality" (Lanham 1993, 189). With this renewed sense of democratic debate as formative of a socially created truth, "rhetoric" thus becomes essential in creating a dialogue between public and civic space.

While many of the early debates over civic/public space were focused on expanding professional and pedagogical responsibilities within the classroom, more recently writing studies has taken to "the streets" (Mathieu 2005), encouraging students to actively participate in the public sphere to enhance their understanding of "civic" practices. Thus, while a longstanding tension between *public* (representing the larger social and political context) and *civic* (standing for cultural and legal institutions/practices) has remained fairly constant, there has been a massive shift in how that tension is being worked out. Whereas in the 1960s and 1970s there was a working assumption that the federal government was the "appeal" of last resort, from approximately 1980 to the present a neoliberal sense of public space has taken over. Here the individual volunteer stands in as the model citizen, with a sense that volunteering coupled with nongovernment-sponsored programming is the best way to achieve equity in the public sphere.

Writing studies is still grappling with how to respond to these "new" definitions of public and civic space, with this shift from a civic space dominated by requests for federal intervention to one dominated by volunteerism. Bruce Herzberg (1994), for instance, has argued that students bring this volunteerist ethos into classroom/**community** work, suggesting that specific strategies have to be developed to undercut it.

Other scholars, such as Nancy Welch (2009), have argued that there is a need to return students to earlier versions of public/civic engagement, citing the history of labor unions and other collective movements for social justice as a means to demonstrate other possible definitions and ways to engage in civic action/debate. John Ackerman (2010) problematizes the entire enterprise of such publicly engaged work, noting that to leave the classroom means intentionally subsuming the progressive politics of civic engagement within the fast-capitalism policies of the United States as a geo-political power.

It should be noted, though, that an engagement with the categories of civic/public does not necessarily imply a critique of neoliberalism or a call to work within social justice movements. Focusing on the ability of such work to provide **personal** affirmation of an individual's voice, David Coogan works toward the formation of a "middle space" that can rhetorically enable "publics," which can allow communities "to address their own social problems" (Coogan 2006, 159). In a similar fashion, Linda Flower (2008) has argued that there is a need to model forms of civic debate based upon intercultural dialogues, conversations that are structured around different rhetorical strategies and that call upon individuals to situate themselves within the argument of their interlocutor. Training in these strategies is designed to produce temporary new "civic" spaces where formerly excluded individuals can gain **agency**—an agency specifically framed to avoid altering existing social policy. The goal is to model a new form of civic dialogue, not necessarily to use that space for specific changes in civic policies.

Michael Warner (2002) likewise complicates the meanings of these keywords, urging us to understand *publics* as poetic creations in which discourse must endlessly circulate, and to imagine the creation of a "non-political counter public" where members can talk openly about their marginalized experience. Similarly, he portrays such communities as existing along an extended timeline. Cushman (2011) demonstrates the difficulty of forming such an extended public—particularly one in a counter-public position—through her examination of Cherokee writing/literacy practices. In fact, a focus on **literacy** within writing studies has been a consistent space in which counter-public community language practices have been examined for their relationship to the dominant public (see Gilyard 1997; Goldblatt 2007; Heath 1983; Parks 2010; Royster 2000).

Finally, recent developments in writing studies continue to complicate the meanings of *civic* and *public* in our professional discourse. The emphasis on global English, for instance, has led to the insight that any public **identity** for a "writer" must be understood to occur within a global context (Canagarajah 2002), while ESL scholarship maintains that a person's public identity should be understood to represent a continuum of geographies, ethnicities, and language patterns. Geography, itself, has also been questioned as a basis for delimiting a "public." **Technical communication** has asked the field to consider how the ability of software to process data creates an ability to create local publics based upon a variety of criteria (Diehl et al. 2008). Moreover, with the emergence of social media, meanings of *public* have expanded to include non-geographical online and social media publics (Banks 2011; Grabill 2007), publics that offer both activist and non-activist possibilities. As scholars and teachers, then, we must continually assess which understanding of these key terms cannot only be generative of our research, but enable the education of our students as well.

Acknowledgments. I thank Tim Dougherty for his insights on classical rhetoric and pedagogy.

References

Ackerman, John M. 2010. "Rhetorical Engagement in the Cultural Economies of Cities." In *The Public Work of Rhetoric: Citizen-Scholars and Public Engagement*, ed. John Ackerman and David Coogan, 175–92. Columbia: University of South Carolina Press.

Banks, Adam. 2011. *Digital Griots: African American Rhetoric in a Multimedia Age.* Urbana: Southern Illinois University Press.

Berlin, James. 1987. *Rhetoric and Reality: Writing Instruction in American Colleges, 1900–1985.* Carbondale: Southern Illinois University Press.

Blackmon, Samantha, Cristina Kirklighter, and Steve Parks. 2011. *Listening to Our Elders: Writing and Working for Change.* Logan: Utah State University Press.

Canagarajah, A. Suresh. 2002. *A Geopolitics of Academic Writing.* Pittsburgh: University of Pittsburgh Press.

Conference on College Composition and Communication. 1974. *Students' Right to Their Own Language.* http://www.ncte.org/cccc/resources/positions/srtolsummary.

Conference on College Composition and Communication. 1988. *CCCC Guideline on the National Language Policy.* http://www.ncte.org/cccc/resources/positions/national-langpolicy.

Coogan, David. 2006. "Service-Learning and Social Change: The Case for a Materialist Rhetoric." *College Composition and Communication* 57: 667–93.

Corbett, Edward. 1969. "The Rhetoric of the Open Hand and the Rhetoric of the Closed Fist." *College Composition and Communication* 20 (5): 288–96. http://dx.doi.org/10.2307/355032.

Cushman, Ellen. 2011. *The Cherokee Syllabary: Writing the People's Perseverance.* Norman: University of Oklahoma Press.

Davis, Marianna. 1994. *History of the Black Caucus of the National Council of Teachers of English.* Urbana: NCTE.

Diehl, Amy, Jeffery T. Grabill, William Hart-Davidson, and Vishal Iyer. 2008. "Grassroots: Supporting the Knowledge of Everyday Life." *Technical Communication Quarterly* 17 (4): 413–34. http://dx.doi.org/10.1080/10572250802324937.

Dwyer, Carlotta Cardenas. 2011. "Chicana Trailblazer in NCTE/CCCC: An Interview with Carlota C'ardenas Dwyer." Interview by Itzcóatl Tlaloc Meztli. In *Listening to Our Elders: Working and Writing for Change*, ed. Samantha Blackmon, Cristina Kirklighter, and Steve Parks, 122–33. Philadelphia: New City Community Press.

Flower, Linda. 2008. *Community Literacy and the Rhetoric of Public Engagement.* Carbondale: Southern Illinois University Press.

Fraser, Nancy. 1990. "Rethinking the Public Sphere: A Contribution to the Critique of Actually Existing Democracy." *Social Text* 25/26 (25/26): 56–80. http://dx.doi.org/10.2307/466240.

Gilyard, Keith. 1997. *Voices of the Self: A Study of Language Competence.* Detroit: Wayne State University Press.

Goldblatt, Eli. 2007. *Because We Live There: Sponsoring Literacy beyond the College Curriculum.* New York: Hampton Press.

Grabill, Jeffery T. 2007. *Writing Community Change: Designing Technologies for Citizen Action.* New York: Hampton Press.

Heath, Shirley. 1983. *Ways with Words.* Cambridge: Cambridge University Press.

Herzberg, Bruce. 1994. "Community Service and Critical Teaching." *College Composition and Communication* 45 (3): 307–19. http://dx.doi.org/10.2307/358813.

Lanham, Richard. 1993. "The 'Q' Question." In *The Electronic Word: Democracy, Technology, and the Arts*, 154–194. Chicago: University of Chicago Press.

Mathieu, Paula. 2005. *Tactics of Hope: The Public Turn in Composition.* Portsmouth, NH: Boynton Cook.

National Council of Teachers of English (NCTE). 1958. *National Interest and the Teaching of English.* Champaign, IL: NCTE.

Parks, Steve. 2010. *Gravyland: Writing beyond the Curriculum in the City of Brotherly Love.* Syracuse: Syracuse University Press.

Royster, Jacqueline Jones. 2000. *Traces of A Stream: Literacy and Social Change among African American Women.* Pittsburgh: University of Pittsburgh Press.

Smitherman, Geneva. 1977. *Talkin and Testifyin: The Language of Black America.* Detroit: Wayne State University Press.

Warner, Michael. 2002. *Publics and Counterpublics.* New York: Zone Books.

Welch, Nancy. 2009. *The Living Room: Teaching Public Writing in a Privatized World.* Portsmouth, NH: Boynton Cook.

CLASS

Julie Lindquist

At one level, every conversation about the project of first-year writing—an institutional practice designed to help students acquire academic **literacy**, and an experience located at the point of entry to higher education—is a conversation about class. However, these various conversations employ the term *class* more or less explicitly as a **discourse** or as a thematic. Given that questions about what *class* means and how it works are important to **research** and scholarship across disciplines, what do those of us with an investment in writing studies talk about when we talk about class?

In writing studies, the idea of class has expressed itself in multiple ways: in inquiries into the terms and stakes of access (to higher education, to academic literacies and codes of schooling, to social mobility); in research and scholarship on Freirian critical pedagogy and associated conversations; in **work** in cultural studies of writing; in educational sociology and philosophy; and in ethnographies of communication and everyday rhetorical practices. A thriving line of inquiry has emerged that takes as its explicit focus working-class culture and language. Even those writing about class, therefore, have had various avenues of disciplinary influence as well as theoretical and methodological points of entry. Theories of class experience are active both in discussions of teaching and learning and in broader inquiries into culture, discourse, and power in rhetorical studies.

Hence, writing studies sustains a pragmatic interest in understanding how class operates within educational institutions and in the lives of the students they serve. Writing researchers and scholars interested in the area of basic writing, for example, are explicitly concerned with issues of educational preparedness, social power, and institutional access (e.g., Bartholomae 1985; Bizzell 1986; Fox 1999; Lu 1987; Parks 2000; Rose 1983; 1989; Shaunessey 1979). Since access to the promises of social mobility higher education offers is itself a function of social class, it follows that social structures, institutional practices, and cultural

DOI: 10.7330/9780874219746.c005

experiences of students are subjects of inquiry for those interested in basic writing programs and curricula. Mike Rose's (1989) *Lives on the Boundary* was a hugely important text in calling the field's attention to, as the book's subtitle indicates, "the struggles and achievements of the underprepared." Written from Rose's perspective as a student relegated to remedial courses in high school, *Lives on the Boundary* exposed the socially immobilizing effects of institutional tracking and the potential of education to replicate and stabilize existing class divisions. While Rose's memoir constituted a powerful critique of schooling, other scholars (e.g., Beech 2004; Bloom 1996; Lindquist 1999; 2004; Watkins 1992; Zebroski 1990; 2006) have questioned the classed practices—and class aspirations—of English and composition as disciplinary (and institutional) cultures.

Alongside inquiries into institutional processes and educational access, much scholarship been produced on the nature and responsibilities of class-conscious literacy education, a line of work developed in response to the claims of critical pedagogy as conceived by Marxist educator Paulo Freire (1970) in *Pedagogy of the Oppressed*. Inquiry inaugurated by Freirian philosophy has perhaps been the most generative in treating the FYC classroom as a space in which social class is experienced and enacted. Proponents (and critics) of critical pedagogy have explored the nature of class experience, the motives of working-class students, the ethics of Marxist approaches to instruction in literacy, and the stakes of education for those seeking upward mobility. Freirian critical pedagogy has attracted the interest of many working in composition studies and related areas: Ira Shor (1987) and James Berlin (1996), for example, have been strong advocates for—and have written extensively about—applications of Frierian educational philosophy to the education of students in American colleges and universities. Other scholars (including Bean 2003; Ellsworth 1989; Mack 2006; Seitz 2004; Trainor 2008; Zebroski 1990; 2006) have questioned the methods and ethics of Freirian approaches to teaching American college students. The fundamental premise of critical pedagogy—that the project of literacy education should and can be devoted to the social "empowerment" of students via practices of rational critique—has animated debates in composition studies for over four decades.

Other educational researchers and philosophers motivated by an interest in social power and stratification (such as Anyon 1980; Aronowitz 2004; Giroux 1988; 2011; Weis 1988) have advanced critiques and investigations of the relationship between educational practices and social mobility. Some of these scholars, such as Aronowitz and Giroux, have delivered critiques of educational institutions on the grounds that these serve the interests of dominant groups and participate in the unequal distribution of social privileges. Educational researcher Jean Anyon makes the case that school curricula are themselves of expressions of class codes, regardless of the "content" they deliver. The claims and findings of Anyon, Weis, and others have influenced researchers and scholars in composition studies seeking to situate the work of FYC in larger **contexts** of educational history, practice, and value.

Much of the thinking about social structures and the classed subjectivities they produce has come by way of research and scholarship inspired by, or within the tradition of, European cultural studies. Sociologists such as Bourdieu and Nice (1987) and Jurgen Habermas (1991) have studied the cultural means by which social structures are reproduced. Those associated with the Centre for Contemporary Culture Studies (CCCS) at Birmingham investigated the relationship between social structures and cultural forms. Paul Willis' (1981) *Learning to Labor*, a study of the class aspirations and loyalties of English schoolboys, for example, established a tradition of inquiry into the relationship between socioeconomic structures and class experience. British and North American scholars influenced by the CCCS have continued to explore questions about the relationships of social structures and institutions (including educational institutions) to cultural practices in defining and maintaining class divisions (see, for example, Bettie 2003; Foley 1990; Fox 2002; Hartigan 1999).

Another line of American-born inquiry in writing studies has sought to understand the cultural practices and value systems of groups with less economic power, with the goal of changing practices within educational institutions. Studies such as *Ways With Words* by linguistic anthropologist Shirley Heath (1983) produce ethnographic stories of class experience as it relates to literacy and schooling. Heath's work has inspired generations of researchers seeking to understand the relationship between education as a social practice and site of middle-class cultural activity and the cultural norms and expectations of working-class communities. Informed by culture studies and inspired by Heath's work, researchers in writing studies—such as Ralph Cintron (1998), Julie Lindquist (2001), Jabari Mahiri (1998), Beverly Moss (2002), David Seitz (2004), and Jennifer Trainor (2008)—have conducted extended ethnographic inquiries into the value systems and discourses of cultural groups with working-class histories and identifications.

While many scholars working in writing studies have investigated questions of institutional power and the nature of students' experiences within educational institutions, others have focused on the experiences of those who have succeeded in securing middle-class positions as academics. Upwardly mobile academics with working-class origins have generated a significant corpus of autobiographical narratives about their experiences in moving from working- to middle-class academic cultures. These stories of the vexations of upward mobility comprise the substance of several edited collections, including *Strangers In Paradise: Academics from the Working Class* (Ryan and Sackrey 1984), *This Fine Place So Far From Home* (Dews and Law 1995), *Working-Class Women in the Academy: Laborers in the Knowledge Factory* (Tokarczyk and Fay 1993), and *Liberating Memory: Our Work and Our Working-Class Consciousness* (Zandy 1994). Class functions psychologically in these narratives, a key factor in their authors' experiences of loss, alienation, and displacement.

References

Anyon, Jean. 1980. "Social Class and the Hidden Curriculum of Work." *Journal of Education* 162 (2): 67–92.

Aronowitz, Stanley. 2004. "Against Schooling: Education and Social Class." *Social Text* 22 (2): 13–35. http://dx.doi.org/10.1215/01642472-22-2_79-13.

Bartholomae, David. 1985. "Inventing the University." In *When a Writer Can't Write: Studies in Writer's Block and Other Composing Problems*, ed. Mike Rose, 134–65. New York: The Guilford Press.

Bean, Janet. 2003. "Manufacturing Emotions: Tactical Resistance in the Narratives of Working-Class Students." In *A Way to Move: Rhetorics of Emotion and Composition Studies*, ed. Laura Micciche and Dale Jacobs, 101–12. Portsmouth, NH: Heinemann.

Beech, Jennifer. 2004. "Redneck and Hillbilly Discourse in the Writing Classroom: Classifying Critical Pedagogies of Whiteness." *College English* 67 (2): 172–86. http://dx.doi.org/10.2307/4140716.

Berlin, James. 1996. *Rhetorics, Poetics, Cultures: Refiguring College English Studies*. Urbana: NCTE Press.

Bettie, Julie. 2003. *Women without Class: Girls, Race, and Identity*. Berkeley: University of California Press.

Bizzell, Patricia. 1986. "What Happens When Basic Writers Come to College?" *College Composition and Communication* 37 (3): 294–301. http://dx.doi.org/10.2307/358046.

Bloom, Lynn. 1996. "Freshman Composition as a Middle-Class Enterprise." *College English* 58 (6): 654–75. http://dx.doi.org/10.2307/378392.

Bourdieu, Pierre, and Richard Nice. 1987. *Distinction: A Social Critique of the Judgment of Taste*. Cambridge: Harvard University Press.

Cintron, Ralph. 1998. *Angels Town: Chero Ways, Gang Life, and the Rhetorics of the Everyday*. Boston: Beacon.

Dews, C. L. Barney, and Carolyn Leste Law. 1995. *This Fine Place So Far From Home: Voices of Academics from the Working Class*. Philadelphia: Temple University Press.

Ellsworth, Elizabeth. 1989. "Why Doesn't This Feel Empowering? Working Through the Repressive Myths of Critical Pedagogy." *Harvard Educational Review* 59 (3): 297–324.

Foley, Douglas. 1990. *Learning Capitalist Culture: Deep in the Heart of Tejas*. Philadelphia: University of Pennsylvania Press.

Fox, Aaron A. 2002. *Real Country: Music and Language in Working-Class Culture.* Raleigh: Duke University Press.

Fox, Tom. 1999. *Defending Access: A Critique of Standards in Higher Education.* Portsmouth, NH: Boynton/Cook.

Freire, Paulo. 1970. *Pedagogy of the Oppressed.* Trans. Myra Bergman Ramos. New York: Continuum.

Giroux, Henry. 1988. *Teachers as Intellectuals: Toward a Critical Pedagogy of Learning.* Westport, CT: Praeger.

Giroux, Henry. 2011. *On Critical Pedagogy.* New York: Continuum Press.

Habermas, Jurgen. 1991. *The Structural Transformation of the Public Sphere: An Inquiry into a Category of Bourgeois Society.* Boston: MIT Press.

Hartigan, John. 1999. *Racial Situations: Class Predicaments of Whiteness in Detroit.* Princeton: Princeton University Press.

Heath, Shirley Brice. 1983. *Ways with Words: Language, Life, and Work in Communities and Classrooms.* Cambridge: Cambridge University Press.

hooks, bell. 1994. *Teaching to Transgress: Education as the Practice of Freedom.* New York: Routledge.

Lindquist, Julie. 1999. "Class Ethos and the Politics of Inquiry: What the Barroom Can Teach Us about the Classroom." *College Composition and Communication* 51 (2): 225–47. http://dx.doi.org/10.2307/359040.

Lindquist, Julie. 2001. *A Place to Stand: Politics and Persuasion in a Working-Class Bar.* New York: Oxford University Press.

Lindquist, Julie. 2004. "Class Affects, Classroom Affectations: Working Through the Paradoxes of Strategic Empathy." *College English* 67 (2): 187–209. http://dx.doi.org/10.2307/4140717.

Lu, Min-Zhan. 1987. "From Silence to Words: Writing as Struggle." *College English* 49 (4): 437–48. http://dx.doi.org/10.2307/377860.

Mack, Nancy. 2006. "Ethical Representation of Working-Class Lives: Multiple Genres, Voices, and Identities." *Pedagogy* 6 (1): 53–78. http://dx.doi.org/10.1215/15314200-6-1-53.

Mahiri, Jabari. 1998. *Shooting for Excellence: African-American and Youth Culture in New Century Schools.* Urbana: NCTE Press.

Moss, Beverly. 2002. *A Community Text Arises.* New York: Hampton Press.

Parks, Stephen. 2000. *Class Politics: The Movement for the Students' Right to Their Own Language.* Urbana: NCTE Press.

Rose, Mike. 1983. "Remedial Writing Courses: A Critique and a Proposal." *College English* 45 (2): 109–28. http://dx.doi.org/10.2307/377219.

Rose, Mike. 1989. *Lives on the Boundary: The Struggles and Achievements of America's Underprepared.* New York: Free Press.

Ryan, Jake, and Charles Sackrey. 1984. *Strangers in Paradise: Academics from the Working Class.* London: South End Press.

Seitz, David. 2004. *Who Can Afford Critical Consciousness? Practicing a Pedagogy of Humility.* New York: Hampton Press.

Shaunessey, Mina. 1979. *Errors and Expectations.* Oxford: Oxford University Press.

Shor, Ira. 1987. *Critical Teaching and Everyday Life.* Chicago: University of Chicago Press.

Tokarczyk, Michelle, and Elizabeth Fay. 1993. *Working-Class Women in the Academy: Laborors in the Knowledge Factory.* Amherst: University of Massachusetts Press.

Trainor, Jennifer. 2008. *Rethinking Racism: Emotion, Persuasion, and Literacy Education in an All-White High School.* Carbondale: Southern Illinois University Press.

Watkins, Evan. 1992. *Work Time: English Departments and the Circulation of Cultural Value.* Palo Alto: Stanford University Press.

Weis, Lois, ed. 1988. *Class, Race, and Gender in American Education.* Albany: SUNY Press.

Willis, Paul. 1981. *Learning to Labour: How Working Class Kids Get Working Class Jobs.* New York: Columbia University Press.

Zandy, Janet. 1994. *Liberating Memory: Our Work and Our Working-Class Consciousness.* New Brunswick, NJ: Rutgers University Press.

Zebroski, James Thomas. 1990. "The English Department and Social Class: Resisting Writing." In *The Right to Literacy,* ed. Andrea A. Lunsford, Helene Moglen, and James Slevin, 81–87. New York: MLA.

Zebroski, James Thomas. 2006. "Social Class as Discourse: Mapping the Landscape of Class in Rhetoric and Composition." *JAC* 26 (3–4): 513–84.

COMMUNITY

Paul Prior

The word *community* functions as what Susan Star and James Griesemer call a "boundary object" (Star and Griesemer 1989, 393), something fluid, adaptable, and robust enough to weave together different **discourses** and worlds. An everyday term in civic, religious, and Internet contexts, *community* also serves as a specialized term in multiple disciplines, including sociology, **ecology**, linguistics, education, and writing studies. The Oxford English Dictionary (2012) highlights that, over six centuries of use, *community* tends to signify a locale or locus of interaction and/or to mark some type of unity, commonality, sharing, or integration. Reflecting on this history, Raymond Williams (1983) famously noted that community is a "warmly persuasive word" and that "unlike all **other** terms of social organization (*state, nation, society,* etc.) it seems never to be used unfavourably, and never to be given any positive opposing or distinguishing term" (76, emphasis in original). Ferdindand Tönnies (1957) offered an influential account that contrasted *gemeinschaft* (translated as community, *gemein* in German meaning "common") with *gesellschaft* (translated as society). For Tönnies, family was the prototype of community, a form of social bonding that was fundamental, organic, intimate, and always positive. Brint (2001) argues that Tönnies's notion of community mistakenly aggregated features—concentration in space, holding common beliefs, participating in common activity, and frequency of interaction—that, when treated as independent variables, offer a more realistic taxonomy of multiple types of community. In writing studies, *community*—especially *discourse community*—became warmly persuasive at a critical juncture in the 1980s, as formation of the new discipline solidified but its initial cognitive emphasis was challenged by socially-oriented theories (Nystrand 2005).

John Swales (1988) recalls that, when he first heard the term *discourse community* in a 1986 talk by Lillian Bridwell-Bowles, he "adopted it immediately" (197). What makes a theoretical notion instantly adoptable? Bizzell (1982) apparently coined the term. Without explicit definition,

DOI: 10.7330/9780874219746.c006

she described discourse communities in terms of shared "discourse conventions," "habits of language use," "expectations," "ways of understanding experience," and patterns of "interaction with the material world" (217–218, 226). Between 1981 and 1983, some notion of literate communities was clearly in the air: David Bartholomae (1983), Charles Bazerman (1981), Shirley Brice Heath (1982), and Martin Nystrand (1982) all published texts that related the social contexts of writing/literacy to some notion of community. The intellectual grounds for such notions varied: Stanley Fish's (1980) interpretive communities, Michel Foucault's (1972) discourses, Dell Hymes' (1971) speech communities, Thomas Kuhn's (1962) paradigms, and Stephen Toulmin's (1972) argument fields. Yet each invocation of community seemed to challenge an authoritative unity like Standard **English**, good writing, logic, or disciplinary knowledge, offering instead fluid maps shaped by multiple, smaller communities. Tensions between different theoretical grounds were nevertheless visible. For example, in the textual debate between Swales (1988) and Bizzell (1992) about what constitutes a discourse community, Swales defines discourse communities as textually-mediated and offers criteria grounded in sociolinguistic concerns whereas Bizzell focuses on **ideology** and material practice.

As the notion of discourse community seemed poised to organize theory, research, and pedagogy for the socially-oriented writing studies of the late 1980s, critical views emerged. Swales (1988) had already noted problems of scale as *community* was applied to academic discourse, divisions like humanities and science, a particular discipline, a particular department, or even a particular classroom. Mary Louise Pratt suggested that linguistic and discursive communities—whether broad communities of national languages, the situated speech communities of sociolinguistics, or Fish's (1980) interpretive communities—were constructed on the nationalist model Benedict Anderson (1991) identified as *imagined communities*, "discrete, sovereign, fraternal—a linguistic utopia" (Pratt 1987, 50). She argued instead for a heterogeneous linguistics focused on language mixing and conflict in **contact zones**. Joseph Harris described discussions of discourse communities as "sweeping" but "vague," portraying communities as fuzzy, homogeneous "discursive utopias" (Harris 1989, 12). Marilyn Cooper (1989) noted that discourse communities are typically conceived as stable entities that govern individuals and events. She argued for seeing discourse communities instead as ways of being in the world, products of continual hermeneutic **work** in which varied values and practices intersected. It is instructive to note that the use of *community* in ecology has been troubled by strikingly

similar conundrums. Looijen and van Andel (1999) note that definition of an ecological community has proven elusive because different
theories of community co-exist in the literature, the notion is applied to
phenomena at wildly different scales, and community boundaries seem
relatively arbitrary.

In 1991, Jean Lave and Etienne Wenger addressed such critiques as
they offered another variant of community:

> In using the term community, we do not imply some primordial culture-
> sharing entity. We assume that members have different interests, make
> diverse contributions to activity, and hold varied viewpoints. In our view,
> participation at multiple levels is entailed in membership in a *community
> of practice.* Nor does the term community imply necessarily co-presence,
> a well-defined, identifiable group, or socially visible boundaries. It does
> imply participation in an activity system about which participants share
> understandings concerning what they are doing and what that means in
> their lives and for their communities. (Lave and Wenger 1991, 97–98,
> emphasis in original)

Anchored in practice, this notion of community seemed modest,
less idealized, less utopian, and more attuned to change, and it was
adopted by a number of writing researchers. For example, Patrick Dias
et al. (1999) adopted communities of practice as they contrasted literate worlds of school and work. However, it also met serious critiques.
After using the notion briefly in earlier work, Ron Scollon rejected it
and proposed an alternative: "The concept of the nexus of practice is
unbounded (unlike the more problematical community of practice)
and takes into account that at least most practices (ordering, purchasing, handing, and receiving) can be linked variably to different practices in different sites of engagement and among different participants"
(Scollon 2001, 5). Emphasizing interaction and co-presence in contrast
with Lave and Wenger's (1991) original formulation, Wenger (1998)
sought a tighter definition of *communities of practice* by focusing on three
characteristics: mutual engagement, an enterprise, and a shared repertoire. Vann and Bowker (2001) suggest that Lave proposed *communities
of practice* to critique schooling and psychological theories that rest on
notions of decontextualized skills, whereas Wenger used the term to
promote new capitalist work policies.

As 2000 approached, the notion of discourse communities continued to be refined, critiqued, and used in its earliest sense. Swales
(1998) distinguished *place discourse communities* (local groups involved
in some mutual project that brings about such things as shared lexis,

regular communicative **genres**, and recognized—though not necessarily consensual—senses of purpose and role) from *focus discourse communities* (not defined by mutual engagement, but consisting of individuals who co-participate in discursive practices with some purposeful focus even when separated by time, language, geography, and so on). Arguing that discourse community theory blended structuralist practices of abstraction and decontextualization with the folk model of communication known as the conduit metaphor, Prior (1998) pointed to dialogic and actor-**network** theories (Bakhtin 1981; Latour 1987; Voloshinov 1973) in proposing alternative notions of disciplinarity and functional systems (see also Cole and Engestrom 1993; Hutchins 1995). Yet, in the same period, Anne Beaufort (1997) articulated a strong notion of unified discourse communities that included both local sites (a particular non-profit **agency**) and large entities like businesses or the federal government. One new development in this period was the emerging focus on digital online communities (see Feenberg and Barney 2004).

Community has been deployed to do other important work in writing studies. In a field formed with a strong orientation to writing in school, *community* became a term in disciplinary boundary work to signify writing outside of school or outside of school and the workplace. David Barton and Roz Ivanič's 1991 collection served as an early announcement of this categorization; in his chapter, Barton emphasized the "everyday" character of ordinary writing and suggested three key domains: "home, school, and work" (Barton 1991, 1, 5). *Community* has come to signify writing that takes place in homes, churches, hobby groups, organizations, and other everyday activities outside of work and school (e.g., Fishman 1988; Grabill 2007; Heath 1982; Sheridan-Rabideau 2008).

Since 2000, the patterns of the first twenty years of uses of *community* in writing studies have continued. *Discourse communities, communities of practice*, and *virtual communities* are terms that have variously been critiqued, refined, and taken as givens. *Community* continues to name literate practices "outside" of schools and workplaces. In spite of pressures for tighter definition, when examples of discourse communities, communities of practices, or virtual communities are listed, they inevitably, if at different scales, seem to be named social entities (e.g., physics, company employees, a family, city government, the military, bikers, garage bands, Facebook friends, World of Warcraft players, etc.). In the typifications of our languages, communities appear to be warmly and persuasively always already there.

References

Anderson, Benedict. 1991. *Imagined Communities: Reflections on the Origin and Spread of Nationalism.* 2nd ed. London: Verso.

Bakhtin, Mikhail. 1981. *The Dialogic Imagination: Four Essays by M. M. Bakhtin,* ed. Michael Holquist, trans. Caryl Emerson and Michael Holquist. Austin: University of Texas Press.

Bartholomae, David. 1983. "Writing Assignments: Where Writing Begins." In *Forum: Essays on Theory and Practice in Writing,* ed. Patricia Stock, 300–311. Upper Montclair, NJ: Boynton/Cook.

Barton, David. 1991. "The Social Nature of Writing." In *Writing in the Community,* ed. David Barton and Roz Ivanič, 1–13. Newbury Park: Sage.

Barton, David, and Roz Ivanič, eds. 1991. *Writing in the Community.* Newbury Park: Sage.

Bazerman, Charles. 1981. "What Written Knowledge Does: Three Examples of Academic Discourse." *Philosophy of the Social Sciences* 11 (3): 361–87. http://dx.doi.org/10.1177/00483931101100305.

Beaufort, Anne. 1997. "Operationalizing the Concept of Discourse Community: A Case Study of One Institutional Site of Composing." *Research in the Teaching of English* 31 (4): 486–529.

Bizzell, Patricia. 1982. "Cognition, Convention, and Certainty: What We Need to Know about Writing." *PRE/TEXT* 3 (3): 213–243.

Bizzell, Patricia. 1992. *Academic Discourse and Critical Consciousness.* Pittsburgh: University of Pittsburgh Press.

Brint, Steven. 2001. "Gemeinschaft Revisited: A Critique and Reconstruction of the Community Concept." *Sociological Theory* 19 (1): 1–23. http://dx.doi.org/10.1111/0735-2751.00125.

Cole, Michael, and Yrjö Engestrom. 1993. "A Cultural-Historical Approach to Distributed Cognition." In *Distributed Cognition: Psychological and Educational Considerations,* ed. Gavriel Saloman, 1–46. Cambridge: Cambridge University Press.

Cooper, Marilyn. 1989. "Why Are We Talking about Discourse Communities? Or Functionalism Rears its Ugly Head Once More." In *Writing as Social Action,* ed. Mariyln Cooper and Michael Holzman, 202–20. Portsmouth: Boynton/Cook.

Dias, Patrick, Aviva Freedman, Peter Medway, and Anthony Pare. 1999. *Worlds Apart: Acting and Writing in Academic and Workplace Contexts.* Mahwah: Lawrence Erlbaum.

Feenberg, Andrew, and Darin Barney, eds. 2004. *Community in the Digital Age: Philosophy and Practice.* Lanham, MD: Rowman and Littlefield.

Fish, Stanley. 1980. *Is There a Text in This Class? The Authority of Interpretive Communities.* Cambridge: Harvard University Press.

Fishman, Andrea. 1988. *Amish Literacy: What and How it Means.* Portsmouth: Heinemann.

Foucault, Michel. 1972. *The Archaeology of Knowledge and the Discourse on Language.* Trans. A. M. Sheridan Smith. New York: Pantheon Books.

Grabill, Jeffrey. 2007. *Writing Community Change: Designing Technologies for Citizen Action.* Cresskill: Hampton Press.

Harris, Joseph. 1989. "The Idea of Community in the Study of Writing." *College Composition and Communication* 40 (1): 11–37. http://dx.doi.org/10.2307/358177.

Heath, Shirley Brice. 1982. "What No Bedtime Story Means: Narrative Skills at Home and School." *Language in Society* 11 (01): 49–76. http://dx.doi.org/10.1017/S0047404500009039.

Hutchins, Edwin. 1995. *Cognition in the Wild.* Cambridge: MIT Press.

Hymes, Dell. 1971. "Competence and Performance in Linguistic Theory." In *Language Acquisition: Models and Methods,* ed. Renira Huxley and Elisabeth Ingram, 3–28. London: Academic Press.

Kuhn, Thomas. 1962. *The Structure of Scientific Revolutions.* Chicago: University of Chicago Press.

Latour, Bruno. 1987. *Science in Action: How to Follow Scientists and Engineers through Society.* Cambridge: Harvard University Press.

Lave, Jean, and Etienne Wenger. 1991. *Situated Learning: Legitimate Peripheral Participation.* Cambridge, UK: Cambridge University Press. http://dx.doi.org/10.1017/CBO978 0511815355.

Looijen, Rick, and Jelte van Andel. 1999. "Ecological Communities: Conceptual Problems and Definitions." *Perspectives in Plant Ecology, Evolution and Systematics* 2 (2): 210–22. http://dx.doi.org/10.1078/1433-8319-00071.

Nystrand, Martin. 1982. "Rhetoric's 'Audience' and Linguistics' 'Speech Community': Implications for Understanding Writing, Reading and Text." In *What Writers Know: The Language, Process, and Structure of Written Discourse,* ed. Martin Nystrand, 1–28. New York: Academic Press.

Nystrand, Martin. 2005. *The Social and Historical Context for Writing Research. Handbook of Writing Research.* Ed. Charles MacArthur, Steve Graham, and Jill Fitzgerald, 11–27. New York: Guilford.

Oxford English Dictionary. 2012. Oxford: Oxford University Press.

Pratt, Mary Louise. 1987. "Linguistic Utopias." In *The Linguistics of Writing: Arguments between Language and Literature,* ed. Nigel Fabb, Derek Attridge, Alan Durant, and Colin McCabe, 48–66. New York: Methuen.

Prior, Paul. 1998. *Writing/Disciplinarity: A Sociohistoric Account of Literate Activity in the Academy.* Mahwah, NJ: Erlbaum.

Scollon, Ron. 2001. *Mediated Discourse: The Nexus of Practice.* London: Routledge.

Sheridan-Rabideau, Mary. 2008. *Girls, Feminism, and Grassroots Literacies.* Albany: State University of New York Press.

Star, Susan Leigh, and James Griesemer. 1989. "Institutional Ecology, 'Translations' and Boundary Objects: Amateurs and Professionals in Berkeley's Museum of Vertebrate Zoology, 1907–1939." *Social Studies of Science* 19 (3): 387–420. http://dx.doi.org /10.1177/030631289019003001.

Swales, John. 1988. "Discourse Communities, Genres, and English as an International Language." *World Englishes* 7 (2): 211–20. http://dx.doi.org/10.1111/j.1467-971X .1988.tb00232.x.

Swales, John. 1998. *Other Floors, Other Voices: A Textography of a Small University Building.* Mahwah, NJ: Lawrence Erlbaum.

Tönnies, Ferndinand. 1957. *Community and Society (Gemeinschaft and Gesellschaft).* Ed. and trans. Charles Loomis. East Lansing: Michigan State University Press.

Toulmin, Stephen. 1972. *Human Understanding.* Princeton, NJ: Princeton University Press.

Vann, Katie, and Geoff Bowker. 2001. "Instrumentalizing the Truth of Practice." *Social Epistemology* 15 (3): 247–62. http://dx.doi.org/10.1080/02691720110076567.

Voloshinov, Valentin. 1973. *Marxisim and the Philosophy of Language.* Trans. L. Matejka and I. R. Titunik. Cambridge: Harvard University Press.

Wenger, Etienne. 1998. *Communities of Practice: Learning, Meaning, and Identity.* Cambridge: Cambridge University Press.

Williams, Raymond. 1983. *Keywords: A Vocabulary of Culture and Society,* revised edition. New York: Oxford University Press.

COMPUTER

Cynthia L. Selfe

In writing studies, computers have been understood both as machines that help us compute *and* machines that help us communicate, fundamentally different conceptions that have shaped our deployment of these devices within writing classrooms. Computers and US composition instruction grew up together in the cultural milieu of the mid-twentieth century and the Second World War, inflected by a set of common cultural values and formations—a modernist belief in science and its link to progress, an ideologically informed commitment to education, and a belief in individual accomplishment—that have assured and shaped a complicated set of ongoing relationships. Some humanists, language scholars, and writing scholars have always mistrusted computers—considering these machines dehumanizing influences (Selfe 1999). Many have also understood computers, almost since their inception, as tools that can aid scholars in the study and the **production** of language and meaning or as environments that can point the way toward emergent and creative language practices. Similarly, while we have also always projected onto computers some version of our own professional understanding of what it means to study language use, teach writing, and compose meaning, we have also looked to computers and their rapidly changing features for glimpses of new possibilities for writing instruction and the composition of meaning.

In the 1950s and 1960s, historical phenomena such as the post-WWII arms and space races, the Cold War, and the launch of Sputnik helped fuel and inflect the invention of early programmable computers like the Harvard Mark 1 by Howard Aiken and Grace Hopper. Within this ideological context, the field of **English** studies worked to apply the objectivity and tools of technological progress to the study of language and translation. In linguistics, for instance, an important goal was to use advanced approaches in mathematics to pursue accurate, machine-based translations from one language to another (a pursuit which had its roots in military projects), developing, as Noam Chomsky observed,

DOI: 10.7330/9780874219746.c007

an "understanding of how a language can (in Humboldt's words) 'make infinite use of finite means'" (Chomsky 1965, 8). Language scholars thus came to understand mainframe computers as powerful tools for analyzing the language features of large-scale corpuses, efforts which led to the formation of computational linguistics as a field and to the invention of mainframe-based tools for parsing grammar, creating concordances, conducting stylistic analysis, and machine translating. As a result of this **work**, by 1967, Walter Ong could write in a lead *PMLA* article, "The computer has opened whole new fields of humanistic research . . . we can welcome" (Ong 1967, 6). One important goal growing out of these early efforts was the development of computer-based analysis and essay scoring, a goal pursued by the Educational Testing Service (Shermis and Burstein 2003) that continues to influence writing studies today.

Our profession's understanding of the word *computer*—and indeed our larger cultural understanding—began to change dramatically during the late 1960s and 1970s, in light of the rapid innovations in the production of microprocessors and smaller workstations. *Computer*—in addition to referring to large-mainframe machines—began appearing with the prefix "micro" attached to it or modified by the adjective *personal*, in reference to small-scale, desktop machines that could be purchased and used flexibly by families and individuals. In writing studies, when computers became commercial products available to individuals, rather than limited to organizations, institutions, and research groups, increasing numbers of teachers and students of composition recognized and embraced them as sophisticated tools of language instruction, production, and circulation.

Software development in the 1980s—which included What-You-See-Is-What-You-Get (WYSIWYG) page-layout programs like Pagemaker in 1985, multi-featured word processing programs such as Microsoft Word released in 1983, early versions of Photoshop first released in 1989, as well as line art (MacPaint) and vector art (Illustrator) programs released in 1984 and 1986, respectively—also changed what *computer* meant and could mean. These software packages, with increasing sophistication, allowed for the reproduction of art elements as well as alphabetic text in student compositions. Along with early hypertext programs such as Hypercard in 1987 and, in the 1990s, the opening of the World Wide Web and the introduction of web-editing software like Dreamweaver, composition teachers and students came to understand *computer* to signify creative composing environments within which they could render words and images, and later video and audio elements, in richly textured multimedia (Hocks 1998; Wysocki 2001) and hypertextual compositions (Coover 1992; Joyce 1987).

Despite these developments, the term *computer* marked a site of contestation. Some scholars argued both that computers themselves were dangerous to the core values of humanism (Birkerts 1994) and that the values commonly associated with computer deployment in the academy—especially the desire for automation and the pursuit of efficiencies—clashed with "some of our basic beliefs about the nature of classroom instruction, in all its communal richness and face-to-face complexity" (Anson 1999, 263). **Other** scholars found in computers productive opportunities to enact critical pedagogies (see Blair, Gajjala, and Tulley 2008; DeVoss, Cushman, and Grabill 2005; Hawisher and Selfe 1999; LeCourt 1998; and Sullivan and Porter 1997). As LeCourt (1998) noted, "Computer Mediated Communication (CMC) and hypertext . . . can support (a) a critical examination of how discursive contexts position authors in potentially oppressive ways, and (b) help highlight how discursive **agency** might be constructed so that students might see their cultural difference as potential for intervening into ideology" (275).

These educational arguments notwithstanding, writers inside and outside the academy have moved much of their own self-sponsored composing online and into computer-based environments that support multimedia composing, such as public repositories for vernacular video (YouTube), photography (Flickr), and audio texts (Napster and its descendants), as well as Twitter, Facebook, and blogs/vlogs. For many individuals, computers (and their integrated systems of telecommunication) have become the primary semiotic environments for making and circulating meaning, much as envisioned by two early pioneers in the field of information **technology**—Vannevar Bush and Theodor Nelson—who understood computers not *only* as tools for scientists, but rather as vehicles for extending the thinking and communicative capacity of *all* humans. Vannevar Bush, for example, in his 1945 publication "As We May Think," predicted modern computers by describing the "memex" as an electronic personal device for saving, storing, analyzing, and circulating knowledge that was characterized by "exceeding speed and flexibility," one that provided an "enlarged intimate supplement" to human memory (Bush 1945, 6). Similarly, Theodor Nelson gave a glimpse of the modern Internet by describing the power of a web-like structure of "all embracing data" connecting information in a "cats'-cradle of linkages" (Nelson 1974, x).

The idea that computers were social devices that could support the productivity, **creativity**, and connectivity of all writers continued to develop during the last decades of the twentieth century and the first decades of the twenty-first. Of late, scholars in writing studies have come to understand *computer* to reference not only powerful tools that (1) support the digitization of humanities resources like archives and online presses (Fitzpatrick 2011; Skinnell 2010), (2) foster language learning in diverse populations (Liu et al. 2003; MacArthur and Cavalier 2004), (3) support richly embroidered **networks** of transnational communicative exchange (Berry, Hawisher, and Selfe 2012), and (4) offer new approaches to rhetorical invention and insight (Delagrange 2011), but also—importantly—machines that reflect the existing cultural divisions around race, **class**, **gender**, accessibility, and geography (Grabill 2003; Haas 2012; Yergeau et al. forthcoming); the products of a consumerist, throw-away culture (Apostle and Apostle 2009); and devices that pose serious ethical challenges to conventional concepts of intellectual property, originality, and authorship (Johnson-Eilola and Selber 2007).

Andersen et al. (1993) asserted that "Computers . . . are sign-producing machines, semiotic systems, semiotic technologies" (2). As writing studies continues to evolve, then, we can only expect the meanings of *computer* to expand as well.

References

Andersen, Peter Bøgh, Berit Holmqvist, Jens F. Berit, and Jens F. Jensen. 1993. *The Computer as Medium.* Cambridge: Cambridge University Press.

Anson, Chris. 1999. "Distant Voices: Teaching and Writing in a Culture of Technology." *College English* 61 (3): 261–80. http://dx.doi.org/10.2307/379069.

Apostle, Shawn, and Kristi Apostle. 2009. "Old World Successes and New World Challenges: Reducing the Computer Waste Stream in America." In *Technological Ecologies and Sustainability*, ed. D. DeVoss, H. McKee, and R. Selfe. Logan: Computers and Composition Digital Press/Utah State University Press.

Berry, Patrick W., Gail E. Hawisher, and Cynthia L. Selfe. 2012. *Transnational Literate Lives in Digital Times.* Logan, UT: Computers and Composition Digital Press/Utah State University Press.

Birkerts, Sven. 1994. *The Gutenberg Elegies: The Fate of Reading in an Electronic Age.* Boston: Faber and Faber.

Blair, Kristine, Radhika Gajjala, and Kristine Tulley. 2008. *Webbing Cyberfeminist Practice: Communities, Pedagogies, and Social Action.* NY: Hampton Press.

Bush, Vannevar. 1945. "As We May Think." *The Atlantic Monthly,* July: 101–108.

Chomsky, Noam. 1965. *Aspects of the Theory of Syntax.* Cambridge: MIT.

Coover, Robert. 1992. "The End of Books." *New York Times Book Review* (1): 8–12.

DeVoss, Dànielle, Ellen Cushman, and Jeffrey T. Grabill. 2005. "Infrastruction and Composing: The When of New Media Writing." *College Composition and Communication* 57 (1): 14–44.

Delagrange, Susan. 2011. *Technologies of Wonder: Rhetorical Practice in a Digital World.* Logan: Computers and Composition Digital Press/Utah State.

Fitzpatrick, Kathleen. 2011. *Planned Obsolescence: Publishing, Technology, and the Future of the Academy.* New York: NYU Press.

Grabill, Jeffrey. 2003. "On Divides and Interfaces: Access, Class, and Computers." *Computers and Composition* 20 (4): 455–72. http://dx.doi.org/10.1016/j.compcom.2003.08.017.

Haas, Angela. 2012. "Race, Rhetoric, and Technology: A Case Study of Decolonial Technical Communication Theory, Methodology, and Pedagogy." *Journal of Business and Technical Communication* 26 (3): 277–310. http://dx.doi.org/10.1177/10506519 12439539.

Hawisher, Gail E., and Cynthia L. Selfe. 1999. *Passions, Pedagogies, and 21st Century Technologies*. Logan: Utah State University Press.

Hocks, Mary. 1998. "'Building a Writing-Intensive Multimedia Curriculum,' with Daniele Bascelli." In *Electronic Communication Across the Curriculum*, ed. Richard J. Selfe, Donna Reiss, and Art Young, 40–56. Urbana, IL: National Council of Teachers of English.

Johnson-Eilola, Johndan, and Stuart A. Selber. 2007. "Plagiarism, Originality, Assemblage." *Computers and Composition* 24 (4): 375–403. http://dx.doi.org/10.1016 /j.compcom.2007.08.003.

Joyce, Michael. 1987. *afternoon, a story*. Watertown, MA: Eastgate.

LeCourt, Donna. 1998. "Critical Pedagogy in the Computer Classroom: Politicizing the Writing Space." *Computers and Composition* 15 (3): 275–95. http://dx.doi.org/10 .1016/S8755-4615(98)90002-0.

Liu, Min, Zena Moore, Leah Graham, and Shinwoong Lee. 2003. "A Look at Computer-Based Technology Use in Second Language Learning: A Review of the Literature from 1990–2000." *Journal of Research on Technology in Education* 34 (3): 250–73. http://dx.doi.org/10.1080/15391523.2002.10782348.

MacArthur, Charles, and Albert R. Cavalier. 2004. "Dictation and Speech Recognition Technology as Test Accommodations." *Exceptional Children* 71 (1): 43–58. http://dx.doi.org/10.1177/001440290407100103.

Nelson, Theodor. 1974. *Literary Machines: The Report on, and of, Project Xanadu Concerning Word Processing, Electronic Publishing, Hypertext, Thinkertoys, Tomorrow's Intellectual Revolution, and Certain Other Topics Including Knowledge, Education, and Freedom.* Sausalito, California: Mindful Press.

Ong, Walter J. 1967. "The Expanding Humanities and the Individual Scholar." *PMLA* 82 (4): 1–7. http://dx.doi.org/10.2307/1261204.

Selfe, Cynthia L. 1999. "Technology and Literacy: A Story about the Perils of Not Paying Attention." *College Composition and Communication* 50 (3): 411–36.

Shermis, Mark D., and Jill Burstein, eds. 2003. *Automated Essay Scoring: A Cross-Disciplinary Perspective*. Mahwah, NJ: Lawrence Erlebaum.

Skinnell, Ryan. 2010. "Circuitry in Motion: Rhetoric(al) Moves in YouTube's Archive." *Enculturation* 8. http://www.enculturation.net/circuitry-in-motion.

Sullivan, Patricia, and James E. Porter. 1997. *Opening Spaces: Writing Technologies and Critical Research Practices*. Westport, CT: Greenwood.

Wysocki, Anne F. 2001. "Impossibly Distinct: On Form/Content and Word/Image in Two Pieces of Computer-Based Interactive Multimedia." *Computers and Composition* 18 (2): 137–62. http://dx.doi.org/10.1016/S8755-4615(01)00053-6.

Yergeau, Melanie, Elizabeth Brewer, Stephanie Kerschbaum, Sushil Oswal, Margaret Price, Michael Salvo, Cynthia Selfe, and Franny Howes. "Multimodality in Motion: Disability and Kairotic Spaces." *Kairos: A Journal of Rhetoric, Technology, and Pedagogy* 18.1 (Fall 2013). http://kairos.technorhetoric.net/18.1/coverweb/yergeau-et-al/index.html.

CONTACT ZONE

Cynthia Fields

Mary Louise Pratt introduced the term *contact zone* to writing studies in 1991, defining contact zones as "social spaces where cultures meet, clash, and grapple with each other, often in contexts of highly asymmetrical relations of power, such as colonialism, slavery, or their aftermaths as they are lived out in many parts of the world today" (Pratt 1991, 34). Pratt also associated various "literate arts" with the contact zone, including "autoethnography, transculturation, parody, denunciation, imaginary dialogue, [and] vernacular expression." However, Pratt noted, the "perils" of writing in the contact zone include "miscomprehension, incomprehension, dead letters, unread masterpieces, [and] absolute heterogeneity of meaning" (37).

Contact zones have been imagined as "a cluster of symbolic and material spaces" (Mullen 2005, 22), "spatial, temporal locations" (Singh and Doherty 2004, 11), "intensely contested political and cultural space[s]," and "physical and imagined terrains of concurrent colonial appropriation and negation" (Negash 2009, 76, 79). The term seems to embody a dual ethos of danger and opportunity, suggesting that contact zones are "uneven terrain" (Yeoh and Willis 2005, 282): "transformative, generative, and disruptive" (West 1996, 147); "potentially powerful" (Miller 1994, 407); "oppositional" and "slantwise" (Ingberg 1995, 601); and "challenging" and "destabilizing" (Chidester 2008, 64). Contact zones have thus been portrayed as "unsolicited **discourse**" (Ingberg 1995, 601) that resists the "temptation either to **silence** or to celebrate the voices that seek to oppose, critique and/or parody" (Miller 1994, 407), and as a "game" from which "no one [is] excluded, and no one [is] safe" (Pratt 1991, 38–39).

Scholars have theorized contact zones as sites facilitating conflicts, movement, and understanding, and as sites of "struggle" (Miller 1994, 391) for "negotiating difference" (Bizzell 1994, 168) and analyzing "everyday encounters and everyday experiences of sameness and difference" (Yeoh and Willis 2005, 271). The "transient" nature (Yeoh and

DOI: 10.7330/9780874219746.c008

Willis 2005, 282) of contact zones produce "cross-fertilization and dialogue" (Khanmohamadi 2010, 177), "boundary crossing" (Manathunga 2009, 169), "cultural negotiation" (Taylor 2010, 38), "intercultural import-export" (Singh and Doherty 2004, 12), and "mutual resistances and subversions" (Coldiron 2004, 214). Contact zones are also a mode for increased comprehension: a heuristic (West 1996, 145) for interpreting "a mutual entanglement of cultural practices and modes of representing cultural **identity** with disputes and struggles over interpretative power" (Singh and Doherty 2004, 12).

The term *contact zone* has thus come to signify widely across writing studies and related fields; it is used to describe a broad range of discursive contexts: the "**public** space," the "political public sphere," and the "electronic public sphere (Canagarajah 1997, 179, 129, 134); the "public sphere of early print" (Coldiron 2004, 208); the "globalizing city" (Yeoh and Willis 2005, 270); the meeting of "lesbian/gay and straight culture" (Peele and Ryder 2003, 7); travel writing (Pratt 1991); tourism (Picard 2007; Richards 2005); sacred music (Vázquez 2004, 195); foreign languages (West 1996, 151); religions (Chidester 2008, 36); the Bible (Dallas and Marwitz 2003, 439); national borders (Mendoza 1994; Ram 2007, 63; Taylor 2010, 26); interspecies interaction (Whitlock 2010, 472); and science fiction, in which contact zones operate in the "collectively imagined future, a symbolic space where utopia, Armageddon, and other powerful scenarios compete" (Attebery 2005, 385).

Within the **context** of education, *contact zone* has been deployed to discuss the academy itself (Canagarajah 1997, 184), **research** (Manathunga 2009, 165), English studies in general (Bizzell 1994, 164), **English** as a second language in particular (Singh and Doherty 2004, 12), international students in the "global university" (Singh and Doherty 2004, 9), national conferences (Miller 1994, 391), writing centers (Brice 1996, 2), and peer response writing groups (Rios 2005, 33). Invoking the English classroom as a contact zone has been used as a basis for curricular decisions, as "a way of organizing literary study" (Bizzell 1994, 164), and especially as "a rationale for integrating English studies multiculturally" (167) through the "juxtaposition of canonical and noncanonical" literature and discourses (Munn 1995, 601) and "diverse *world* literatures" (van Slyck 1997, 154, emphasis in original). Miller argues that the "central activity" of the classroom as contact zone is "investigating the range of literate practices available to those within asymmetrical power relationships" (Miller 1994, 399). For Pratt, teaching practices in a contact zone classroom could include exercises in storytelling and in identifying with the ideas, interests, histories, and attitudes of others; experiments in transculturation and collaborative work and in the arts of critique, parody, and comparison (including unseemly comparisons between elite and vernacular forms); the redemption of the oral; ways for people to engage with suppressed aspects of history (including their own histories); ways to move *into and out of* rhetorics of authenticity; ground rules for communication across lines of difference and hierarchy that go beyond politeness but maintain mutual respect; [and] a systematic approach to the all-important concept of *cultural mediation.* (Pratt 1991, 33, emphasis in original)

In composition studies, *contact zone* has frequently been associated with efforts to improve students' reflection and critical consciousness. Contact zones are thus construed as places "where students of different cultures, attitudes, and values meet to interact," to continually "reflect on their own reading, writing, and interpretive practices" (West 1996, 144, 145) in order to discern "layers of meaning" (Mullen 2005, 22) in the "colliding voices" (Lu 1994, 448), and to discover how their choices "are limited by the normalizing and marginalizing effects of discursive formations" (West 1996, 147). The contact zone classroom thus constitutes a site of *epistemological* struggle, a "social space where the culture of authority differ[s] from what they [students] had been given as the truth about themselves and the world" (Dallas and Marwitz 2003, 439). The "antagonistic epistemology" (West 1996, 146) of a contact zone classroom can thus threaten the "identity of these students and their sense of **community** solidarity" (Canagarajah 1997, 179).

Nonetheless, contact zones are also understood as opportunities for empowering students to resist dominant discourses. Scholars suggest that students can act "as agents *of* the contact zone" to "communicate across lines of difference" (Burns 1999, 139) and explore "how a subordinate group should represent itself to a dominant group" (Peele and Ryder 2003, 7). Maxson likewise argues that contact zone pedagogy "should induce students to draw on resources from their home languages and cultures, combining these with resources from school languages and cultures, to perform a critique of the latter" (Maxson 2005, 25). Despite its apparent potential to radically refigure educational spaces, contact zone pedagogy also has been critiqued as potentially "normative" with a "homogenizing effect" (Ingberg 1995, 600), as a "New Hegemony in English studies" (Munn 1995, 227), as "intellectual slumming" that produces "hyperconformity" (Miller 1994, 399, 396), and as "allow[ing] most faculty to go on functionally doing what they have always been doing, albeit now with the added glamour of being 'political'" (Mullen 2005, 21). The contact zone classroom, in fact, may be tame in its transformative effects. For instance, Miller argues it may merely be a "contestatory space where the vertiginous possibilities of the multivalent, multivocal text become at least a momentary reality in the hands of a loosely federate, heterogeneous group with widely divergent reading abilities and political commitments" (Miller 1994, 402).

Finally, and not surprisingly, contact zones are frequently represented as emotionally volatile spaces, as places where things happen with "unpredictability and novelty" (Khanmohamadi 2010, 186). As Pratt puts it, "[a]long with rage, incomprehension, and pain there [are] exhilarating moments of wonder and revelation, mutual understanding, and new wisdom—the joys of the contact zone" (Pratt 1991, 39). As writing studies extends its reach, scholars will surely encounter additional contact zones—additional powerful, unpredictable, and even precarious opportunities for discovery.

References

Attebery, Brian. 2005. "Aboriginality in Science Fiction." *Science Fiction Studies* 32 (3): 385–405.

Bizzell, Patricia. 1994. "'Contact Zones' and English Studies." *College English* 56 (2): 163–69. http://dx.doi.org/10.2307/378727.

Brice, Jennifer. 1996. "Northern Realities, Northern Literacies: The Writing Center in the 'Contact Zone.'" *Writing Lab Newsletter* 20 (8): 1–4.

Burns, Philip J. 1999. "Supporting Deliberative Democracy: Pedagogical Arts of the Contact Zone of the Electronic Public Sphere." *Rhetoric Review* 18 (1): 128–46. http://dx.doi.org/10.1080/07350199909359260.

Canagarajah, A. Suresh. 1997. "Safe Houses in the Contact Zone: Coping Strategies of African-American Students in the Academy." *College Composition and Communication* 48 (2): 173–96. http://dx.doi.org/10.2307/358665.

Chidester, David. 2008. "Dreaming in the Contact Zone: Zulu Dreams, Visions, and Religion in Nineteenth-Century South Africa." *Journal of the American Academy of Religion* 76 (1): 27–53. http://dx.doi.org/10.1093/jaarel/lfm094.

Coldiron, A. E. B. 2004. "Public Sphere/Contact Zone: Habermas, Early Print, and Verse Translation." *Criticism: A Quarterly for Literature and the Arts* 46 (2): 207–22. http://dx.doi.org/10.1353/crt.2004.0040.

Dallas, Phyllis Surrency, and Mary Marwitz. 2003. "Community or Contact Zone? Deconstructing an Honors Classroom." *Pedagogy* 3 (3): 435–40. http://dx.doi.org/10.1215/15314200-3-3-435.

Ingberg, Alfhild. 1995. "A Comment on 'Contact Zones' and English Studies." *College English* 57 (5): 599–602. http://dx.doi.org/10.2307/378833.

Khanmohamadi, Shirin. 2010. "Casting a 'Sideways Glance' at the Crusades: The Voice of the Other in Joinville's *Vie de Saint Louis*." *Exemplaria* 22 (3): 177–99. http://dx.doi.org/10.1179/104125710X12670930868252.

Lu, Min-zhan. 1994. "Professing Multiculturalism: The Politics of Style in the Contact Zone." *College Composition and Communication* 45 (4): 442–58.

Manathunga, Catherine. 2009. "Research as an Intercultural 'Contact Zone.'" *Discourse (Abingdon)* 30 (2): 165–77. http://dx.doi.org/10.1080/01596300902809161.

Maxson, Jeffrey. 2005. "Government of da Peeps, for da Peeps, and by da Peeps: Revisiting the Contact Zone." *Journal of Basic Writing* 24 (1): 24–47.

Mendoza, Louis. 1994. "The Border between Us: Contact Zone or Battle Zone?" *MFS: Modern Fiction Studies* 40 (1): 119–39.

Miller, Richard E. 1994. "Fault Lines in the Contact Zone." *College English* 56 (4): 389–408. http://dx.doi.org/10.2307/378334.

Mullen, Mark. 2005. "Cultural Studies, Composition, and Pedagogy." *CLCWeb: Comparative Literature and Culture* 7 (3): 19–27.

Munn, Paul. 1995. "A Comment on 'Contact Zones' and English Studies." *College English* 57 (2): 226–27. http://dx.doi.org/10.2307/378819.

Negash, Ghirmai. 2009. "Native Intellectuals in the Contact Zone: African Responses to Italian Colonialism in Tigrinya Literature." *Biography: An Interdisciplinary Quarterly* 32 (1): 74–88. http://dx.doi.org/10.1353/bio.0.0075.

Richards, Sandra L. 2005. "What Is to Be Remembered?: Tourism to Ghana's Slave Castle-Dungeons." *Theatre Journal* 57 (4): 617–37. http://dx.doi.org/10.1353/tj.2006.0044.

Peele, Thomas, and Mary Ellen Ryder. 2003. "Belief Spaces and the Resistant Writer: Queer Space in the Contact Zone." *Journal of Basic Writing* 22 (2): 27–46.

Picard, David. 2007. "Friction in a Tourism Contact Zone: Ethnographic Field Notes from a Malagasy Village." *Suomen Antropologi/Antropologi i Finland/The Journal of the Finnish Anthropological Society* 32 (2): 96–109.

Pratt, Mary Louise. 1991. "Arts of the Contact Zone." *Profession* 91: 33–40.

Ram, Harsha. 2007. "Towards a Cross-Cultural Poetics of the Contact Zone: Romantic, Modernist, and Soviet Intertextualities in Boris Pasternak's Translations of T'itsian T'abidze." *Comparative Literature* 59 (1): 63–89. http://dx.doi.org/10.1215/-59-1-63.

Rios, Lori Smith. 2005. "Making Contact Zones Matter in the Composition Classroom: Grappling to Negotiate Understanding in Peer-Response Groups." *EAPSU Online: A Journal of Critical and Creative Work* 2: 33–42.

Singh, Parlo, and Catherine Doherty. 2004. "Global Cultural Flows and Pedagogic Dilemmas: Teaching in the Global University Contact Zone." *TESOL Quarterly* 38 (1): 9–42. http://dx.doi.org/10.2307/3588257.

Taylor, Christopher. 2010. "North America as Contact Zone: Native American Literary Nationalism and the Cross-Cultural Dilemma." *Studies in American Indian Literatures: The Journal of the Association for the Study of American Indian Literatures* 22 (3): 26–44. http://dx.doi.org/10.1353/ail.2010.0015.

van Slyck, Phyllis. 1997. "Repositioning Ourselves in the Contact Zone." *College English* 59 (2): 149–70. http://dx.doi.org/10.2307/378546.

Vázquez, Louis. 2004. "Go and Make Disciples: An Analysis of the *Salsa Evangélica* Movement in Puerto Rico." *Centro Journal* 16 (2): 195–225.

West, Thomas. 1996. "Beyond Dissensus: Exploring the Heuristic Value of Conflict." *Rhetoric Review* 15 (1): 142–55. http://dx.doi.org/10.1080/07350199609359211.

Whitlock, Gillian. 2010. "Remediating Gorilla Girl: Rape Warfare and the Limits of Humanitarian Storytelling." *Biography: An Interdisciplinary Quarterly* 33 (3): 471–97. http://dx.doi.org/10.1353/bio.2010.0994.

Yeoh, Brenda S. A., and Katie Willis. 2005. "Singaporean and British Transmigrants in China and the Cultural Politics of 'Contact Zones.'" *Journal of Ethnic and Migration Studies* 31 (2): 269–85. http://dx.doi.org/10.1080/1369183042000339927.

CONTEXT

Jason Swarts

Context can be understood as "the words and sentences that surround any part of **discourse** and help to determine its meaning; also, the rhetorical situation and background of an issue that help to determine the meaning of any text" (Crowley and Hawhee 1999, 430). The multiplicity of this definition points to a range of ways that the term *context* has been used in writing studies to talk about settings of **work** and learning.

Often, *context* is used synonymously with *rhetorical situation*, because, like contexts, Gerard Hauser notes, we intuitively understand situations to have meaningful "spatio-temporal" qualities that shape how we utilize discourse to bring about an effect in the world (Hauser 2002, 42–44). This is true for oral discourse as well as print, where contexts and rhetorical situations combine as "rhetorical contexts," the **locations** of "appropriate interpersonal and intertextual relationships" (Hyland 1998, 438; Odell 1986). Rhetorical context is a "consequence of **literacy**," the development of "context-free" language (Ong 2002, 76). Yet, given the oral origins of rhetoric, Lloyd Bitzer (1968) and Richard Vatz (1973) provide reasons not to conflate these concepts.

Definitions of context that incorporate the notion of a rhetorical situation implicitly reference Bitzer's tripartite construction of the rhetorical situation: exigence, audience, and constraints (Bitzer 1968, 8). The glue holding these ideas together stems from a writer's tendency to understand rhetorical situations as problems to be solved by discourse, problems that entail coordinating events, objects, and people that could very well be materially as well as textually real (Hauser 2002, 42–43). Bitzer did not equate "meaning context" with context, "social context," or "historical context" (Bitzer 1968, 3). Instead, he defined *context* as an arrangement of elements, a reality in which a rhetorical act does work "not by the direct application of energy to objects, but by the creation of discourse which changes reality through the mediation of thought and action" (3). While Bitzer claims the constraints of context are "objective and observable" (3), critics like (Vatz 1973) disagree, noting that such a

DOI: 10.7330/9780874219746.c009

claim means that a rhetorical situation grounded in a context is always "real or genuine—that our critical examination will certify its existence." Contexts are more complex, and "it is hard to see how [their] 'existence' can be certified" (155). The situation does not precede rhetoric, but is instead constructed by it.

I. A. Richards' work motivates still **other** uses of context, underpinned by a commitment to a broader understanding of context as "a whole cluster of events that occur together" (Bizzell and Herzberg 2001, 978), a reading that points to the meaning context of a word and its historical context while moving beyond either as solely determining meaning. Richards' definition addresses the material complexity of context, which Valentin Voloshinov argues accounts for an attendant rhetorical complexity, noting that while the "multiplicity of meanings is the constitutive feature of word," its meaning "is inseparable from the concrete situation of its implementation" (Voloshinov 1986, 101). This characteristic of context is central to the influential notion of an "utterance," which Mikhail Bakhtin says is the basis of language: "language is realized in the form of concrete utterances (oral and written) by participants in the various areas of human activity. These utterances reflect the specific conditions and goals of each such area" (Bakhtin 1986, 60), meaning that the context of interpretation includes both awareness of form and conditions influencing its "uptake," the relationships and actions established through an utterance (Freadman 2002, 40).

The range of contexts addressed within writing studies is broad, including medical (Barton and Eggly 2009; Mirel et al. 2008), financial (Devitt 1991; Smart 1999), and engineering (Bucciarelli 1996; Selzer 1983; Winsor 1996). Most uses of *context* refer to a complex account of the symbolic, historical, and social contexts of meaning. As Colomb and Williams (1986) note, context refers to "not just physical text but also the human context in which the text functions," to a "complex web of intentions" that the writer and reader bring (87). Expanding this general definition, Berkenkotter, Huckin, and Ackerman (1988) define context as a social and symbolic space shaped by the "conventions and conversations [of a] discourse **community**" (10), conventions and conversations that solidify and stabilize as they become "institutional and historical" (Berkenkotter and Ravotas 1997, 256) and instantiated in artifacts associated with those contexts (Berkenkotter 2001). Collectively, these artifacts form "material contexts" that may be "fleeting or durable" but that always mediate how one perceives a task (Prior and Shipka 2003). Increasingly, these contexts are thought of as complex and distributed, overflowing across material and virtual space, across texts, people, interfaces, and other objects (Johnson-Eilola 2005, 59–88). We experience these overflows as "laminated" (Prior and Shipka 2003).

Contexts are also invoked as frames of action that describe the materials appearing with a text. These materials include other symbolic content or machines and the people to whom words are addressed. Context in this sense is an ontological construct. Contexts as frames of meaning are epistemological constructs that point to motives that are never discrete but always hybrid. Conceptually, Bakhtin argues that contexts are "populated . . . with the intentions of others" (Bakhtin 1982, 294, 304), which are sometimes literally written onto the interfaces through which people encounter and navigate space.

Some research in **technical communication** draws upon sociology and cognitive science (e.g., Goodwin and Goodwin 1996; Hutchins 1995) to describe contexts as bounded systems or **networks** of people, events, and objects that interrelate and coordinate around activities that are at once independent while also coordinated and shaped by shared values and modes of thinking. Contexts, as systems, are "structures [that] shape the way writers and readers cope in organizations" (Schryer et al. 2003, 69). Dorothy Winsor describes such contexts as created, "distributed," and maintained through communication tools, which are "the essential means by which [a] system function[s] and . . . [are] the essential means by which [writers] could be plugged into the network" (Winsor 2001, 25).

Similarly, contexts are sometimes treated as ecologies, similar to systems and networks but less rigidly bounded and stable. In an **ecology**, the focus is on the "system of people, practices, values, and technologies in a particular local environment" (Nardi and O'Day 2000, 49; see also Cooper 1986, 369–370) that is contingent and subject to reframing through a shifting lens of values. Instead of seeing context as given or stable, an ecological perspective emphasizes embodiment in a living, evolving situation made up of "interrelated group[s] of **genres** (artifact types and the interpretive habits that have developed around them) used to jointly mediate the activities that allow people to accomplish complex objectives" (Spinuzzi and Zachry 2000, 172).

Other formulations of context emphasize still greater indeterminacy and fluidity. In various places, contexts are described as flows in which "neither boundaries nor relations mark the difference between one place and another. Instead, sometimes boundaries come and go, allow leakage or disappear altogether, while relations transform themselves without fracture" (Mol and Law 1994, 643). A single context might be the meeting place for multiple contexts of rhetorical action, a place where systems or networks of actors meet and "enact" an object of concern (Mol 2002, 32–33). These enactments may have affinities or they may contradict; however, one does not cancel another so much as they bleed together. More recent research on context has started to examine how mobile technologies influence perceptions of where and how contexts overlap. While mobile technologies move us through contexts of action (Swarts and Kim 2009) and, perhaps, remove us from them, other scholars argue that these technologies make us simultaneously aware of global and local contexts (Gordon 2008).

References

Bakhtin, Mikhail M. 1982. "Discourse in the Novel." In *The Dialogic Imagination*, ed. Michael Holquist, 259–422. Austin: University of Texas Press.

Bakhtin, Mikhail M. 1986. "The Problem of Speech Genres." In *Speech Genres and Other Late Essays*, 60–102. Austin: University of Texas Press.

Barton, Ellen, and Susan Eggly. 2009. "Ethical or Unethical Persuasion?: The Rhetoric of Offers to Participate in Clinical Trials." *Written Communication* 26 (3): 295–319. http://dx.doi.org/10.1177/0741088309336936.

Berkenkotter, Carol. 2001. "Genre Systems at Work: DSM-IV and Rhetorical Recontextualization in Psychotherapy Paperwork." *Written Communication* 18 (3): 326–49. http://dx.doi.org/10.1177/0741088301018003004.

Berkenkotter, Carol, and Doris Ravotas. 1997. "Genre as Tool in the Transmission of Practice over Time and across Professional Boundaries." *Mind, Culture, and Activity* 4 (4): 256–74. http://dx.doi.org/10.1207/s15327884mca0404_4.

Berkenkotter, Carol, Thomas N. Huckin, and John Ackerman. 1988. "Conventions, Conversations, and the Writer." *Research in the Teaching of English* 22 (1): 9–44.

Bitzer, Lloyd F. 1968. "The Rhetorical Situation." *Philosophy & Rhetoric* 1 (1): 1–14.

Bizzell, Patricia, and Bruce Herzberg. 2001. *The Rhetorical Tradition*. Boston: Bedford/St. Martin's.

Bucciarelli, Louis L. 1996. *Designing Engineers*. Cambridge, MA: The MIT Press.

Colomb, Gregory G., and Joseph M. Williams. 1986. "Perceiving Structure in Professional Prose: a Multiply Determined Experience." In *Writing in Non-Academic Settings*, ed. Lee Odell and Dixie Goswami, 87–128. New York: Guilford Press.

Cooper, Marilyn. 1986. "The Ecology of Writing." *College English* 48 (4): 364–75. http://dx.doi.org/10.2307/377264.

Crowley, Sharon, and Deborah Hawhee. 1999. *Ancient Rhetorics for Contemporary Students*. Needham Heights, MA: Allyn and Bacon.

Devitt, Amy J. 1991. "Intertextuality in Tax Accounting: Generic, Referential, and Functional." In *Textual Dynamics of the Professions: Historical and Contemporary Studies of Writing in Professional Communities*, ed. Charles Bazerman and James Paradis, 336–357. Madison: University of Wisconsin Press.

Freadman, Ann. 2002. "Uptake." In *The Rhetoric and Ideology of Genre*, ed. Richard Coe, Lorelei Lingard, and Tatiana Teslenko, 39–53. Cresskill, NJ: Hampton Press.

Goodwin, C., and M. H. Goodwin. 1996. "Seeing as Situated Activity: Formulating Planes." *Cognition and Communication at Work*, 61–95.

Gordon, Eric. 2008. "Towards a Theory of Network Locality." *First Monday* 13 (10). http://journals.uic.edu/ojs/index.php/fm/article/view/2157/2035.

Hauser, Gerard A. 2002. *Introduction to Rhetorical Theory*. Long Grove, IL: Waveland Press.

Hutchins, Edwin. 1995. *Cognition in the Wild*. Cambridge, MA: MIT Press.

Hyland, Ken. 1998. "Persuasion and Context: The Pragmatics of Academic Meta-discourse." *Journal of Pragmatics* 30 (4): 437–55. http://dx.doi.org/10.1016/S0378-2166(98)00009-5.

Johnson-Eilola, Johndan. 2005. *Datacloud: Toward a New Theory of Online Work*. Cresskill, NJ: Hampton Press.

Mirel, Barbara, Ellen Barton, and Mark Ackerman. 2008. "Researching Telemedicine: Capturing Complex Clinical Interactions with a Simple Interface Design." *Technical Communication Quarterly* 17 (3): 358–78. http://dx.doi.org/10.1080/105722508 02100477.

Mol, Annemarie. 2002. *The Body Multiple: Ontology in Medical Practice*. Durham, NC: Duke University Press Books. http://dx.doi.org/10.1215/9780822384151.

Mol, Annemarie, and John Law. 1994. "Regions, Networks and Fluids: Anaemia and Social Topology." *Social Studies of Science* 24 (4): 641–71. http://dx.doi.org/10.1177/030631279402400402.

Nardi, Bonnie A., and Vicki O'Day. 2000. *Information Ecologies: Using Technology with Heart*. Cambridge, MA: The MIT Press.

Odell, Lee. 1986. "Beyond the Text: Relations between Writing and Social Context." In *Writing in Non-Academic Settings*, ed. Lee Odell and Dixie Goswami, 249–80. New York: Guilford Press.

Ong, Walter J. 2002. *Orality and Literacy: The Technologizing of the Word*. New York: Theatre Arts Books.

Prior, Paul, and Jody Shipka. 2003. "Chronotopic Lamination: Tracing the Contours of Literate Activity." In *Writing Selves, Writing Societies: Research from Activity Perspectives*, ed. Charles Bazerman and David R. Russell, 180–238. Fort Collins, CO: The WAC Clearinghouse and Mind, Culture, and Activity.

Schryer, C. F., L. Lingard, M. Spafford, and K. Garwood. 2003. "Structure and Agency in Medical Case Presentations." In *Writing Selves, Writing Societies: Research from Activity Perspectives*, ed. Charles Bazerman and David R. Russell, 62–96. Fort Collins, CO: The WAC Clearinghouse and Mind, Culture, and Activity.

Selzer, Jack. 1983. "The Composing Processes of an Engineer." *College Composition and Communication* 34 (2): 178–87. http://dx.doi.org/10.2307/357405.

Smart, Graham. 1999. "Storytelling in a Central Bank: The Role of Narrative in the Creation and Use of Specialized Economic Knowledge." *Journal of Business and Technical Communication* 13 (3): 249–73. http://dx.doi.org/10.1177/1050651999 01300302.

Spinuzzi, Clay, and Mark Zachry. 2000. "Genre Ecologies: An Open-System Approach to Understanding and Constructing Documentation." (JCD) *ACM Journal of Computer Documentation* 24 (3): 169–81. http://dx.doi.org/10.1145/344599.344646.

Swarts, Jason, and Loel Kim. 2009. "Guest Editors' Introduction: New Technological Spaces." *Technical Communication Quarterly* 18 (3): 211–23. http://dx.doi.org/10.1080/10572250902941986.

Vatz, Richard E. 1973. "The Myth of the Rhetorical Situation." *Philosophy & Rhetoric* 6 (3): 154–61.

Voloshinov, Valentin. 1986. *Marxism and the Philosophy of Language*. Cambridge, MA: Harvard University Press.

Winsor, Dorothy. 1996. *Writing Like an Engineer: A Rhetorical Education*. Lawrence Erlbaum.

Winsor, Dorothy. 2001. "Learning to Do Knowledge Work in Systems of Distributed Cognition." *Journal of Business and Technical Communication* 15 (1): 5–28. http://dx.doi.org/10.1177/105065190101500101.

CREATIVITY

Tim Mayers

Creativity is arguably one of the most ambiguous words in the **discourse** of writing studies. Michelene Wandor neatly sums up the "oppositional uses" of the "now heavily overused term 'creative,'" when she notes that it means "on the one hand . . . the rare, exceptional (talent, genius) and on the **other**, the democratizing, expanding, enhancing faculty that some argue is possessed by all" (Wandor 2008, 18). Perhaps these opposing views constitute a spectrum of meaning; the words *creative* and *creativity* are used in a wide range of overlapping and contradictory senses. Raymond Williams (1983) noted that "[*creative*] in modern **English** has a general sense of original and innovating, and an associated special sense of productive. It is also used to distinguish certain kinds of **work**, as in creative writing" (82).

"Creative writing" is also the name of an academic subfield of English studies that emerged in the late nineteenth and early twentieth centuries in the United States, and more recently (though along somewhat different lines) in Australia, the United Kingdom, and parts of Europe. In academic settings, when *creative* functions as an adjective to *writing*, it signifies the composition of three traditional literary **genres**—poetry, fiction, and drama—and sometimes also "creative" or "literary" nonfiction, like memoir. According to D. G. Myers, the term *creative writing* was very likely first used by Ralph Waldo Emerson, though it did not refer to a course of academic study until middle school teacher Hughes Mearns used it that way in 1929 (Myers 1996, 103). Myers argues that creative writing was originally imagined as an integral component of literary study, not as a separate field. Norman Foerster, who first made it possible for graduate students to write "creative" theses at the University of Iowa in the 1930s, held this view. However, after Foerster left Iowa, the Writers' Workshop he had helped to establish moved off in its own direction, largely separate from the interpretive study of literature and the study of rhetoric. And since so many Iowa graduates spread out across the United States and developed new creative writing courses and programs after the middle of

DOI: 10.7330/9780874219746.c010

the twentieth century, the meaning of *creative writing* as literary **production** divorced from interpretation became widely entrenched in the American academic scene.

These developments probably exacerbated a commonly held distinction between *creative writing* and *expository writing*, with the former term understood to refer to a type of art and the latter used almost exclusively to represent communication or information transfer. Frequently, it was believed that students needed to master the essentials of expository writing before being allowed to progress into creative writing, and in some cases creative writing was reserved as the province of those relatively few students believed to have the requisite talent and skill.

The meaning of *creativity* as a special or different capability held only by a few has roots in the ancient concept of inspiration—the notion that poets were possessed by gods or some type of divine madness. This very quality in poets, argued Plato's Socrates, made them unfit for citizenship in the ideal republic. The battle between poetry (loosely aligned with rhetoric) and philosophy (loosely aligned with science) has been a feature of the Western intellectual landscape since the time of Plato, with philosophy and science almost always holding the upper hand. The ancient concept of inspiration gradually became embodied by the term *creativity*, which began to take on a more noticeably modern form, in the English-speaking world, during the Romantic period. Percy Bysshe Shelley (2010), in *A Defense of Poetry*, argued that language originated in a human striving after harmony, order, and beauty, and that poets—those individuals possessing "the most delicate sensibility and the most enlarged imagination" (610)—were most keenly in touch with that striving. Shelley's contemporary, Samuel Taylor Coleridge (2010), argued in *Biographia Literaria* for the importance of *the imagination*, a phrase that would develop a close linguistic association with *creativity*. Widely read in the works of German idealist philosophers like Kant and Schelling, Coleridge theorized the imagination (sometimes in unclear or even contradictory ways) as the spark of the divine present within poets and other creative individuals.

Invested with romantic inflections, *creativity* held great sway in the late nineteenth and early twentieth centuries, in both the United Kingdom and the United States, as literary criticism began to replace philology as the center of academic English studies. But, although both the "liberal humanism" prevalent in the United Kingdom and the "new criticism" prevalent in the United States were deeply compatible with the meaning *creativity* acquired during the Romantic period, the scholars who legitimized literary criticism as an academic discipline tended in practice to focus on the *interpretation* of established literary works as opposed to any analysis of their *production*. The creativity of literary artists was assumed, but rarely ever explained or theorized. (A similar dynamic operated within creative writing courses as well—even though such courses ostensibly focused on the production rather than the interpretation of student texts, in practice they operated via the workshop method, where completed drafts of student work were analyzed by the class in terms of the "craft" elements through which these texts might be made more polished or publishable.) By the latter half of the twentieth century, liberal humanism and new criticism gave way to newer theories of literary interpretation—many of them influenced by developments in philosophy, sociology, and other disciplines—that tended to downplay the role of the creative individual in the composition of literary works, focusing instead on the larger social, ideological, and economic forces that influence the production of literary texts.

Also, in the latter half of the twentieth century in the United States, scholarship and research began to gel around postsecondary writing instruction. The field at its outset was deeply tied to the required FYC course, and much of its early research was geared toward developing new and more effective pedagogies for this course. The "process movement" shifted the focus of writing instruction away from the assessment and correction of static, finished student texts and toward the dynamic processes through which those texts had come into being. "Process, not product" was the motto. Process-oriented teachers believed writing processes could be analyzed and understood, and that teachers could intervene in students' processes to help them become better writers. A key strand within the process movement, which came to be known as "expressivism" following the epistemological categories named by James Berlin (1982), posited a deep connection between the act of writing and students' "selves"— their perceived uniqueness and individuality. Like many of their colleagues in creative writing, expressivist composition teachers believed in their students' creativity. Unlike many of their creative writing colleagues, though, expressivists believed that *all* students were endowed with creativity, not just a select few. For expressivists, those students who initially appeared to be void of creativity simply needed to have their creativity sparked or awakened.

Creativity has long been a term in tension with itself, its usage marked by key questions: Is creativity the province of special, gifted individuals— a personality trait that is inborn, mysterious, largely impervious to analysis? Or is it a quality all humans possess? Do creative writers work largely in isolation from the world around them? Or does that world exert a powerful, perhaps unconscious, influence? There have not been any final or definitive answers to these questions; debate continues to rage. Psychologist Mihaly Csikszentmihalyi's (1996) case studies demonstrate a powerful and decisive role for both the writer *and* the environment. Dianne Donnelly, a writing studies scholar, offers an excellent "Taxonomy of Creative Writing Pedagogies," illustrating how modes of assignment **design**, along with the response to and assessment of student writing, are underwritten by different—and at times contradictory—meanings of the word *creative* (Donnelly 2012, 22–70). These contradictions can be pedagogically productive, claims Donnelly: while the "Romantic myth" of inspired, effortless composition may initially "motivate students," it also opens the door for teachers to demonstrate that "'creativity' is . . . serious business" that necessarily "requires work, practice, [and] reading" (50). Anis Bawarshi's investigations in genre theory have traced how the meaning of *creativity* has gradually grown from a uniquely individual concept to the notion of a larger "field" beyond, but also including, the individual (Bawarshi 2003, 179). And Graeme Harper's (2010) *On Creative Writing* rigorously questions a series of propositions about what *creative* might mean when applied to writing, demonstrating that now, in the second decade of the twenty-first century, its meaning may be more contested—and more important—than ever before.

References

Bawarshi, Anis S. 2003. *Genre and the Invention of the Writer: Reconsidering the Place of Invention in Composition*. Logan: Utah State University Press.

Berlin, James A. 1982. "Contemporary Composition: The Major Pedagogical Theories." *College English* 44 (8): 765–77. http://dx.doi.org/10.2307/377329.

Coleridge, Samuel Taylor. (1817) 2010. "From Biographia Literaria." In *The Norton Anthology of Theory & Criticism*, 2nd ed., ed. Vincent B. Leitch, William E. Cain, Laurie A. Finke, Barbara E. Johnson, John McGowan, T. Denean Sharpley-Whiting, Jeffrey J. Williams, 584–91. New York: Norton.

Csikszentmihalyi, Mihaly. 1996. *Creativity: Flow and the Psychology of Discovery and Invention*. New York: HarperCollins.

Donnelly, Dianne. 2012. *Establishing Creative Writing Studies as an Academic Discipline*. Bristol, UK: Multilingual Matters.

Harper, Graeme. 2010. *On Creative Writing*. Bristol, UK: Multilingual Matters.

Myers, D. G. 1996. *The Elephants Teach: Creative Writing Since 1880*. Englewood Cliffs, NJ: Prentice Hall.

Shelley, Percy Bysshe. (1821) 2010. "From a Defence of Poetry." In *The Norton Anthology of Theory and Criticism*, 2nd ed., ed. Vincent B. Leitch, William E. Cain, Laurie A. Finke, Barbara E. Johnson, John McGowan, T. Denean Sharpley-Whiting, and Jeffrey J. Williams, 595–613. New York: Norton.

Wandor, Michelene. 2008. *The Author is Not Dead, Merely Somewhere Else: Creative Writing Reconceived*. New York: Palgrave Macmillan.

Williams, Raymond. 1983. *Keywords: A Vocabulary of Culture and Society*, revised edition. New York: Oxford University Press.

DESIGN

Melanie Yergeau

Design, much like *writing*, has a wide intersection of meanings. Although its prominence in the field is more generally associated with the emergence of **computers** and writing scholarship in the 1980s (Knievel 2009), *design* has an extensive and polysemous history. *Design* has variously referred to—or invoked—items that include instructional design, process and postprocess pedagogies, visual rhetoric and multimodality, theories of space and embodiment, and the reimagining of traditional literacies and cultural practices. Given its wide range of signification, writing scholars often struggle to justify the place of design in the discipline. As Banks (2006) remarks, "the field still grapples with just how and to what extent [design] belong[s]" (119). Is designing writing? Is writing designing? At what points do these taxonomies diverge, and at what point do we teach one at the expense of another? Or, as Bruce Horner (2000) might ask, is "expense" even the right question? In many respects, design theory recalls writing studies' long-held treatment of process and/versus product (Marback 2009, 397). Do we theorize *design* as a verb, as a noun, or both?

As early as the 1940s, compositionists began exploring design's import to writing studies, albeit primarily in terms of course planning and research methodology. Essays such as Minton's (1941) "Design for Composition" and Steinberg and Forehand's (1964) "Problems of Testing and Research Design in Curriculum Study in **English**" identify design as a sort of pedagogical bricolage. The authors variously focus on tasks such as scaffolding assignments or the ethical execution of teacher-based research. But a fully realized definition of *design* appears elusive here, with Minton's essay foreshadowing items central to present-day conversations in **Writing across the Curriculum/Writing in the Disciplines**, **technical communication**, and multimodal composition alike:

> The broadest objective is the satisfaction of the claims of basic mental processes as they operate in the act of expression—processes of purpose-forming, of selection, of arrangement, and of symbolization. . . . Consideration of

DOI: 10.7330/9780874219746.c011

those relations and of the conditions of the teaching problem has led to the statement of certain concepts that are suited to give firm direction to expression on the learning level. (Minton 1941, 146)

Although contemporary debates are less concerned with cognitive psychology than is Minton, questions concerning the "teaching problem," assessment, and modality inflect, however tangentially, scholarship related to design. Implicit in these discussions is an understanding of design as tinkering (Ballentine 2009) and design as an action or product with modal layers beyond that of traditional, text-based writing (Handa 2003). But this conception of design also highlights the interplay of bodies and spaces—what Minton and contemporary scholars like Porter (2009), Stolley (2011), and Vandenberg, Hum, and Clary-Lemon (2006) describe as "relations" and "conditions."

Beyond composition studies, design has a long and storied history within theories of education. Buzzwords like *instructional design* or *design for learning* frequently circulate on writing program listservs and at conferences. The WAC Clearinghouse, the WPA Council, and the College Conference on Composition and Communication all have statements addressing the design of writing curricula, and with it the *implementation* of such designs in first-year and advanced writing courses. Purposing design within a more curricular framework, Sean Williams (2008) describes design as an "assemblage" and "an instructional paradigm that helps students weave multiple content forms together" (469). While more technology-focused approaches like those of Yancey (2008) or Wysocki (2002) have centered on the potentialities of non-print media, **other** writing scholars—especially those within the purview of cultural studies—have long considered instructional design within the context of systems change and cultural transformation (Alexander and Rhodes 2012; Banks 2006; Walls 2008). Marilyn Cooper claimed in 1986 that "textual forms are just as easily used as barriers to **discourse** as they are used as means to discourse" (Cooper 2006, 188), suggesting the cross-modal possibilities of design as a discursive framework and a means of access. And, as Scott DeWitt (2001) suggests, such theories of access invoke questions concerning existing designs, the barriers inherent in these designs, and the ethical means of reinventing these designs.

In this reinvention sense, then, *design* as a keyword straddles both the concrete and the abstract. When we talk about design, are we talking about the bodies within (and outside of) our classrooms? Are we talking about the built environment and the physical arrangement of classroom spaces? Are we talking about writing program administration and assignment sequencing? Are we talking about access and inclusion? Are we talking about arranging paragraphs on a screen, or organizing images and hypertextual nodes? To what end are we assembling? *What* or *whom* are we assembling?

Perhaps one of the more visible discussions concerning the role of design is the New London Group's (NLG) theory of Design, so capitalized to signify a "meta-language of multiliteracies" (New London Group 2000, 19). The NLG defines *Design* as both a process and a product, as an event and destination that embraces multimodality: "Every moment of meaning involves the transformation of the available resources of meaning. Reading, seeing, and listening are all instances of Designing" (22). Like Cooper, the NLG stresses that postsecondary writing instruction "has been a carefully restricted project" (9). The NLG contends that current semiotic theories revolve around verbal language, thereby neglecting other forms of meaning-making. Patricia Dunn (2001), for instance, has long argued for a more robust approach to the teaching of writing, encouraging curricular design that incorporates talking, sketching, and moving. Cheryl Ball (2006) and Anne Wysocki (2002), among others, present *design*—and another keyword, **production**—as the twenty-first-century analogues to writing, using *production* to signify (the assemblage of) already-made artifacts and *design* to imply recursive process. Wysocki further suggests that traditional writing itself *is* design, albeit design that has traditionally subjugated visual rhetorical concepts such as color theory and page layout. Jay David Bolter (2001) has taken a similar approach, historicizing writing and design in the context of medieval manuscripts, the advent of the printing press, and the evolution of the book.

These and other **technology**-imbued **reflections** on design have inspired a myriad of conversations about access and methodology. Whether our focus is local or global, it is evident that our methods of design contribute to "a larger cultural system of differential power that has resulted in the systematic domination and marginalization of certain groups" (Selfe and Selfe 1994, 40). **Technical communication** and cultural studies theorists alike have sought to establish more "democratic" (Salvo 2001) structures in both the execution and the consumption of design. Whose bodyminds are centered in the design of our field, and how might we enable broader participation? In response to such questions, Dolmage (2009) and Slatin (2001) exhort us to call upon cross-disciplinary methods of design and practice. What technical communication, then, has brought us are theories such as universal design or participatory design. Participatory design, for example, foregrounds users as co-producers or co-designers (Bowie 2009). Participatory theories of design assert that users of a given product should be involved in the very process of creating that product. Similar sentiments vis-à-vis participation pervade scholarship on universal design (UD), which entails designing for the widest array of users possible (Dunn and De Mers 2002). Historically specific to architecture, UD in contemporary scholarship considers the design of both material and conceptual spaces—whether sidewalks, computer programs, or lesson plans.

There are, of course, differences between UD and participatory design. As Price (2009) argues, UD is often a gesture made by able, normative designers who attempt to anticipate as many users' needs as possible. Conversely, participatory design necessitates the involvement of a product's constituency, including marginalized users. Participatory design can be a lead designer's headache—a difficult project to execute, especially when collaborating with multiple users or co-producers. And, as Seelman (2005) has implied, universal design tends to represent design monolithically, as product rather than process. The scholarly enterprise of design, whether it involves new media or teacher training, struggles with this duality of user and use, of production and producing.

The complexity of design is palpable. As noted in this essay's introduction, to suggest that design is largely a technology-centric concept would be false. While design invariably calls upon multimodality, multimodality is by no means restricted to conversations on the digital, the technical, or even the architectural. As a trope, design brings into focus questions concerning the very purpose and intent of writing curricula. When is a writing course about writing? Is writing designing? Is designing writing? To what end do we tinker, produce, and problematize what it is that we do?

References

Alexander, Jonathan, and Jacqueline Rhodes. 2012. "Queer Rhetoric and the Pleasures of the Archive." *Enculturation* 13. http://www.enculturation.net/queer-rhetoric-and-the-pleasures-of-the-archive.

Ball, Cheryl E. 2006. "Designerly ≠ Readerly: Re-Assessing Multimodal and New Media Rubrics for Writing Studies." *Convergence* 12: 393–412.

Ballentine, Brian. 2009. "Hacker Ethics and Firefox Extensions: Writing and Teaching the 'Grey' Areas of Web 2.0." *Computers and Composition Online.* http://www2.bgsu.edu/departments/english/cconline/Ballentine/

Banks, Adam. 2006. *Race, Rhetoric, and Technology: Searching for Higher Ground.* Mahwah, NJ: Lawrence Erlbaum and National Council on Teaching English.

Bolter, Jay David. 2001. *Writing Space: Computers, Hypertext, and the Remediation of Print.* Mahwah, NJ: Lawrence Earlbaum.

Bowie, Jennifer. 2009. "Beyond the Universal: The Universe of Users Approach to User-Centered Design." In *Rhetorically Rethinking Usability,* ed. Susan Miller-Cochran and Rochelle L. Rodrigo, 135–63. Cresskill, NJ: Hampton Press.

Cooper, Marilyn. (1986) 2006. "The Ecology of Writing." In *Relations, Locations, Positions: Composition Theory for Writing Teachers*, ed. Peter Vandenberg, Sue Hum, and Jennifer Clary-Lemon, 181–97. Urbana, IL: NCTE.

DeWitt, Scott. 2001. *Writing Inventions: Identities, Technologies, Pedagogies.* Albany: SUNY.

Dolmage, J. 2009. "Disability, Usability, Universal Design." In *Rhetorically Rethinking Usability*, ed. Susan Miller-Cochran and Rochelle L. Rodrigo, 167–90. Cresskill, NJ: Hampton Press.

Dunn, Patricia A. 2001. *Talking, Sketching, Moving: Multiple Literacies in the Teaching of Writing.* Portsmouth, NH: Boynton/Cook Heinemann.

Dunn, Patricia A., and K. Dunn De Mers. 2002. "Reversing Notions of Disability and Accommodation: Embracing Universal Design in Writing Pedagogy and Web Space." *Kairos: A Journal of Rhetoric, Technology, and Pedagogy* 7 (1). http://kairos.technorhetoric.net/7.1/coverweb/dunn_demers/index.html.

Handa, Carolyn. 2003. "Teaching with the World Wide Web: Transforming Theory, Pedagogy, and Practice." In *Teaching Writing with Computers*, ed. Pamela Takayoshi and Brian Huot, 166–81. Boston: Houghton Mifflin.

Horner, Bruce. 2000. *Terms of Work for Composition: A Materialist Critique of Writing.* Albany: SUNY Press.

Knievel, Michael. 2009. "What Is Humanistic about Computers and Writing? Historical Patterns and Contemporary Possibilities for the Field." *Computers and Composition* 26 (2): 92–106. http://dx.doi.org/10.1016/j.compcom.2009.02.002.

Marback, Richard. 2009. "Embracing Wicked Problems: The Turn to Design in Composition Studies." *College Composition and Communication* 61 (2): 397–419.

Minton, A. 1941. "Design for Composition." *English Journal* 30 (2): 136–46. http://dx.doi.org/10.2307/805841.

New London Group. 2000. "A Pedagogy of Multiliteracies Designing Social Features." In *Multiliteracies: Literacy Learning and the Design of Social Futures*, ed. Bill Cope and Mary Kalantzis, 9–39. London: Routledge.

Porter, James E. 2009. "Recovering Delivery for Digital Rhetoric." *Computers and Composition* 26 (4): 207–24. http://dx.doi.org/10.1016/j.compcom.2009.09.004.

Price, Margaret. 2009. "Access Imagined: The Construction of Disability in Conference Policy Documents." *Disability Studies Quarterly* 29 (1). http://dsq-sds.org/article/view/174/174.

Salvo, Michael J. 2001. "Ethics of Engagement: User-Centered Design and Rhetorical Methodology." *Technical Communication Quarterly* 10 (3): 273–90. http://dx.doi.org/10.1207/s15427625tcq1003_3.

Seelman, K. D. 2005. "Universal Design and Orphan Technology: Do We Need Both?" *Disability Studies Quarterly* 25 (3). http://www.dsq-sds.org/article/view/584/761.

Selfe, Cynthia L., and Richard J. Selfe. 1994. "The Politics of the Interface: Power and Its Exercise in Electronic Contact Zones." *College Composition and Communication* 45 (4): 480–504. http://dx.doi.org/10.2307/358761.

Slatin, John. 2001. "The Art of the Alt: Toward a More Accessible Web." *Computers and Composition* 18 (1): 73–81. http://dx.doi.org/10.1016/S8755-4615(00)00049-9.

Steinberg, E. R., and G. A. Forehand. 1964. "Problems of Testing and Research Design in Curriculum Study in English." Paper presented at the Research, Design, and the Teaching of English proceedings of the San Francisco Conference, San Francisco.

Stolley, Karl. 2011. *How to Design and Write Web Pages Today.* Santa Barbara, CA: Greenwood.

Vandenberg, Peter, Sue Hum, and Jennifer Clary-Lemon, eds. 2006. *Relations, Locations, Positions: Composition Theory for Writing Teachers.* Urbana, IL: National Council of Teachers of English.

Walls, Douglas. 2008. "An 'A' Word Production: Authentic Design." *Kairos: A Journal of Rhetoric, Technology, and Pedagogy* 13 (1). http://kairos.technorhetoric.net/13.1/disputatio/walls/index.htm

Williams, Sean D. (2001) 2008. "Toward an Integrated Composition Pedagogy in Hypertext." In *Computers in the Composition Classroom*, ed. Michelle Sidler, Elizabeth Overman Smith, and Richard Morris, 469–81. Boston: Bedford/St. Martin's.

Wysocki, Anne F. 2002. "With Eyes that Think, and Compose, and Think: On Visual Rhetoric." In *Teaching Writing with Computers*, ed. Pamela Takayoshi and Brian Huot, 182–201. Boston: Houghton Mifflin.

Yancey, Kathleen B. (2001) 2008. "Looking for Sources of Coherence in a Fragmented world: Notes Toward a New Assessment Design." In *Computers in the Composition Classroom*, ed. Michelle Sidler, Elizabeth Overman Smith, and Richard Morris, 293–307. Boston: Bedford/St. Martin's.

DISABILITY

Cynthia Lewiecki-Wilson

Rosemarie Garland-Thomson, alluding to Foucault, notes that "the archive . . . determines what we can know" and, until recently, "there has been no archive . . . for understanding disability" (Garland-Thomson 2002, 2). Is *disability* understood as defined by the Americans with Disabilities Act (ADA): a condition that interferes with a major life function, and, whether real or imputed, a label that may trigger discrimination? (ADA 2009) Is disability a relationship between a **body** and its environment, as maintained by the United Nations (2006)? Is disability historically and culturally produced, as disability studies theories posit?

In the academy, *disability* functions through a range of meanings: as an absent presence; as a perceived insufficiency in students, requiring either programs of side-streaming or individual remediation; as constructed by the metaphor of the "level playing field," a condition applied to individuals judged to meet the legal threshold of minimal accommodation; as an aspect of **identity** and contributor to diversity; as a phenomenon of digital mediation; as a rhetoric for analysis; and as an interdisciplinary studies area aligned with **other** areas, such as feminism or **queer** theory, offering a critical perspective on the academy and field.

Searching for *disability* does not yield much within the early decades of composition studies, although the same tensions now apparent in conjunction with disability are seen in debates on the access and inclusion of previously excluded groups, whether based on differences of **class**, race, nation/language, or preparation for college (e.g., debates on basic writing and the label *basic writers*, mainstreaming and tracking, error and remediation). Regardless of the label, a focus on "diagnosing" learning differences—grouping students accordingly and devising remedies to "cure" them and return them to the mainstream—metaphorically treats those students as disabled and in need of rehabilitation. Early approaches to teaching writing to students with disabilities followed this pattern of side-streaming students based on a diagnostic category, or devising specialized teaching strategies for students in mainstream classes based on

DOI: 10.7330/9780874219746.c012

an informal teacher diagnosis. These approaches still exist, as does criticism of teachers taking a diagnostic and therapeutic stance toward students (Jurecic 2007; Lewiecki-Wilson and Dolmage 2008).

The tradition of specialized strategies also contributed to the development and use of assistive **technology** (Li and Hamel 2003), including technological accommodations that influence the meanings of *disability* in twenty-first century new media classrooms (e.g., screen readers, talk-to-text programs, etc.). While popular culture dreams that technology may erase disability, more often technology offers better accommodations for some, which helps to mediate relationships between the non-disabled and certain populations of disabled people (for instance, communication access real-time translation [CART] for deaf students in a writing and discussion class). Nonetheless, emerging writing technologies are also producing new barriers for the disabled, such as when blind students face video composition assignments.

After passage of the ADA and the Individuals with Disability Education Act (IDEA) in 1990, more students with disabilities began appearing in college, although not necessarily claiming a disability identity. Brenda Brueggemann et al. (2001) note this absent presence, the operations of this dominant metaphor of visibility/invisibility, in their widely cited piece, "Becoming Visible: Lessons in Disability." In like manner, disability in writing studies has long been construed as an issue of equity and diversity. Patricia Dunn's (1995) *Learning Re-abled* features the experiences of learning-disabled writers, told in their own words, and teaching practices that can help them. That book and her next, *Talking, Sketching, Moving* (Dunn 2001), draw on many bodily modalities (oral, visual, kinesthetic) and a more expansive view of "writing" (including, for example, oral journals). Acceptance of disability differences as important aspects of diversity has grown slowly. Activists, scholars, and allies continue to advocate that disability differences bring valuable viewpoints and add diversity to the academy. In a recent exchange in *College English*, for instance, Paul Heilker (2008) makes the case that autism should not be considered a disability issue but a diversity issue.

Disability studies has influenced the meanings of *disability* in writing studies through its emphasis on the social dimensions of disability. For instance, Lennard Davis (1995) introduced writing scholars to the idea of disability as a critical mode of analysis, while Brueggemann (1997) highlighted disability identity issues such as "passing." As a result, writing scholars have increasingly turned their attention to the role of **discourses** of education, language, and cultural practice in constructing disability. Brueggemann's (1999) *Lend Me Your Ears*, for instance, studies the rhetoric of deafness—examining both the ways that teachers construct deaf student writers and the students' own accounts of their **literacy** practices—and finds that, contrary to assumptions that deaf students achieve low levels of literacy, deaf literacy practices are, in fact, rich and complex. In like manner, Wilson and Lewiecki-Wilson (2002) point out that society, and especially the academy, traditionally discusses equity using the rhetoric of the "norm" (imagined as the majority) and "fairness" (imagined as sameness), arguing that we should therefore develop a transformative "third space" pedagogy that moves us beyond binary oppositions such as abled/disabled. Barber-Fendley and Hamel (2004) examine how the metaphor of the "level playing field" simultaneously creates and justifies the idea of a normative student body that ought to be treated in a standardized way, thereby constructing disability as non-standard and individual accommodations as threatening the norm. Julie Jung (2007) examines disability narratives in composition anthologies and analyzes the ways they reinforce the "belief that accommodation is an individualized process" rather than a "shared social responsibility" (160, 175).

In like manner, Garland-Thomson (2002) understands disability/ability as a broad *system* of underlying practices of normativity and exclusion. In this vein, Robert McRuer (2004) compares the systems of heteronormativity and compulsory ablebodiedness, noting that both structuring systems reinforce university and employer demands for normed and composed bodies. Amy Vidali (2007) similarly examines a range of required university documents (e.g., student application statements and letters of recommendation) to explicate how disability is forced into particular kinds of spaces and representational narratives, such as the overcoming narratives of student essays (see also Wood 2011). Jay Dolmage (2008) links the physical access of the academy (steep steps, retrofitted ramp, or universally-designed building) to the pedagogical access teachers can provide by adopting flexible universal **design** teaching principles (see also Dunn and DeMers 2002), a move that reconstructs *all* students as needing flexible accommodations. In sum, Lewiecki-Wilson and Brueggemann (2008) present disability as epistemically important, not peripheral, to the teaching of writing and the training of writing teachers, while Dolmage (2011) coins the term *discomposition* to express the perspective and understanding that ability/disability functions as a deep structure and episteme of the academy and the field.

The coining of new terms underscores that scholars and activists have long understood disability as a rhetorical phenomenon. For instance, activists have deployed neologisms to call attention to the rhetoric of ableist language: *neurodiversity* highlights the positive aspects of autism as a usefully different way of experiencing and understanding the world, while *neurotypical*, an ironic term used to describe non-autistics, highlights the assumptions and forces of containment in labels. Recent rhetorical scholarship on the meanings of *disability* include Duffy and Dorner's (2011) analysis of how the concept of "mindblindness" functions in science writing as a rhetoric of sadness that mourns the loss of the autistic, while also justifying his exclusion as not fully human; Shannon Walters's (2010) redefinition of autistic women writers as not deficient, but instead skilled in the rhetorical facility of *metis*; Margaret Price's (2011) *Mad at School*, which examines the common *topoi* that constitute those with mental disabilities as invisible and unwelcome in the academy; and Jay Dolmage's (2014) locating of disability in the earliest formation period of classical rhetoric, and the subsequent history of its—and the divergent body's—containment or erasure.

References

ADA. 2009. "Americans with Disabilities Act of 1990, as Amended." March 25. http://www.ada.gov/pubs/ada.htm.

Barber-Fendley, Kimber, and Chris Hamel. 2004. "A New Visibility: An Argument for Alternative Assistance Writing Programs for Students with Learning Disabilities." *College Composition and Communication* 55 (3): 504–35. http://dx.doi.org/10.2307/4140697.

Brueggemann, Brenda Jo. 1997. "On (Almost) Passing." *College English* 59 (6): 647–60. http://dx.doi.org/10.2307/378278.

Brueggemann, Brenda Jo. 1999. *Lend Me Your Ears: Rhetorical Constructions of Deafness.* Washington, DC: Gallaudet University Press.

Brueggemann, Brenda Jo, Linda Feldmeier White, Patricia A. Dunn, Barbara Heifferon, and Johnson Cheu. 2001. "Becoming Visible: Lessons in Disability." *College Composition and Communication* 52 (3): 368–98. http://dx.doi.org/10.2307/358624.

Davis, Lennard J. 1995. "Deafness and Insight: The Deafened Moment as a Critical Modality." *College English* 57 (8): 881–900. http://dx.doi.org/10.2307/378619.

Dolmage, Jay. 2008. "Inviting Disability in the Front Door." In *Composing Other Spaces*, ed. John Tassoni and Douglas Reichert-Powell, 121–44. Cresskill, NJ: Hampton Press.

Dolmage, Jay. 2011. "Discomposition: 'I Had to Throw in a Few, So They'd Know It Was Me.'" Paper presented at Composing Disability, a George Washington University Symposium, Washington, DC.

Dolmage, Jay. 2014. *Disability Rhetoric.* Syracuse: Syracuse University Press.

Duffy, John, and Rebecca Dorner. 2011. "The Pathos of 'Mindblindness': Autism, Science, and Sadness in 'Theory of Mind' Narratives." *Journal of Literary and Cultural Disability Studies* 5 (2): 201–15. http://dx.doi.org/10.3828/jlcds.2011.16.

Dunn, Patricia A. 1995. *Learning Re-Abled: The Learning Disability Controversy and Composition Studies.* Portsmouth, NH: Boynton/Cook.

Dunn, Patricia A. 2001. *Talking, Sketching, Moving: Multiple Literacies in the Teaching of Writing.* Portsmouth, NH: Heineman-Boynton/Cook.

Dunn, Patricia A., and Kathleen Dunn DeMers. 2002. "Reversing Notions of Disability and Accommodation: Embracing Universal Design in Writing Pedagogy and Web

Space." *Kairos: A Journal of Rhetoric, Technology, and Pedagogy* 7 (1). http://english.ttu .edu/kairos/7.1.

Garland-Thomson, Rosemarie. 2002. "Integrating Disability, Transforming Feminist Theory." *NWSA Journal* 14 (3): 1–32. http://dx.doi.org/10.2979/NWS.2002.14.3.1.

Heilker, Paul. 2008. "Two Comments on Neurodiversity." *College English* 70 (3): 314–25.

Jung, Julie. 2007. "Textual Mainstreaming and Rhetorics of Accommodation." *Rhetoric Review* 26 (2): 160–78. http://dx.doi.org/10.1080/07350190709336707.

Jurecic, Ann. 2007. "Neurodiversity." *College English* 69 (5): 421–42.

Lewiecki-Wilson, Cynthia, and Brenda Jo Brueggemann, with Jay Dolmage. 2008. *Disability and the Teaching of Writing: A Critical Sourcebook*. Boston: Bedford/St. Martin's.

Lewiecki-Wilson, Cynthia, and Jay Dolmage. 2008. "Two Comments on Neurodiversity." *College English* 70 (3): 314–25.

Li, Huijun, and Christine M. Hamel. 2003. "Writing Issues in College Students with Learning Disabilities: A Synthesis of the Literature from 1990 to 2000." *Learning Disability Quarterly* 26 (1): 29–46. http://dx.doi.org/10.2307/1593683.

McRuer, Robert. 2004. "Composing Bodies; or, De-composition: Queer Theory, Disability Studies, and Alternative Corporealities." *JAC: Rhetoric, Writing, Multiple Literacies, and Politics* 24 (1): 47–78.

Price, Margaret. 2011. *Mad at School: Rhetorics of Mental Disability and Academic Life*. Ann Arbor: University of Michigan Press.

United Nations. 2006. "Convention on the Rights of Persons with Disabilities." http:// www.un.org/disabilities/convention/conventionfull.shtml.

Vidali, Amy. 2007. "Performing the Rhetorical Freak Show: Disability, Student Writing, and College Admisssions." *College English* 69 (6): 615–41.

Walters, Shannon. 2010. "Animal Athena: The Interspecies Metis of Women Writers with Autism." *JAC: Rhetoric, Writing, Multiple Literacies, and Politics* 30 (3–4): 683–711.

Wilson, James C., and Cynthia Lewiecki-Wilson. 2002. "Constructing a Third Space: Disability Studies, the Teaching of English, and Institutional Transformation." In *Disability Studies: Enabling the Humanities*, ed. Brenda Jo Brueggemann, Sharon Snyder, and Rosemarie Garland-Thomson, 296–307. New York: MLA.

Wood, Tara. 2011. "Overcoming Rhetoric: Forced Disclosure and the Colonizing Ethic of Evaluating Personal Essays." *Open Words: Access and English Studies* 5 (1): 38–52.

DISCOURSE

Christine M. Tardy

The many layers of meaning that circulate around the term *discourse* within writing studies illustrate at once its complexity, multidisciplinarity, and productive nature. At its most general level, the term alludes to the socially situated nature of meaning in or through language, but more precise theoretical orientations emphasize different elements of this simplified characterization. As a lay term, *discourse* commonly carries both a general meaning of verbal communication and the notion of a philosophical treatise associated with French philosophical thought (Mills 1997). In writing studies, the word variously attends more or less to text, **context**, and social and ideological ways of being, as well as the intertwining of these layers. The *discourse* in *academic discourse*, for example, differs from that in the *discourse of neoliberalism*, yet both uses share an acknowledgment that discourse takes into account language, context, and social structures.

The first use of the term within the pages of *College Composition and Communication* is found in the journal's inaugural 1950 volume, within a summary report of a workshop (College Composition and Communication 1950). Reference is made to students working with "argumentative discourse," seemingly invoking discourse as a type of writing characterized by its overall aim. The importance of purpose in defining and classifying discourse types is later expanded on in James Kinneavy's (1971) influential **work**, which outlined four primary aims of discourse (referential, persuasive, literary, and expressive) and discussed for each the characteristic logic, organizational patterns, and stylistic features. By 1984, Louise Wetherbee Phelps had summarized modern discourse studies as "see[ing] language as *ecological* or *contextualized*; *constructive*, *functional* and *strategic*, *holistic*, with a strong *tacit* component; *dynamic*; and *interactive*" (Phelps 1984, 34, emphasis in original).

At least three theoretical approaches to discourse can be found within contemporary writing studies, though classifying definitions and orientations belies the instability and layered uses of the term.

DOI: 10.7330/9780874219746.c013

Indeed, these characterizations might be best configured as lying on a continuum or as embedded circles rather than as distinct categories. Norman Fairclough (1992), for example, represents discourse as a three-dimensional concept, including "discourse as text," which is embedded within "discursive practice," which is then encompassed by "discourse as social practice."

Drawing heavily from linguistics, a "discourse as text" orientation defines *discourse* as a coherent unit of analysis beyond the sentence—an approach that James Paul Gee (1989) refers to as little "d" discourse. This sense of the term must be understood historically, as it was specifically used to distinguish a focus on broader, contextualized textual units (e.g., conversations, letters, research articles) from the formerly prevailing linguistic focus on decontextualized linguistic features within sentences and clauses. With this shift in focus, traditional tools of linguistic analysis became less relevant and language researchers began to look at new features, investigating "what gives stretches of language unity and meaning" (Cook 1989, 13). Features such as parallelism, politeness markers, and organizational patterns became new analytic tools for identifying some of the ways in which speakers and authors shape discourse types in order to achieve particular aims. Though text is a primary focus in this approach, it is always analyzed with sensitivity (of varying degrees) to context, including the interlocutors and their aims (Brown and Yule 1983). While this orientation is not prominent in contemporary writing studies, it is important for its early influence in expanding the analytic lens beyond sentence grammar to texts as whole, meaningful, socially-situated units.

One of the most common orientations to discourse within writing studies emphasizes social context and the ways in which writers and speakers make meaning (through language but also **other** resources) within social environments—roughly what Fairclough (1992) refers to as a "discursive practice" approach. This context-oriented definition of *discourse* often assumes discourse to be "a dynamic, temporal process of negotiation" among participants, "semiotically mediat[ing] interactions" (Nystrand, Greene, and Wiemelt 1993, 300). In a seminal article published in 1989, Gee similarly emphasized the broad range of semiotic resources that construct discourses, defining (big "D") Discourses as "*saying(writing)-doing-being-valuing-believing combinations*" (Gee 1989, 6, emphasis in original). They are, he argued, "ways of being in the world . . . forms of life which integrate words, acts, values, beliefs, attitudes, and social identities as well as gestures, glances, **body** positions, and clothes" (6–7). Here, the meaning of discourse expands rather significantly beyond text. A chemist, for example, adopts a certain discourse not just through her use of passive voice or particular written **genres**, but also through her actions within a laboratory, the possession of protective eyewear, the presence of a periodic table in her office, and the array of journals that line her bookshelves. Discourse has therefore been described by Gee as an "**identity** kit" (Gee 1989, 7), or a way of projecting oneself as a certain kind of person performing a particular role within a specific social setting (Gee 2010).

Also influential within writing studies is view of discourse as a set of values that structure how we understand and act within the world—an orientation that might be termed "discourse as social structure." This approach is heavily associated with Michel Foucault's conception of discourse as "practices that systematically form the objects of which they speak" (Foucault 1972, 49). Foucault's "objects," however, are not as tangible as those to which Gee refers; rather, Foucault refers to objects of knowledge, such as mental illness or race. Discourses shape, produce, and reproduce such objects, ultimately structuring society's values, assumptions, and even behaviors. Foucault's interest in discourse is not in identifying a "true" representation of objects, but rather in understanding how certain discourses become dominant, normalized, supported, and reinforced by social structures. Working from a slightly more text-based orientation but still foregrounding social structure, Fairclough defines discourses as "ways of representing aspects of the world" (Fairclough 2003, 124), serving as one resource through which people relate to one another. For Fairclough, discourses are understood through analysis of the parts of the world (or their main themes) and the perspectives they represent. While a Foucauldian approach to discourse may examine institutionalized societal structures such as the healthcare system, a Faircloughian approach would more likely examine how such social structures are represented through language, such as political speeches, editorials, or policy documents.

In writing studies, discourse has not only provided theoretical frameworks for understanding writing and the contexts of written language, but has also served as a valuable analytic tool. Both discourse analysis and critical discourse analysis are used to understand better how texts (broadly construed) operate within and are co-constitutive of social domains. Approaches to discourse analysis vary in relation to the discourse theory researchers adopt and the analytic tools they deploy. Approaches may, for example, examine patterns of lexico-grammatical features across academic disciplines (Hyland 2000); semantic relations and grammatical features that shape a discourse's representations of the world (Fairclough 2003); rhetorical features in public texts (Fahnestock and Secor 2002); multimodal features of public texts (Levine and Scollon 2004); or even the roles and subjectivities taken on within mental health discourses (Emmons 2009) [see Barton and Stygall 2002 for more examples of discourse analysis in writing studies]. Discourse analysis that takes an explicitly critical lens—that is, seeking to uncover the ways in which dominant discourses have served to marginalize certain groups over others—is referred to as critical discourse analysis (CDA). Most approaches to CDA draw upon linguistic and contextual analysis to examine social issues and imbalances of power (van Dijk 1986; Wodak and Meyer 2001), such as discourses surrounding racism (van Dijk 1986) or homelessness (Huckin 2002).

The concept of discourse **community** has also played an important role in writing studies. In the early 1980s, Patricia Bizzell used the term to emphasize the shared patterns of language use that exist within a specific community (Bizzell 1982). She later expanded on the term, noting that such shared patterns may include both stylistic conventions as well as canonical knowledge (Bizzell 1992). John Swales' (1990) work has also been influential in developing the concept of discourse community. While he originally treated shared language patterns as a central defining feature, he later drew on James Porter's work to account for different types of discourse communities, which may be bound together variously by physical space (such as a workplace) or by shared goals and interests (such as an academic discourse community) (Swales 1998). Criticisms notwithstanding, the concept of discourse community has played an important role in theorizing and researching the challenges students face when learning academic discourse (see, for example, Bartholomae 1985; Berkenkotter, Huckin, and Ackerman 1987).

Despite—or perhaps because of—its layered and contested meanings, *discourse* remains a remarkably productive term within writing studies, bringing the interests of student writers, classroom teachers, and scholarly researchers together around central issues of language, meaning, and social context.

References

Bartholomae, David. 1985. "Inventing the University." In *When a Writer Can't Write*, ed. Mike Rose, 134–65. New York: Guilford.

Barton, Ellen, and Gail Stygall, eds. 2002. *Discourse Studies in Composition*. Creskill, NJ: Hampton Press.

Berkenkotter, Carol, Thomas Huckin, and John Ackerman. 1987. "Conventions, Conversations, and the Writer: Case Study of a Student in a Rhetoric PhD Program." *Research in the Teaching of English* 22: 9–44.

Bizzell, Patricia. 1982. "Cognition, Convention, and Certainty: What We Need to Know about Writing." *Pre/Text* 3: 213–243.

Bizzell, Patricia. 1992. *Academic Discourse and Critical Consciousness*. Pittsburgh: University of Pittsburgh Press.

Brown, Gillian, and George Yule. 1983. *Discourse Analysis*. Cambridge: Cambridge University Press. http://dx.doi.org/10.1017/CBO9780511805226.

College Composition and Communication. 1950. "Objectives and Organization of the Communication Course: The Report of Workshop No. 4." *College Composition and Communication* 1: 15–18.

Cook, Guy. 1989. *Discourse*. Oxford: Oxford University Press.

Emmons, Kimberly K. 2009. "Uptake and the Biomedical Subject." In *Genre in a Changing World*, ed. Charles Bazerman, Adair Bonini, and Déborah Figueiredo, 134–57. West Lafayette, IN: Parlor Press.

Fahnestock, Jeanne, and Marie Secor. 2002. "Rhetorical Analysis." In *Discourse Studies in Composition*, ed. Ellen Barton and Gail Stygall, 177–200. Creskill, NJ: Hampton Press.

Fairclough, Norman. 1992. *Discourse and Social Change*. Malden, MA: Polity.

Fairclough, Norman. 2003. *Analysing Discourse: Textual Analysis for Social Research*. London, New York: Routledge.

Foucault, Michel. 1972. *The Archaeology of Knowledge and the Discourse on Language*. New York: Pantheon Books.

Gee, James Paul. 1989. "Literacy, Discourse, and Linguistics: Introduction." *Journal of Education* 171 (1): 5–17.

Gee, James Paul. 2010. *An Introduction to Discourse Analysis: Theory and Method*, 3rd ed. New York: Routledge.

Huckin, Thomas. 2002. "Critical Discourse Analysis and the Discourse of Condescension." In *Discourse Studies in Composition*, ed. Ellen Barton and Gail Stygall, 155–76. Creskill, NJ: Hampton Press.

Hyland, Ken. 2000. *Disciplinary Discourses: Social Interactions in Academic Writing*. London: Longman.

Kinneavy, James. 1971. *Theory of Discourse: The Aims of Discourse*. Englewood Cliffs, NJ: Prentice-Hall.

Levine, Philip, and Ron Scollon, eds. 2004. *Discourse and Technology: Multimodal Discourse Analysis*. Washington, DC: Georgetown University Press.

Mills, Sarah. 1997. *Discourse*. London: Routledge.

Nystrand, Martin, Stuart Greene, and Jeffrey Wiemelt. 1993. "Where Did Composition Studies Come From?: An Intellectual History." *Written Communication* 10 (3): 267–333. http://dx.doi.org/10.1177/0741088393010003001.

Phelps, Louise Wetherbee. 1984. "Cross-Sections in an Emerging Psychology of Composition." In *Research in Composition and Rhetoric*, ed. Michael G. Morgan and Ronald F. Lunsford, 27–69. Westport, CT: Greenwood.

Swales, John M. 1990. *Genre Analysis: English in Academic and Research Settings*. Cambridge: Cambridge University Press.

Swales, John M. 1998. *Other Floors, Other Voices: A Textography of a Small University Building*. Mahwah, NJ: Lawrence Erlbaum Associates.

van Dijk, Teun A. 1986. *Racism in the Press*. London: Arnold.

Wodak, Ruth, and Michael Meyer, eds. 2001. *Methods of Critical Discourse Analysis*. Thousand Oaks, NJ: Sage.

ECOLOGY

Christian R. Weisser

Like many of the keywords in writing studies, *ecology* is an imported term with divergent significations and various meanings. The term comes from the natural sciences, where it is used to explain the biological relationships between living organisms and their environments. Ecologists study how organisms interact and interconnect with each **other**, the ways in which species adapt to and create systems, and the processes through which energy and materials move through systems. In lay terms, *ecology* tends to be used to describe the environments in which these relationships take place, often with an implicit concern for the preservation of "natural" environments. This difference between the specialized conception of *ecology* as a scientific field of study and its more generalized association with environments and their preservation mirrors the various connotations of the term within contemporary writing studies.

The term *ecology* first appears in writing studies in the 1980s, in conjunction with the shift away from examining the individual writer's cognitive process and toward a conception of writing as both a social phenomenon and a complex system. As part of this postprocess movement, writing theorists began to define writing as an ecological act, one that is bound up in, influenced by, and relational to spaces, places, **locations**, environments, and the interconnections among the entities they contain. Within writing studies, the word *ecology* carries a close association with systems of thinking and an interconnected, dynamic conception of writing. In fact, since its earliest usage, *ecology* has often served as a near synonym to the terms *system* and *complexity*. For example, Richard M. Coe's "Eco-Logic for the Composition Classroom" includes the first direct reference to ecology in writing studies, asserting an "eco-logical" conception of writing, which emphasizes "systemic interrelations instead of analytic separations" (Coe 1975, 237). Coe's usage of the term anticipates later discussions of ecology, complexity, and systems theories in composition by arguing that traditional, reductionist approaches to writing are "inadequate for discussing the more

DOI: 10.7330/9780874219746.c014

complex phenomena which are increasingly relevant to contemporary realities" (232).

In some ways, the term *ecology* stands in dichotomy to a keyword in writing studies from an earlier time, *process*. Most current references to writing as a process critique its static and simplistic categories of contextual models, while an ecological conception of writing emphasizes complex adaptation and the constant motion of discursive systems. Marilyn Cooper's "The Ecology of Writing" is a principal source for most definitions of the term in writing studies, and her notion of ecology, along with other postprocess **work**, marks a clear break from earlier process-based models. Cooper proposes an ecological model of writing, "whose fundamental tenet is that writing is an activity through which a person is continuously engaged with a variety of socially constituted systems" (Cooper 1986, 366). That is, Cooper suggests that writing not be examined as an individual process, but as an ecological activity reliant upon complex relationships and dynamic connections. She argues that

> All the characteristics of any individual writer or piece of writing both determine and are determined by the characteristics of all the other writers and writings in the systems. An important characteristic of ecological systems is that they are inherently dynamic; though their structures and contents can be specified at a given moment, in real time they are constantly changing, limited only by parameters that are themselves subject to change over longer spans of time. . . In place of the static and limited categories of contextual models, the ecological model postulates dynamic interlocking systems which structure the social activity of writing. (Cooper 1986, 368)

In this way, Cooper defines an ecology of writing as both relational and fluid, and this conception permeates writing studies' current usages of *ecology*. More elaborate and detailed definitions of *ecology* follow Cooper's conception, shifting the focus away from individuals and texts and toward the complex systems of writing. For example, Margaret Syverson describes four attributes of ecological systems: distribution, emergence, embodiment, and enaction. According to Syverson, writing is a "complex system of self-organizing, adaptive, and dynamic interactions [that are] situated in an ecology, a larger system" (Syverson 1999, 5). Though Syverson's conception is more detailed, she extends Cooper's use of the term *ecology* to distinguish between a static, process-based conception of writing and a more complex notion that emphasizes systems.

Other references to *ecology* emerged in writing studies at about the same time, and it is worth noting that the word is often intermingled and occasionally conflated with other spatial terms like *environment, place,* and *location* in writing. These other terms are more likely to refer to physical and literal spaces, while ecology typically connotes a metaphorical or theoretical conception of writing itself, though there is some overlap between them. This intermingling of terms has been fueled by the subfield of *ecocomposition,* which draws upon the eco-prefix to consider the ecological properties of writing and investigate the ways in which places of all types are discursively constructed (Dobrin and Weisser 2002). Ecocomposition is concerned with the spatial aspects of **discourse**, and much of its scholarly focus has been upon place and location as a critical category (alongside race, **class**, **gender**, and culture) in understanding how texts are created and distributed. In other words, ecocomposition incorporates the ecological emphasis on location and relationships into conversations about how writing is created and distributed. In this way, ecocomposition positions composition as "an ecological endeavor in that writing and rhetoric cannot be separated from place, from environment, from nature, or from location" (Dobrin 2001, 13).

Though ecocomposition brought further consideration to the role of ecology in writing studies, it has been critiqued for its over-attention to the pedagogical applications of environmentalist concerns (i.e., nature writing in the composition classroom) rather than the ways in which writing itself is an ecological inquiry. In some ways, this critique is due to the conflation of the term *ecology*—which generally conveys a theoretical emphasis on the **production** of texts—with terms like *environment* and *environmental writing*, which often deal with the development of place-based composition courses or other more practical, tangible, or pedagogical topics within writing studies. These related terms both fragment and expand an ecological sensibility in writing studies, and they have been central to inquiries involving environmental rhetoric (see Herndl and Brown 1996, Killingsworth and Palmer 1992, and Waddell 1998) sustainability (see Owens 2001 and Patrick 2012) and place and location (see Fleckenstein et al. 2008, Keller and Weisser 2007, and Reynolds 2004).

Many of the recent incorporations of ecology in writing studies have drawn upon the term to help explain the intricacies and interconnectedness of writing in the digital age. Without a doubt, the development of networked communication technologies after the turn of the millennium has revealed much about the ways in which writing is systemic and ecological, and the term *ecology* has been closely linked with electronic media. The thrust of this work focuses on the properties of the **networks** themselves, emphasizing the transitory, emergent, and situational properties of writing systems. Complex ecologies suggest an understanding of writing as a "self-organizing system responsive to, but neither designed nor controlled by writers" (Cooper 2011, 444). In many ways, then, these discussions move writing studies further beyond the individual or even the group as the locus of the writing equation, looking instead to patterns and fluctuations in the system. Byron Hawk, among others, addresses the "hyper-circulatory" interactions between **technology**, agents, and language, suggesting that "network culture puts the importance of ecology and immersion in sharp relief" (Hawk 2007, 166).

In this sense, ecology becomes a means of explaining the inseparability of writing and technology, of identifying the systems of interaction inherent in the network (see Brooke 2009, Devoss, McKee, and Selfe 2009, and Spinuzzi 2008). In addition, these recent moves emphasize the limits of previous ecological conceptions of writing as overly static or stable, recognizing that the complexities of writing "are so diverse and divergent that we may never be able to fully account for all of the facets and functions of writing, particularly as writing endlessly fluctuates as a system" (Dobrin 2011, 143; see also Edbauer 2005; Rivers and Weber 2011). In other words, the most recent ecological conceptions of writing emphasize the situational, fluid patterns through which meaning arises, highlighting the complex systems that writing saturates. The term *ecology* becomes a vehicle to unpack the complexity, interconnectedness, fluidity, and motion of discursive networks.

Though *ecology* has been a keyword in writing studies for nearly three decades, most sources continue to characterize it as an imported term associated with the natural sciences. Consequently, the term is often used in a referential or metaphorical way rather than as a naturalized part of the vocabulary. Similar to other keywords, *ecology* may become a normalized term through continued use. It seems likely that the concepts and terminology of ecology will continue to influence the direction of future theoretical models in writing studies, though such models will transform and develop in unexpected ways. Writing studies, like the field of ecology, has only scratched the surface in mapping out the intricacies of these complex systems. Questions remain about how ecologies of writing emerge, transform, interact with, and are differentiated from other human and nonhuman systems.

References

Brooke, Collin Gifford. 2009. *Lingua Fracta: Towards a Rhetoric of New Media*. Cresskill, NJ: Hampton Press, Inc.

Coe, Richard M. 1975. "Eco-logic for the Composition Classroom." *College Composition and Communication* 26 (3): 232–37. http://dx.doi.org/10.2307/356121.

Cooper, Marilyn. 1986. "The Ecology of Writing." *College English* 48 (4): 364–75. http://dx.doi.org/10.2307/377264.

Cooper, Marilyn. 2011. "Rhetorical Agency as Emergent and Enacted." *College Composition and Communication* 62 (3): 420–49.

Devoss, Dànielle Nicole, Heidi A. McKee, and Richard (Dickie) Selfe, eds. 2009. *Technological Ecologies and Sustainability.* Computers and Composition Digital Press Online. Accessed February 14, 2012.

Dobrin, Sidney I. 2001. "Writing Takes Place." In *Ecomposition: Theoretical and Pedagogical Approaches*, ed. Christian R. Weisser and Sidney I. Dobrin, 11–25. Albany: State U of New York P.

Dobrin, Sidney I. 2011. *Postcomposition.* Carbondale: Southern Illinois UP.

Dobrin, Sidney I., and Christian R. Weisser. 2002. *Natural Discourse: Toward Ecocomposition.* Albany: State U of New York P.

Edbauer, Jenny. 2005. "Unframing Models of Public Distribution: From Rhetorical Situation to Rhetorical Ecology." *Rhetoric Society Quarterly* 35 (4): 5–24. http://dx.doi.org/10.1080/02773940509391320.

Fleckenstein, Kristie S., Clay Spinuzzi, Rebecca J. Rickly, and Carole Clark Papper. 2008. "The Importance of Harmony: An Ecological Metaphor for Writing Research." *College Composition and Communication* 60 (2): 388–419.

Hawk, Byron. 2007. *A Counter History of Composition: Toward Methodologies of Complexity.* Pittsburgh: UP of Pittsburgh.

Herndl, Carl G., and Stuart Brown, eds. 1996. *Green Culture: Environmental Rhetoric in Contemporary America.* Madison: U of Wisconsin P.

Keller, Christopher J., and Christian R. Weisser, eds. 2007. *The Locations of Composition.* Albany: State U of New York P.

Killingsworth, M. Jimmie, and Jacqueline S. Palmer. 1992. *Ecospeak: Rhetoric and Environmental Politics in America.* Carbondale: Southern Illinois University Press.

Owens, Derek. 2001. *Composition and Sustainability: Teaching for a Threatened Generation.* Urbana, IL: NCTE.

Patrick, Amy M. 2010. "Sustaining Writing Theory." *Composition Forum* 21 (Spring). Accessed October 15, 2012.

Reynolds, Nedra. 2004. *Geographies of Writing: Inhabiting Places and Encountering Difference.* Carbondale, IL: Southern Illinois UP.

Rivers, Nathaniel A., and Ryan P. Weber. 2011. "Ecological, Pedagogical, Public Rhetoric." *College Composition and Communication* 63 (2): 187–218.

Spinuzzi, Clay. 2008. *Network: Theorizing Knowledge Work in Telecommunications.* New York: Cambridge UP. http://dx.doi.org/10.1017/CBO9780511509605.

Syverson, Margaret. 1999. *The Wealth of Reality: An Ecology of Composition.* Carbondale, IL: SIU Press.

Waddell, Craig, ed. 1998. *Landmark Essays on Rhetoric and the Environment.* Mahwah, NJ: Lawrence Erlbaum Associates.

ENGLISH

A. Suresh Canagarajah

The grammar and values attached to *English* have been changing in
relation to social and philosophical developments. It is difficult to talk
about *English* without clarifying what we mean by *language*, an orientation shaped by the ways communities have related to each **other** in
social history.

Many people think of languages as separate from each other, each
with its own grammar, vocabulary, and other structural features forming a tightly woven system that determines meaning and communication. While there are different varieties of a language (dialects, registers,
and **discourses**), they are considered to derive from the one underlying
system, finding manifestation in a shared standard language, to which
everyone should adhere. However, this idea of language is recent. It is
attributed to European modernity, to Johannes Herder, who connected
language, place, and **community**, giving a bounded and territorial **identity** to each of them (Blommaert 2010). This language **ideology** is different from orientations in other places and times. In precolonial South
Asia, for example, people thought of languages as resources they could
freely borrow from and adopt as part of their own repertoire, giving
them meanings related to their own interests (Khubchandani 1997),
an orientation to language that is becoming relevant again as people
shuttle between languages, constructing hybrid communicative practices in late modernity. Sociolinguist Jan Blommaert therefore calls for
a shift in perspective from "immobile languages" to "mobile resources"
(Blommaert 2010, 43).

If we consider English from this point of view, it was already a set
of mobile and fragmented semiotic resources, already lacking unitary
identity, in its very inception. As Fennell notes, English emerged from
the tribal dialects of Angles, Jutes, and Saxons that migrated to England
from the European mainland around 449 AD. It then combined with
local language resources from Frisian and Celtic tribes, which were
themselves already influenced by Latin colonization, to gain an identity

DOI: 10.7330/9780874219746.c015

as English. English was gradually standardized through technological developments such as printing, the political imposition of rulers such as King Alfred, and lexicographical efforts of scholars like Samuel Johnson (1755). Even as Johnson tried to systematize English, he acknowledged the importance of migration and contact that would continue to hybridize English (Blommaert 2010, 3).

Though the rise of English from a rustic dialect to a vernacular that gained its own national identity against imperial Latin was slow, it quickly developed its own imperial identity in the seventeenth century (see Fennell 2001). The values motivating this language are clear in Thomas Macaulay's (1965) *Minute on India Education*, where he proposed to the British parliament that English should be taught to Indians above the local vernaculars and other regional *linguae francae* such as Sanskrit or Arabic. In Macauley's text, English is represented as a language of science, modernity, and progress; valued for its ability to connect people to other global communities and provide access to information and knowledge; and held up as a superior language on which local peoples should model their own.

What Macaulay didn't anticipate was that the natives would not only use English to refashion their languages, but also shape English to suit their own identities and values. English became increasingly hybrid during the British colonial expansion as it came in contact with ever more disparate communities and languages. Over time, this contact has spawned distinct varieties, with their own identities and functions. In 1986, Indian linguist Braj Kachru coined the term *World Englishes* to capture the notion that English is a multinational language comprising many varieties. He modeled the diversity of English according to its spread and functions in three concentric circles. The Inner Circle, which consists of those who speak English as their native language, is labeled "norm providing," privileging the owners of the language. The Outer Circle, which is constituted by former British colonies where English is spoken as a second language for intra-community purposes, is considered "norm developing," as these communities have their own grammatical norms, different from those of native speakers. Kachru (1986) contended that outer circle varieties such as Sri Lankan, Nigerian, or Singaporean English should not be considered deficient or unsystematic ("broken" in popular parlance), but rule-governed in their own ways. The Expanding Circle consists of communities that speak English as a foreign language, for functional contact purposes with those outside their communities. Kachru maintained that countries in South America, East Asia, and Europe did not have community-internal uses of English, and were thus "norm dependent" on native speakers.

Recent developments in **technology**, migration, and communication have further pluralized *English*, motivating a critique of World Englishes. Scholars now point out that communities in the Expanding Circle have considerable local uses of English and are developing their own norms, leading to varieties such as Mexican English (Clemente and Higgins 2008) and German English (Erling 2002). Empirical studies also show that multilinguals in contact situations are not deferring to native speaker norms but constructing their own *lingua franca* norms (Seidlhofer 2004). More significantly, scholars have come to doubt whether native speaker communities are at the center of these developments anymore, determining the spread, functions, and norms of English. They point out that multilinguals who use English as an additional language far exceed native speakers in number—they have thus shifted the power in their favor as they creatively use English for their own purposes and values, reconfiguring the language (Graddol 1999). For this reason, scholars of English as an International Language (EIL) do not model global English into three-tiered circles, but adopt a flat plane where all varieties share the same status (Crystal 2004; McArthur 1987; Modiano 2004). For EIL, English is "a family of languages" (Crystal 2004, 49).

The debate now centers on how speakers of these diverse varieties will talk to each other in the future. While some fear the fragmentation of English, others are not so pessimistic. Those in the EIL school predict that a neutral global norm will arise to help multinational people communicate. A more empirical project to describe this evolving global norm is the English as a Lingual Franca (ELF) school (see Jenkins 2006 and Seidlhofer 2004). These scholars are identifying the bare minimum grammatical and lexical resources one needs to communicate in English. They claim that ELF is free of values and voices and thus serves as a "language for communication" rather than a "language for identification" (House 2003, 561). In other words, these scholars assert that ELF is an instrumental and functional variety that doesn't pose identity and power threats.

Others question whether a neutral global norm is possible or desirable, whether eliminating identity and voice in certain forms of communication is a proper goal. Besides, the neutral norm might develop alternate identities, perhaps bland, mechanical, or impersonal ones, which also present problems for those who value aesthetic and cultural richness in a language (Tibor 2004). More importantly, there is empirical evidence to show that multilinguals do not rely on a uniform norm, but rather on situational co-construction of meaning from the diverse resources they bring with them (Canagarajah 2007; Meierkord 2004). What this means is that multilinguals (and often native speakers in contact situations) collaborate in defining their norms and meanings interpersonally through the mix of languages they bring with them. This practice-based orientation to communication differs from the traditional assumption that a predefined grammar determines meaning. Scholars are now moving away from trying to codify the grammar and system of global English and are instead searching for the practices that help people negotiate meaning and grammar from ground up in situated interactions (Pennycook 2010).

There are many terms being deployed to describe this orientation to English as a set of mobile semiotic resources. In the field of composition, terms such as *codemeshing* (Canagarajah 2006; Young 2004) and *translingual practice* (Canagarajah 2011; Horner et al. 2011) are becoming familiar. This orientation has implications not only for **multilingual** writers but native speakers as well. Compositionists have started questioning if teaching a single norm as the target is helpful to students, and, indeed, if a monolithic and neutral variety of Standard Written English even exists. Compositionists are now exploring how they can develop the metalinguistic awareness and communicative practices for all students to shuttle between language resources as they construct texts that negotiate the relevant norms of the respective **contexts** and audiences.

References

Blommaert, Jan. 2010. *A Sociolinguistics of Globalization*. Cambridge: Cambridge University Press. http://dx.doi.org/10.1017/CBO9780511845307.

Canagarajah, A. Suresh. 2006. "The Place of World Englishes in Composition: Pluralization Continued." *College Composition and Communication* 57 (4): 586–619.

Canagarajah, A. Suresh. 2007. "Lingua Franca English, Multilingual Communities, and Language Acquisition." *Modern Language Journal* 91 (5): 921–37.

Canagarajah, A. Suresh. 2011. "Codemeshing in Academic Writing: Identifying Teachable Strategies of Translanguaging." *Modern Language Journal* 95 (3): 401–17. http://dx.doi.org/10.1111/j.1540-4781.2011.01207.x.

Clemente, Angeles, and Michael Higgins. 2008. *Performing English with a Postcolonial Accent*. London: Tufnell.

Crystal, David. 2004. *The Language Revolution*. Cambridge, UK: Polity.

Erling, Elizabeth. 2002. "'I Learn English Since Ten Years': The Global English Debate and the German University Classroom." *English Today* 70: 8–13.

Fennell, Barbara. 2001. *A History of English: A Sociolinguistic Approach*. Oxford: Blackwell.

Graddol, David. 1999. "The Decline of the Native Speaker." *AILA Review* 13: 57–68.

Horner, Bruce, Min-Zhan Lu, Jacqueline Jones Royster, and John Trimbur. 2011. "Language Difference in Writing: Toward a Translingual Approach." *College English* 73 (3): 303–21.

House, Julianne. 2003. "English as a Lingua Franca: A Threat to Multilingualism?" *Journal of Sociolinguistics* 7 (4): 556–78. http://dx.doi.org/10.1111/j.1467-9841 .2003.00242.x.

Jenkins, Jennifer. 2006. "Current Perspectives on Teaching World Englishes and English as a Lingua Franca." *TESOL Quarterly* 40 (1): 157–81. http://dx.doi.org/10.2307 /40264515.

Johnson, Samuel. 1755. *A Dictionary of the English Language.* London: Strahan.

Kachru, Braj. 1986. *The Alchemy of English: The Spread, Functions and Models of Non-Native Englishes.* Oxford: Pergamon.

Khubchandani, Lachman. 1997. *Revisualizing Boundaries: A Plurilingual Ethos.* New Delhi, India: Sage.

Macaulay, Thomas. (1835) 1965. "Minute by the Hon'ble T. B. Macaulay, dated the 2nd February 1835." In *Bureau of Education: Selections from Educational Records, Part I (1781–1839),* ed. H. Sharp, 107–117. Calcutta: Superintendent, Government Printing, 1920. Reprint, Delhi: National Archives of India. http://www.columbia.edu/itc/mealac /pritchett/00generallinks/macaulay/txt_minute_education_1835.html.

McArthur, Tom. 1987. "The English Languages?" *English Today* 3 (3): 9–13. http:// dx.doi.org/10.1017/S0266078400013511.

Meierkord, Cristina. 2004. "Syntactic Variation in Interactions across International Englishes." *English World-Wide* 25 (1): 109–32. http://dx.doi.org/10.1075/eww.25 .1.06mei.

Modiano, Marko. 2004. "Monoculturalization and Language Dissemination." *Journal of Language, Identity, and Education* 3 (3): 215–27. http://dx.doi.org/10.1207/s153277 01jlie0303_3.

Pennycook, Alastair. 2010. *Language as a Local Practice.* London: Routledge.

Seidlhofer, Barbara. 2004. "Research Perspectives on Teaching English as a Lingua Franca." *Annual Review of Applied Linguistics* 24: 209–39. http://dx.doi.org/10.1017 /S0267190504000145.

Tibor, Frank. 2004. "Supranational English, American Values, and East-Central Europe." *PMLA* 119 (1): 80–91. http://dx.doi.org/10.1632/003081204X23548.

Young, Vershawn. 2004. "Your Average Nigga." *College Composition and Communication* 55 (4): 693–715. http://dx.doi.org/10.2307/4140667.

GENDER

Lorin Shellenberger

Gender's relationship with writing studies has long been complicated. According to Joy Ritchie and Kathleen Boardman, in the 1970s "composition's official published discussions were largely silent on issues of gender," with "little explicit evidence of systematic theorizing about gender from the 1950s to the late 1980s" (Ritchie and Boardman 1999, 586). Despite gender's overwhelming presence in feminist studies during this time period, it was not until 1988, when Elizabeth Flynn examined gender differences in student writing, that gender entered the discussion in composition studies at all (Flynn 1988, 425).

Gender is portrayed as both a "covert category," seemingly "transparent" in human interactions, and yet also "highly visible" in texts (Curzan 2003, 20; Davies 1993, xiv–xv). Suzanne Romaine, for example, claims gender is "a dynamic process that people index, do, display, communicate, or perform," to the extent that "gender itself has become a verb" (Romaine 1999, 4). Judith Butler calls gender "an act which has been rehearsed" and "the vehicle for the phantasmatic transformation of that nexus of race and **class**, the site of its articulation" (Butler 1990, 272; 1993, 130). And, according to Catharine MacKinnon, gender contains a "force" of "biological or mythic or semantic partition, engraved, inscribed, or inculcated by god, nature, society (agents unspecified), the unconscious, the cosmos" (MacKinnon 1987, 32). Scholars disagree about the use of the term: social scientists refer to *gender* as a "'factor' or a 'dimension' of an analysis" or "'a mark' of biological, linguistic, and/or cultural difference," while some feminist scholars understand the term to signify "'a relation,' indeed, a set of relations, and not an individual attribute" (Butler 1990, 13). **Other** scholars equate gender with "psychological functioning" or "a constructivist category," locating it as a site for possible transformation (Grosz 1994, 17–18). Butler even wonders "whether *gender* is the term to be argued about at all, or whether the discursive construction of *sex*, is, indeed, more fundamental, or perhaps *women* or *woman* and/or *men* or *man*" (Butler 1990, 15, emphasis in original).

DOI: 10.7330/9780874219746.c016

These complicated understandings of gender arise, it seems, from its being invoked as both a category with particular characteristics and as a variable liable to change at any moment. Gender is "a social category imposed on a sexed **body**" (Scott 1988, 32) and "a category, a way of making distinctions between people" (Farganis 1989, 215). At the same time, gender "builds on a highly variable and interpretable biological given" (Dimen 1989, 38); is "a performative, fluid and unstable category" (Jones 2011, 170); and is "a fundamental or organic social variable in all human experience" (Showalter 1997, 67), with "no fixed essence" (Flax 1997, 171). Krista Ratcliffe might put it best, identifying *gender* as a "slippery category": "its associated meanings shift across time and place" and "intersect with meanings ascribed to other cultural categories that classify people, such as age, class, race, ethnicity, nationality, and religion" (Ratcliffe 2005, 11).

Indeed, *gender* seems to be always moving and yet always constant: "Gender is a complexity whose totality is permanently deferred, never fully what it is at any given juncture of time" (Butler 1990, 22), it "varies both within and over time" (Flax 1997, 171) and "never exhibits itself in pure form" (Bordo 1990, 147), and yet "gender must be related to a moment in time—now and not then—as well as to a place—here and not there. Gender, variable as it may be, is a constant of history" (Farganis 1989, 215). Gender can be a boundary, creating "lines that separate male and female, feminine and masculine," and it can also be "rhizomatic," with "many ways to be a girl or boy, and in which girls are not limited to femininity and boys are not limited to masculinity" (Blackburn 2005, 406; Rowan et al. 2002, 74). Gender has "both external and internal dimensions" (Farganis 1989, 215) and is seen as both "an interior essence that might be disclosed" and "a free-floating artifice" that can't be contained (Butler 1990, xiv, 10).

Gender also has a wide range of impact. Gender can "mark" people, objects, and cultural positions (Ratcliffe 2005, 11); can affect issues, influence, social expectations, disparity, inequalities, achievement (Peterson and Parr 2011, 152–53), bias, assumptions, problematics (Sullivan 2003, 136–37), pedagogies, and ideologies (Maor 2003, 348); and can influence spaces, **locations**, duties, identities (Enoch 2008, 287), language (Curzan 2003), tropes (Ratcliffe 2005, 9), communicative practices, **discourse**, roles (Sullivan 2003, 133–34), experience (Kirsch and Ritchie 1995, 11), and traits (Grosz 1994, 17). One can have "gender loyalties" (Harding 1986, 138) or be "gender-neutral" (Sullivan 2003, 134), be "gender-blind" or "gender-sensitive" (Peaden 1993, 260).

Gender, bodies, and textuality intersect in complex and powerful ways. On the one hand, Butler (1990) argues, gender is "'prediscursive,' prior to culture, a politically neutral surface *on which* culture acts" and "the very apparatus of **production** whereby the sexes themselves are established" (10, emphasis in original). But she also urges us to think of "gender [as] the repeated stylization of the body, a set of repeated acts within a highly rigid regulatory frame" (43–44). For Butler, "bodies cannot be said to have a signifiable existence prior to the mark of their gender" (Butler 1993, 13), while Elizabeth Grosz claims "the kind of body inscribed makes a difference to the meanings and functioning of gender that emerges" (Grosz 1994, 58). Likewise, Susan Bordo argues the bodies of disordered women are texts that "insist to be read as a cultural statement, a statement about gender" (Bordo 1989, 16).

Gender is also often associated with social, cultural, and political power. According to Cheryl Glenn, gender is a "relationship among distributions of power," "an institution of power relations learned through and perpetuated by culture" (Glenn 1997, 2, 12). Ratcliffe claims gender is "always a question . . . of unearned privilege and power—or lack thereof" (Ratcliffe 2005, 10), and Monique Wittig argues "gender is the linguistic index of the political oppositions between the sexes" (Wittig 1983, 64). According to Muriel Dimen, "gender is the way that consciousness of self, and so one's sense of empowerment, is most immediately experienced" (Dimen 1989, 38).

These many strands of meaning can also be seen operating in the ways *gender* circulates in writing studies. For instance, scholars have identified associations between gender and reading texts (both teachers' readings of student texts and students' readings of texts), gender and writing, and gender and written comments to student writing (Barnes 1990; Gabriel 1990; Rubin 1993). In like manner, our understandings of *writing*, per se, seem strongly inflected by meanings associated with *gender*. David Bleich (1989) argues for an almost inextricable connection between gender and writing, noting the etymological association of *gender* and *genre*. For Bleich, "the genders of writing show significant correspondences to the genders that govern social relations," such that *gender* is used instead of *genre* to "emphasize the political ingredients in the idea of a 'kind' of anything, in this case writing" (13). As Susan Jones explains, "both gender and writing are value-laden concepts," and the gender of the writer is "a possible determiner in both engagement and success," a "variable" that can provide "an advantage," particularly when it comes to writing (Jones 2011, 162–65). Similarly, Gemma Moss notes that "gender is always intersected by the designation of ability," and Elizabeth Dutro portrays gender as a "central tension" in children's reading practices (Moss 2007, 165; Dutro 2002, 383).

Finally, scholars have identified the gendered space of the writing classroom itself as a rich problematic. According to Jessica Enoch, the writing classroom is traditionally considered a "gendered sphere" that results in the "gendered **identity** of the teacher," and Susan Jones argues that writing classrooms must now **work** to "challenge dominant gender discourses and represent gender as a diverse category informed by post-structural perspectives" (Enoch 2008, 285–87; Jones 2011, 170). Susan Jarratt thus identifies the writing classroom as "the starting point for creating a consciousness in students and teachers" about the conflicts often created by gender, race, and class (Jarratt 2003, 275–76).

In sum, as writing studies evolves, the complex ways that *gender* writes and is written in our discourses will surely continue to evolve as well.

References

Barnes, Linda Laube. 1990. "Gender Bias in Teachers' Written Comments." In *Gender in the Classroom*, ed. Susan L. Gabriel and Isaiah Smithson, 140–59. Chicago: University of Illinois Press.

Blackburn, Mollie. 2005. "Disrupting Dichotomies for Social Change: A Review of, Critique of, and Complement to Current Educational Literacy Scholarship on Gender." *Research in the Teaching of English* 39 (4): 398–416.

Bleich, David. 1989. "Genders of Writing." *JAC* 9 (1): 10–25.

Bordo, Susan. 1989. "The Body and the Reproduction of Femininity: A Feminist Appropriation of Foucault." In *Gender/Body/Knowledge*, ed. Alison M. Jaggar and Susan R. Bordo, 13–33. New Brunswick: Rutgers University Press.

Bordo, Susan. 1990. "Feminism, Postmodernism, and Gender-Skepticism." In *Feminism/ Postmodernism*, ed. Linda J. Nicholson, 133–56. New York: Routledge.

Butler, Judith. 1990. *Gender Trouble*. New York: Routledge.

Butler, Judith. 1993. *Bodies that Matter*. New York: Routledge.

Curzan, Anne. 2003. *Gender Shifts in the History of English*. Cambridge: Cambridge University Press. http://dx.doi.org/10.1017/CBO9780511486913.

Davies, Bronwyn. 1993. *Shards of Glass*. Cresskill, NJ: Hampton Press.

Dimen, Muriel. 1989. "Power, Sexuality, and Intimacy." In *Gender/Body/Knowledge*, ed. Alison M. Jaggar and Susan R. Bordo, 34–51. New Brunswick: Rutgers University Press.

Dutro, Elizabeth. 2002. "'But That's a Girls' Book!': Exploring Gender Boundaries in Children's Reading Practices." *Reading Teacher* 55 (4): 376–84.

Enoch, Jessica. 2008. "A Woman's Place is in the School: Rhetorics of Gendered Space in Nineteenth-Century America." *College English* 70 (3): 275–95.

Farganis, Sondra. 1989. "Feminism and the Reconstruction of Social Science." In *Gender/ Body/Knowledge*, ed. Alison M. Jaggar and Susan R. Bordo, 207–23. New Brunswick, NJ: Rutgers University Press.

Flax, Jane. 1997. "Postmodernism and Gender Relations in Feminist Theory." In *Feminisms*, ed. Sandra Kemp and Judith Squires, 170–78. Oxford: Oxford University Press.

Flynn, Elizabeth. 1988. "Composing as a Woman." *College Composition and Communication* 39 (4): 423–35. http://dx.doi.org/10.2307/357697.

Gabriel, Susan L. 1990. "Gender, Reading, and Writing: Assignments, Expectations, and Responses." In *Gender in the Classroom*, ed. Susan L. Gabriel and Isaiah Smithson, 127–39. Chicago: University of Illinois Press.

Glenn, Cheryl. 1997. *Rhetoric Retold*. Carbondale: Southern Illinois University Press.

Grosz, Elizabeth. 1994. *Volatile Bodies*. Bloomington: Indiana University Press.

Harding, Sandra. 1986. *The Science Question in Feminism*. Ithaca: Cornell University Press.

Jarratt, Susan C. 2003. "Feminism and Composition: The Case for Conflict." In *Feminism and Composition: A Critical Sourcebook*, ed. Gesa E. Kirsch, Faye Spencer Maor, Lance Massey, Lee Nickoson-Massey, and Mary P. Sheridan, 140–59. Boston: Bedford/St. Martin's.

Jones, Susan. 2011. "Mapping the Landscape: Gender and the Writing Classroom." *Journal of Writing Research* 3 (3): 161–79.

Kirsch, Gesa, and Joy Ritchie. 1995. "Beyond the Personal: Theorizing a Politics of Location in Composition Research." *College Composition and Communication* 46 (1): 7–29. http://dx.doi.org/10.2307/358867.

MacKinnon, Catherine. 1987. *Feminism Unmodified: Discourses on Life and Law*. Cambridge: Harvard University Press.

Maor, Faye Spencer. 2003. "Gender, Teaching, and Identity: Introduction." In *Feminism and Composition: A Critical Sourcebook*, ed. Gesa E. Kirsch, Faye Spencer Maor, Lance Massey, Lee Nickoson-Massey, and Mary P. Sheridan, 347–50. Boston: Bedford/St. Martin's.

Moss, Gemma. 2007. *Literacy and Gender*. New York: Routledge.

Peaden, Catherine Hobbes. 1993. "Review of *Gender Issues in the Teaching of English*." *Journal of Advanced Composition* 13: 260–63.

Peterson, Shelly Stagg, and Judy M. Parr. 2011. "Gender Literacy Issues and Research: Placing the Spotlight on Writing." *Journal of Writing Research* 3 (3): 151–61.

Ratcliffe, Krista. 2005. *Rhetorical Listening: Identification, Gender, Whiteness*. Carbondale: Southern Illinois University Press.

Ritchie, Joy, and Kathleen Boardman. 1999. "Feminism in Composition: Inclusion, Metonymy, and Disruption." *College Composition and Communication* 50 (4): 585–606. http://dx.doi.org/10.2307/358482.

Romaine, Suzanne. 1999. *Communicating Gender*. Mahwah, NJ: L. Erlbaum Associates.

Rowan, Leonie, Michelle Knobel, Chris Bigum, and Colin Lankshear. 2002. *Boys, Literacies and Schooling*. Buckingham, UK: Open University Press.

Rubin, Donnalee. 1993. *Gender Influences: Reading Student Texts*. Carbondale: Southern Illinois University Press.

Scott, Joan Wallach. 1988. *Gender and the Politics of History*. New York: Columbia University Press.

Showalter, Elaine. 1997. "A Criticism of Our Own: Autonomy and Assimilation in Afro-American and Feminist Literary History." In *Feminisms*, ed. Sandra Kemp and Judith Squires, 58–69. Oxford: Oxford University Press.

Sullivan, Patricia. 2003. "Feminism and Methodology in Composition Studies." In *Feminism and Composition: A Critical Sourcebook*, ed. Gesa E. Kirsch, Faye Spencer Maor, Lance Massey, Lee Nickoson-Massey, and Mary P. Sheridan, 124–39. Boston: Bedford/St. Martin's.

Wittig, Monique. 1983. "The Point of View: Universal or Particular?" *Feminist Issues* 3 (2): 63–69. http://dx.doi.org/10.1007/BF02685543.

GENRE

Amy J. Devitt

The word genre has its origins in a French word for *kind* and a dictionary sense of "kind, sort, style" (*OED Online* 2014). In common parlance it
refers to hip hop music and *Laike Moussike*, to comedy and poetry, to film
noir and chick flick. In the discipline of writing studies, genre has come
to refer to a highly theorized concept of "social action," so that a search
in *College Composition and Communication* for "genre" (since 2005) or even
"the genre of" brings up not labels for or studies of specific genres but
rather discussions of genre in the abstract. The breadth and diversity of
genres as discussed in popular **discourse** make *genre* even more interesting a term to genre theorists.

   Although Aristotle itemized the genres of epic, tragedy, and comedy
and Edwin Black (1965) steered rhetorical criticism toward genres as
situational types in the 1960s, genre scholarship within writing studies
was largely moribund until the 1980s, when an article by Carolyn Miller
built upon Black and **others** to redefine *genre* as "typified rhetorical
actions based in recurrent situations" (Miller 1984, 159). The **work** that
followed from Miller has been aptly termed "rhetorical genre studies"
(RGS) (Freedman 1999, 764) because it treats genres as rhetorically
meaningful actions, not as categories of literary analysis or **creativity**-
constricting formulae. Today, RGS (Miller 1984; see also Bawarshi and
Reiff 2010; Bazerman 2009; Devitt 2009; Russell 1997) is commonly
contrasted with genre work in "**English** for Specific Purposes" (ESP)
(Bhatia 1993; Hyland 1998; Johns 1997; Swales 1990; Tardy 2006) and
the so-called Australian or Sydney School based in "Systemic Functional
Linguistics" (SFL) (Halliday 1978; see also Christie 1987; Cope and
Kalantzis 1993; Martin 1997; Martin and Rothery 1993). Each has different purposes and groundings. Miller and others in RGS base genre
in recurrent rhetorical situations (Bitzer 1968) and apply their work
most commonly to FYC and writing in the professions. John Swales
and others in ESP, building from Swales' foundational book on *Genre
Analysis*, ground genre in communicative purposes and apply their work

DOI: 10.7330/9780874219746.c017

particularly to second language writers. J. R. Martin and others build SFL from Halliday's and Malinowski's context of situation and context of cultures and strive to increase access to academic and workplace genres for marginalized groups. Increasingly, these three "schools" of genre studies have been learning from one another, building on their common grounding of genre in rhetorical contexts and concern for novices learning unfamiliar genres (see Bawarshi and Reiff 2010; Tardy 2009).

At the heart of all these contemporary views of genre lies an understanding of genres as actions that writers perform in similar ways in similar contexts over time. Charles Bazerman describes how far beyond forms genres go when he writes,

> Genres are not just forms. Genres are forms of life, ways of being. They are frames for social action. They are environments for learning. They are **locations** within which meaning is constructed. Genres shape the thoughts we form and the communications by which we interact. Genres are the familiar places we go to [in order] to create intelligible communicative action with each other and the guideposts we use to explore the unfamiliar. (Bazerman 1997, 19)

Because genres are actions embedded in shifting social contexts, they remain dynamic, not static. Catherine Schryer, oft quoted, argues that genres are "stabilized-for-now . . . or stabilized-enough sites of social and ideological action" (Schryer 1994, 108). Genres interact with other genres within these contexts, performing the work of professional communities in genre sets (Devitt 1991) or serving as tools within activity systems (Russell 1997), within other kinds of systems (Bazerman 1994; Yates and Orlikowski 2002), or within a genre **ecology** across systems (Spinuzzi 2003). Besides *tool* and *forms of life*, other common metaphors for genre emphasize different parts of its nature: among other things, genres are imagined as biological species, families, social institutions, speech acts, sites, and, of course, social actions (see Bastian 2007; Fishelov 1993; Swales 2004, 68).

Against the common perception of genres as formulas (mysteries, romance, other "genre writing") and limits (which "creative" writers need to break), genre theory argues that genre clarifies as well as constrains a writer's choices (Christie 1987; Devitt 1997). It also argues that genre's constraints run much deeper than many casual critics realize. Rather than just templates that can produce formulaic writing, genres as social actions limit what writers believe they can do. As Miller points out, "[W]hat we learn when we learn a genre is not just a pattern of forms or even a method of achieving our own ends. We learn, more importantly, what ends we may have" (Miller 1994, 38). Anne Freadman elaborates, in her extended analogy of genres as games, that "To understand the rules of the genre is to know when and where it is appropriate to do and say certain things, and to know that to say and do them at inappropriate places and times is to run the risk of having them ruled out" (Freadman 1994, 59). The ideological nature of genres within their communities has thus been the focus of considerable scholarly attention (see Coe, Lingard, and Teslenko 2002; Freedman and Medway 1994; Paré 2002).

Embedded within communities, schools, and professions, genres become actions that can be fully understood or appropriately enacted only by insiders. Berkenkotter and Huckin (1995) argue that genre knowledge itself is "best conceptualized as a form of situated cognition embedded in disciplinary activities" (477). Given genre's social embeddedness, great debate has raged over the teachability of genres, especially in the classroom apart from the **community**. Aviva Freedman (1993) crystallized the issues in her critical article "Show and Tell? The Role of Explicit Teaching in the Learning of New Genres," arguing for the necessity of immersion over explicit instruction (for challenges to her argument, see Swales 2004; Williams and Colomb 1993). **Others** have developed extensive curricula to teach contextual as well as formal genre knowledge. Most notably, those in the Sydney School since the 1980s have developed a teaching–learning cycle for teaching the textual, and increasingly contextual, traits of powerful school and workplace genres (see Cope and Kalantzis 1993; Feez and Joyce 1998). Those working in ESP teach genre's **context** along with rhetorical moves (see Johns 1997 and Swales 1990 for examples). Working primarily with postsecondary instruction, scholars in RGS have argued for teaching critical genre awareness, an analytic approach that combines rhetorical understanding of a genre's formal traces with critique of a genre's **ideology** (Bawarshi 2003, Devitt 2004; 2009). Christine Tardy (2006; 2009) combines substantial bodies of first and second language **research**, demonstrating that instruction in genres as "typified responses to repeated situational exigencies" crosses language borders (Tardy 2009, 6).

Traditional questions, particularly among some in literary and communication studies, about genres as formal categories—Is this a genre or a subgenre? What formal traits distinguish this genre from others? Is this a genre or some other kind of thing?—tend to be of little interest to contemporary genre scholars within writing studies. Still, specific genres examined within writing studies have ranged from the end comment (Smith 1997) to social workers' assessments (Paré 2002), from blogs (Miller and Shepherd 2004) to experimental articles (Bazerman 1988), from research articles (Swales 2004) to syllabi (Bawarshi 2003).

Contemporary genre scholarship emphasizes community, context, and—increasingly—cognition (see Bazerman 2009, Nowacek 2011, and Reiff and Bawarshi 2011 for examples). Even amidst debates about teaching genres, relatively little has yet been said about the individual's construction of genre or the nature of genre as an individual interpretation. A rich concept, genre still has much to be researched and much to offer writing studies.

References

Bastian, Heather. 2007. "Rethinking Identity through Generic Agency." Conference on College Composition and Communication, New York.

Bawarshi, Anis. 2003. *Genre and the Invention of the Writer: Reconsidering the Place of Invention in Composition.* Logan: Utah State University Press.

Bawarshi, Anis, and Mary Jo Reiff. 2010. *Genre: An Introduction to History, Theory, Research, and Pedagogy.* West Lafayette, IN: Parlor Press.

Bazerman, Charles. 1988. *Shaping Written Knowledge: The Genre and Activity of the Experimental Article in Science.* Madison, WI: University of Wisconsin Press.

Bazerman, Charles. 1994. "Systems of Genres and the Enactment of Social Intentions." In *Genre and the New Rhetoric*, ed. Aviva Freedman and Peter Medway, 79–101. Bristol: Taylor and Francis.

Bazerman, Charles. 1997. "The Life of Genre, the Life in the Classroom." In *Genre and Writing: Issues, Arguments, Alternatives*, ed. Wendy Bishop and Hans Ostrom, 19–26. Portsmouth: Boynton/Cook.

Bazerman, Charles. 2009. "Genre and Cognitive Development: Beyond Writing to Learn." In *Genre in a Changing World*, ed. Charles Bazerman, Adair Bonini, and Débora Figueiredo, 283–98. Fort Collins, CO: The WAC Clearinghouse and Parlor Press.

Berkenkotter, Carol, and Thomas Huckin. 1995. *Genre Knowledge in Disciplinary Communication.* Hillsdale, NJ: Lawrence Erlbaum.

Bhatia, Vijay. 1993. *Analysing Genre: Language Use in Professional Settings.* London: Longman.

Bitzer, Lloyd F. 1968. "The Rhetorical Situation." *Philosophy & Rhetoric* 1: 1–14.

Black, Edwin. 1965. *Rhetorical Criticism: A Study in Method.* New York: Macmillan.

Christie, Frances. 1987. "Genres as Choice." In *The Place of Genre in Learning: Current Debates*, ed. Ian Reid, 22–35. Geelong: Deakin University.

Coe, Richard, Lorelei Lingard, and Tatiana Teslenko, eds. 2002. *The Rhetoric and Ideology of Genre: Strategies for Stability and Change.* New Jersey: Hampton Press.

Cope, Bill, and Mary Kalantzis. 1993. *The Powers of Literacy: A Genre Approach to Teaching Writing.* Pittsburgh: University of Pittsburgh Press.

Devitt, Amy J. 1991. "Intertextuality in Tax Accounting: Generic, Contemporary Studies of Writing in Professional Communities." In *Textual Dynamics of the Professions: Historical and Contemporary Studies of Writing in Professional Communities*, ed. Charles Bazerman and James Paradis, 335–57. Madison: University of Wisconsin Press.

Devitt, Amy J. 1997. "Genre as Language Standard." In *Genre and Writing: Issues, Arguments, Alternatives*, ed. Wendy Bishop and Hans Ostrom, 45–55. Portsmouth, NH: Boynton.

Devitt, Amy J. 2004. *Writing Genres.* Carbondale: Southern Illinois University Press.

Devitt, Amy J. 2009. "Teaching Critical Genre Awareness." In *Genre in a Changing World*, ed. Charles Bazerman, Adair Bonini, and Débora Figueiredo, 342–55. Fort Collins, CO: WAC Clearinghouse and Parlor Press.

Feez, Susan, and H. Joyce. 1998. *Text-Based Syllabus Design.* Sydney: National Center for English Language Teaching and Research.

Fishelov, David. 1993. *Metaphors of Genre: The Role of Analogies in Genre Theory.* University Park: Pennsylvania State University Press.

Freadman, Anne. 1994. "Anyone for Tennis?" In *Genre and the New Rhetoric,* ed. Aviva Freedman and Peter Medway, 43–66. Bristol: Taylor and Francis.

Freedman, Aviva. 1993. "Show and Tell? The Role of Explicit Teaching in the Learning of New Genres." *Research in the Teaching of English* 27: 222–51.

Freedman, Aviva. 1999. "Beyond the Text: Towards Understanding the Teaching and Learning of Genres." *TESOL Quarterly* 33 (4): 764–67. http://dx.doi.org/10.2307/3587890.

Freedman, Aviva, and Peter Medway, eds. 1994. *Learning and Teaching Genre.* Portsmouth, NH: Boynton/Cook.

Halliday, M. A. K. 1978. *Language as Social Semiotic: The Social Interpretation of Language and Meaning.* London: Edward Arnold.

Hyland, Ken. 1998. *Hedging in Scientific Research Articles.* Amsterdam: John Benjamins. http://dx.doi.org/10.1075/pbns.54.

Johns, Ann M. 1997. *Text, Role, and Context: Developing Academic Literacies.* New York: Cambridge University Press. http://dx.doi.org/10.1017/CBO9781139524650.

Martin, J. R. 1997. "Analysing Genre: Functional Parameters." In *Genres and Institutions: Social Processes in the Workplace and School,* ed. Frances Christie and J. R. Martin, 33–69. London: Cassell.

Martin, J. R., and J. Rothery. 1993. "Grammar: Making Meaning in Writing." In *The Powers of Literacy: A Genre Approach to Teaching Writing,* ed. B. Cope and M. Kalantzis, 137–53. Pittsburgh, PA: University of Pittsburgh Press.

Miller, Carolyn R. 1984. "Genre as Social Action." *Quarterly Journal of Speech* 70 (2): 151–67. http://dx.doi.org/10.1080/00335638409383686.

Miller, Carolyn R. 1994. "Rhetorical Community: The Cultural Basis of Genre." In *Genre and the New Rhetoric,* ed. Aviva Freedman and Peter Medway, 67–77. Bristol: Taylor and Francis.

Miller, Carolyn R., and Dawn Shepherd. 2004. "Blogging as Social Action: A Genre Analysis of the Weblog." In *Into the Blogosphere: Rhetoric, Community, and Culture of Weblogs,* ed. Laura J. Gurak, Smiljana Antonijevic, Laurie Johnson, Clancy Ratliff, and Jessica Reyman. http://blog.lib.umn.edu/blogosphere/visual_blogs.html.

Nowacek, Rebecca. 2011. *Agents of Integration: Understanding Transfer as a Rhetorical Act.* Carbondale, IL: Southern Illinois University Press.

OED Online. 2014. "genre, n." Oxford University Press. Accessed December 2014.

Paré, Anthony. 2002. "Genre and Identity: Individuals, Institutions, and Ideology." In *The Rhetoric and Ideology of Genre: Strategies for Stability and Change,* ed. Richard Coe, Lorelei Lingard, and Tatiana Teslenko, 57–71. Creskill, NJ: Hampton Press.

Reiff, Mary Jo, and Anis Bawarshi. 2011. "Tracing Discursive Resources: How Students Use Prior Genre Knowledge to Negotiate New Writing Contexts in First-Year Composition." *Written Communication* 28 (3): 312–37. http://dx.doi.org/10.1177/0741088311410183.

Russell, David. 1997. "Rethinking Genre in School and Society: An Activity Theory Analysis." *Written Communication* 14 (4): 504–54. http://dx.doi.org/10.1177/0741088397014004004.

Schryer, Catherine. 1994. "The Lab vs. the Clinic: Sites of Competing Genres." In *Genre and the New Rhetoric,* ed. Aviva Freedman and Peter Medway, 105–24. London: Taylor and Francis.

Smith, Summer. 1997. "The Genre of the End Comment: Conventions in Teacher Responses to Student Writing." *College Composition and Communication* 48 (2): 249–68. http://dx.doi.org/10.2307/358669.

Spinuzzi, Clay. 2003. *Tracing Genres through Organizations: A Sociocultural Approach to Information Design.* Cambridge, MA: MIT Press.

Swales, John M. 1990. *Genre Analysis: English in Academic and Research Settings.* Cambridge: Cambridge University Press.

Swales, John M. 2004. *Research Genres: Explorations and Applications.* Cambridge: Cambridge University Press. http://dx.doi.org/10.1017/CBO9781139524827.

Tardy, Christine. 2006. "Researching First and Second Language Genre Learning: A Comparative Review and a Look Ahead." *Journal of Second Language Writing* 15 (2): 79–101. http://dx.doi.org/10.1016/j.jslw.2006.04.003.

Tardy, Christine. 2009. *Building Genre Knowledge.* West Lafayette, IN: Parlor Press.

Williams, Joseph, and Gregory G. Colomb. 1993. "The Case for Explicit Teaching: Why What You Don't Know Won't Help You." *Research in the Teaching of English* 27: 252–64.

Yates, JoAnne, and Wanda Orlikowski. 2002. "Genre Systems: Structuring Interaction through Communicative Norms." *The Journal of Business Communication* 39: 13–35.

IDENTITY

Morris Young

Considering *identity* as a keyword in writing studies is a daunting prospect. What is meant by *identity* and how might it differ from terms such as *ethos* (Baumlin and Baumlin 1994), *self* (Brooke 1991), or *subject* (Clifford 1991)? How might *identity* signify in ways similar to **other** expressions such as *voice* (Elbow 2000; Harris 1997), *identification* (Burke 1950; Ratcliffe 2005), *the personal* (Bleich and Holdstein 2001), or any number of related and cognate terms that might overlap or even act synonymously?

In composition studies, the main locus for understanding the significance of identity has been the curricular site of the classroom where, as Michelle Cox et al. (2010) have described, the field has tried "to reconcile the identities students bring with the identities their instructors expect them to occupy—or at least perform—as they develop into academic and professional writers" (xvii). The transformation of the US population throughout the twentieth century was reflected in the college classroom with the entrance of students from more diverse socio-economic, racial, and ethnic backgrounds, including first-generation and nontraditional students (Crowley 1998; Fleming 2010; Shaughnessy 1977; Stanley 2010). This growing sense of heterogeneous language practices, and a necessity to address the range of preparedness of students, made identity an apparent presence in the classroom. Recognizing these changing conditions, the Conference on College Composition and Communication (1974) issued a policy statement, "Students' Right to Their Own Language": "We affirm the students' right to their own patterns and varieties of language—the dialects of their nurture or whatever dialects in which they find their own identity and style" (2). Subsequent research by scholars such as Geneva Smitherman (1986), Shirley Brice Heath (1983), Mina P. Shaughnessy (1977), and David Bartholomae (1985) focused on the development and use of language as informed by social contexts and how this may inform a student's entry into formal educational settings and his or her introduction to academic

DOI: 10.7330/9780874219746.c018

discourses. Identity in these studies functions as a resource and **context** to explain and argue for language use of all varieties as intentional and systematic rather than as deficient and reductively essentializing.

For Roz Ivanič, "Writing is an act of identity in which people align themselves with socio-culturally shaped possibilities for self-hood, playing their part in reproducing or challenging dominant practices and discourses, and the values, beliefs, and interests which they embody" (Ivanič 1998, 32). Similarly, in his **work** on literacy and the use of identity as a frame for educational research, James Paul Gee has described discourse as an "identity kit" (Gee 1989, 7) or as "ways of being certain kinds of people" (Gee 2000, 110). In connecting discourse and identity in this way, Gee theorizes and develops a framework for analyzing language practices as both a **performance** and a socializing experience (Gee 1989, 8). Thus, as Joy Ritchie (1989) has argued, "the personal, educational, and linguistic histories students bring to our classes contribute to the rich texture of possibilities for writing, thinking, and for negotiating personal identity" (157).

The social turn in the human sciences—a shift that foregrounded the social construction of knowledge—situated individual subjectivity within broader social contexts and actions, making identity a key dimension in understanding composing practices (Trimbur 1994). As Bronwyn T. Williams has argued, identity, "as opposed to an internal somewhat stable sense of 'self,' has been recognized as a construction, influenced by culture and **ideology** and changeable depending on the social context" (Williams 2006, 4). Similarly, John Clifford has critiqued traditional and expressive rhetorical theory for its unproblematic assumption that the "individual writer is free, beyond the contingencies of history and language, to be an authentic and unique consciousness" (Clifford 1991, 39). In these contexts, the term *identity* is invested with the political status of the subject—scholars began to consider how language was not only informed by identity but also used as a mode to respond to specific conditions and exigencies experienced by individuals and communities (Berlin 2003; Faigley 1992). Understanding how subjects are located in specific historical, social, cultural, and institutional contexts and the uses of language in these **locations** helped build scholarship about the experiences of writers as informed by **gender**, race and ethnicity, social **class**, sexuality, and other identity positions, and also influenced researchers to look beyond the classroom to what Anne Ruggles Gere has termed "the extracurriculum of composition" (Gere 1994, 79).

In looking at language practices in sites beyond the classroom, scholars have worked to identify, recuperate, and situate the language practices of those who have often been placed on the margins of culture because of their identities, showing how identity and language are co-constitutive and inform the composing practices that are not only shaped by experience but that also provide a means for expression of those identities (e.g., Alexander 2008; Baca 2008; Cintron 1997; Hesford 1999; Logan 1999; Lyons 2000; Moss 1994; Ratcliffe 2005; Rose 1989). For example, in studying the rhetorical work of African American women, Jacqueline Jones Royster argues that "in what may be a non-Westernized sense of the relationships between experience and truth—and between these two concepts and the social roles that such relationships support in one's daily life—African American women invoke 'truth' or experience as a source of both passion and commitment in constructing and presenting the speaking self" (Royster 2000, 67). Similarly, LuMing Mao and Morris Young (2004) have theorized Asian American rhetoric as a "rhetoric of becoming," that is, a "rhetoric that participates in this generative process, yielding an identity that is Asian American and producing a transformative effect that is always occasioned by use" (Mao and Young 2009, 5). Vershawn Ashanti Young (2007) is especially mindful of the problematic equation of language practices and racial identity. He critiques code switching as a way to maintain "authentic" racial identity while acquiring secondary discourses and their attendant cultural capital, and he argues that code meshing more accurately reflects the diverse language practices that are part and parcel of language use and identity performance (7).

Within the social turn in writing studies we have also seen a narrative or **personal** turn, a move to foreground the theorizing of identity and writing through critical **reflection** and the rhetorical construction of the self. As Debra Journet, Beth A. Boehm, and Cynthia E. Britt argue, "The ability to say 'I' is a narrative act, not because of an ontologically prior subject, but because the notion of 'I' only makes sense for something or someone who is located in space and extended through time: engaged, that is, in the narrative act of being a self" (Journet, Boehm, and Britt 2011, 8). David Bleich and Deborah Holdstein explicate "how fundamental it is in humanistic scholarship to take account, in a variety of ways and as part of the subject matter, of the personal and collective experiences of scholars, researchers, critics, and teachers" (Bleich and Holdstein 2001, 1). Scholars such as Keith Gilyard (1991), Donna LeCourt (2004), and Victor Villanueva (1993), among others, have used narrative to interrogate the relationship between identity and language by unpacking the historical, social, and language and **literacy** contexts that have shaped their lives and informed their own theorizing of writing. These studies return us to the pedagogical implications for both teachers and students in their performance and application of identity. As Karen Kopelson writes, "In short, a performative pedagogy endeavors to proliferate innumerable—and in*enumerable*—*possibilities* for identity, rather than to *represent* one bounded identity or the other, ultimately to expose and contest the normalizing processes of identity's construction" (Kopelson 2002, 20, emphasis in original).

Whether we see identity inflected in the registers, styles, or syntax of language or see identity in the tropes and symbolic work as informed by culture and experience, the interaction between identity and writing functions epistemologically to create and express knowledge that is not necessarily located in and limited by identity but rather expands what we understand about how we write and why we write through an awareness of who we are.

References

Alexander, Jonathan. 2008. *Literacy, Sexuality, Pedagogy: Theory and Practice for Composition Studies*. Logan, UT: Utah State University Press.

Baca, Damian. 2008. *Mestiz@ Scripts, Digital Migrations, and the Territories of Writing*. New York: Palgrave MacMillan. http://dx.doi.org/10.1057/9780230612570.

Bartholomae, David. 1985. "Inventing the University." In *When a Writer Can't Write: Studies in Writer's Block and Other Composing Problems*, ed. Mike Rose, 134–65. New York: Guilford.

Baumlin, James S., and Tita French Baumlin, eds. 1994. *Ethos: New Essays in Rhetorical and Critical Theory*. Dallas: Southern Methodist University Press.

Berlin, James. 2003. *Rhetorics, Poetics, Cultures: Refiguring College English Studies*. West Lafayette, IN: Parlor Press.

Bleich, David, and Deborah H. Holdstein. 2001. "Introduction: Recognizing the Human in the Humanities." In *Personal Effects: The Social Character of Scholarly Writing*, ed. Deborah H. Holdstein and David Bleich, 1–24. Logan, UT: Utah State University Press.

Brooke, Robert E. 1991. *Writing and Sense of Self: Identity Negotiation in Writing Workshops*. Urbana, IL: National Council of Teachers of English.

Burke, Kenneth. 1950. *A Rhetoric of Motives*. New York: Prentice Hall.

Cintron, Ralph. 1997. *Angel's Town: Chero Ways, Gang Life, and Rhetorics of the Everyday*. Boston: Beacon Press.

Clifford, John. 1991. "The Subject in Discourse." In *Contending with Words: Composition and Rhetoric in a Postmodern Age*, ed. Patricia Harkin and John Schilb, 38–51. New York: Modern Language Association of America.

Conference on College Composition and Communication. 1974. "Students' Right to Their Own Language." *College Composition and Communication* 25 (3): 1–18.

Cox, Michelle, Jay Jordan, Christina Ortmeier-Hooper, and Gwen Gray Schwartz, eds. 2010. *Reinventing Identities in Second-Language Writing*. Urbana, IL: National Council of Teachers of English.

Crowley, Sharon. 1998. *Composition in the University: Historical and Polemical Essays*. Pittsburgh: University of Pittsburgh Press.

Elbow, Peter. 2000. *Everyone Can Write: Essays Toward a Hopeful Theory of Writing and Teaching Writing*. New York: Oxford University Press.

Faigley, Lester. 1992. *Fragments of Rationality: Postmodernity and the Subject of Composition.* Pittsburgh: University of Pittsburgh Press.

Fleming, David. 2010. *From Form to Meaning: Freshman Composition and the Long Sixties, 1957–1974.* Pittsburgh: University of Pittsburgh Press.

Gee, James Paul. 1989. "Literacy, Discourse, and Linguistics: Introduction." *Journal of Education* 171 (1): 5–17.

Gee, James Paul. 2000. "Identity as an Analytic Lens for Research in Education." *Review of Research in Education* 25: 99–125.

Gere, Anne Ruggles. 1994. "Kitchen Tables and Rented Rooms: The Extracurriculum of Composition." *College Composition and Communication* 45 (1): 75–92. http://dx.doi.org /10.2307/358588.

Gilyard, Keith. 1991. *Voices of the Self: A Study of Language Competence.* Detroit: Wayne State University Press.

Harris, Joseph. 1997. *A Teaching Subject: Composition Since 1966.* Upper Saddle River, NJ: Prentice-Hall.

Heath, Shirley Brice. 1983. *Ways with Words.* New York: Cambridge University Press.

Hesford, Wendy S. 1999. *Framing Identities: Autobiography and the Politics of Pedagogy.* Minneapolis: University of Minnesota Press.

Ivanič, Roz. 1998. *Writing and Identity: The Discoursal Construction of Identity in Academic Writing.* Amsterdam: John Benjamins Publishing Company. http://dx.doi.org/10 .1075/swll.5.

Journet, Debra, Beth A. Boehm, and Cynthia E. Britt, eds. 2011. *Narrative Acts: Rhetoric, Race and Identity, Knowledge.* Creskill, NJ: Hampton Press.

Kopelson, Karen. 2002. "Dis/Integrating the Gay/Queer Binary: 'Reconstructed Identity Politics' for a Performative Pedagogy." *College English* 65 (1): 17–35. http://dx.doi.org /10.2307/3250728.

LeCourt, Donna. 2004. *Identity Matters: Schooling the Student Body in Academic Discourse.* Albany: Statue University of New York Press.

Logan, Shirley Wilson. 1999. *We Are Coming: The Persuasive Discourse of 19th Century Black Women.* Carbondale: Southern Illinois University Press.

Lyons, Scott R. 2000. "Rhetorical Sovereignty: What Do American Indians Want from Writing?" *College Composition and Communication* 51 (3): 447–68. http://dx.doi.org /10.2307/358744.

Mao, LuMing, and Morris Young, eds. 2009. *Representations: Doing Asian American Rhetoric.* Logan: Utah State University Press.

Moss, Beverly J. 1994. *Literacy across Communities.* Cresskill, NJ: Hampton.

Ratcliffe, Krista. 2005. *Rhetorical Listening: Identification, Gender, Whiteness.* Carbondale, IL: Southern Illinois University Press.

Ritchie, Joy S. 1989. "Beginning Writers: Diverse Voices and Individual Identity." *College Composition and Communication* 40 (2): 152–74. http://dx.doi.org/10.2307/358126.

Rose, Mike. 1989. *Lives on the Boundary.* New York: Penguin Books.

Royster, Jacqueline Jones. 2000. *Traces of a Stream: Literacy and Social Change among African American Women.* Pittsburgh: University of Pittsburgh Press.

Shaughnessy, Mina. 1977. *Errors and Expectations: A Guide for Teachers of Basic Writing.* New York: Oxford University Press.

Smitherman, Geneva. 1986. *Talkin and Testifyin: The Language of Black America.* Detroit: Wayne State University Press.

Stanley, Jane. 2010. *The Rhetoric of Remediation: Negotiating Entitlement and Access to Higher Education.* Pittsburgh: University of Pittsburgh Press.

Trimbur, John. 1994. "Taking the Social Turn: Teaching Writing Post Process." *College Composition and Communication* 45 (1): 108–18. http://dx.doi.org/10.2307/358592.

Villanueva, Victor, Jr. 1993. *Bootstraps: From an American Academic of Color.* Urbana, IL: National Council of Teachers of English.

Williams, Bronwyn T., ed. 2006. *Identity Papers: Literacy and Power in Higher Education.* Logan: Utah State University Press.

Young, Morris. 2004. *Minor Re/Visions: Asian American Literacy Narratives as a Rhetoric of Citizenship.* Carbondale, IL: Southern Illinois University Press.

Young, Vershawn Ashanti. 2007. *Your Average Nigga: Performing Race, Literacy, and Masculinity.* Detroit: Wayne State University Press.

IDEOLOGY

Kelly Pender

Ideology became a keyword in writing studies in the early 1990s, when a number of rhetoricians began arguing that the Marxist understanding of the term as "false consciousness" should be replaced with the definition found in Louis Althusser's (1994) essay, "Ideology and Ideological State Apparatuses." Whereas the Marxist understanding held that ideology masked an individual's relationship to real conditions of existence, Althusser argued that ideology represented an individual's *imaginary* relationship to those conditions, that it had a material existence, and that it interpellated individuals as subjects (123, 125, 128). Among **other** things, this definition meant that there was nothing behind ideology— no real self or true knowledge—that could be accessed to catalyze social change. While a number of rhetoricians (e.g., Bizzell 1991, Clifford 1991, and Faigley 1989) worked to popularize this definition of *ideology* in writing studies, no one did more to ensure its keyword status than James Berlin (1988; 1992).

The main source of Berlin's conception of ideology wasn't Althusser per se, but rather the Althusser-influenced **work** of Göran Therborn, who understood the term *ideology* to refer to a dominant way of thinking about what exists, what is good, and what is possible (Berlin 1992, 23). Following Therborn, Berlin argued that ideology interpellates individuals as subjects and, using "strong social and cultural reinforcements," makes those forms of subjectivity—and the "authority regimes" that support them—appear natural while disqualifying others as unnatural (Berlin 1992, 23–24). What is crucial about Berlin's definition is the way it relates ideology to rhetoric. Relying on Therborn and, later, Stuart Hall, Berlin understood ideology as something that is located in **discourse** (Berlin 1992, 681; 1988, 24). If ideology creates subjects and is located in discourse, then it stands to reason that subjects are created discursively. This formulation not only makes rhetoricians critics of ideology *par excellence,* but it also makes their classrooms sites where students can learn to analyze and resist the oppressive discourses that interpellate them.

DOI: 10.7330/9780874219746.c019

Beginning in the late 1990s, this relationship between ideology and rhetoric became a significant source of disagreement regarding the definition and role of ideology in writing studies. One manifestation of this disagreement focused on the issue of interpretation, specifically on the fact that to claim rhetoric is housed in ideology is to suggest that the rhetorician's main function is interpretation. Susan Miller challenged this suggestion in 1997, arguing that Berlin's definition of ideology turned composition into an enterprise of cultural hermeneutics that, despite its cache in **English** departments, could not motivate the literate practices students needed to become effective writers (Miller 1997, 499). In 2001, Raúl Sánchez similarly argued that in order for composition to "begin accounting for the increasingly complex webs of textual relations" in which subjects write, it must develop a textual rhetoric that incorporates *but does not prioritize* a theory of ideology (Sánchez 2001, 742).

A second manifestation of the disagreement about the definition of *ideology* in writing studies centers on the conception of subjectivity operating in Berlin's work. Using psychoanalytic theory, Marshall Alcorn (1995; 2002) and Thomas Rickert (2007) both ask: by what mechanism does someone become a subject of one discourse instead of another? For Berlin, the answer was critical thinking—students change their ideological identifications once critical thinking reveals how oppressive they are. Identifying this reliance on critical thinking as a vestige of liberal humanism, both Alcorn and Rickert sought to complicate the field's understanding of ideology. Alcorn did this in 1995 (and later in 2002) by focusing on the "defensive subject functions"—or libidinal investments—that motivate an individual to "actively process" the discourses to which they are exposed (Alcorn 1995, 338). "Because of a kind of adhesive 'attachment' that subjects have to certain instances of discourse," Alcorn explained, "some discourse structures are 'characteristic' of subjects and have a temporal stability" (339). In other words, subjects will work to defend the discourses that are "symptomatic" of their subjectivity—even if those discourses are oppressive to themselves or others (348). Changing these discourses requires not just critical thinking, Alcorn wrote, but also a "mournful mode of **reflection**" that can address the "unconscious fears and poorly repressed internal conflicts" driving oppression (343, 345).

In 2007, Thomas Rickert also drew attention to the affective and unconscious forces operating in ideology. However, he used the neo-Lacanian theory of Slavoj Žižek (1989) particularly in his *The Sublime Object of Ideology, to* offer two distinct reasons why ideology critique typically fails to produce change: (1) ideology manifests in what one does, not just in what one knows; and (2) it operates in the Lacanian register of the Real, not just in the Imaginary and Symbolic. With regard to the first point, Rickert argued that, whereas Berlin saw ideology as an internal relation to external circumstances, Žižek insists ideology is to be found in what people do, that is, in their practices (Rickert 2007, 117). Thus while Berlin's work would lead us to see a contradiction between someone's actions and beliefs as a sign that ideology critique hasn't gone far enough, Žižek's would suggest that this contradiction between doing and knowing *is* ideology (102). From this perspective, Rickert argued that the critical distance generated by critique often works *not* to dislodge ideology but rather to ensure its survival (124).

The second part of Rickert's claim is harder to explain since it deals with the Real, the most elusive of Lacan's tripartite conception of the psyche. For most theorists, ideology operates in the Symbolic and the Imaginary. However, for Žižek—and for Rickert—ideology also operates in the Real, the realm Lacan associated with a kind of positivity that does not, strictly speaking, exist (and therefore cannot be represented) but yet manifests in our lives in specific forms of fundamental antagonisms. According to Žižek, ideology works to create fantasies that provide a way out of contact with these fundamental antagonisms, or what he calls "traumatic kernel[s]" of the Real (Žižek 1989, 181). As Rickert (2007) explained, these ideological fantasies are not daydreams but rather unconscious fantasies that create and integrate subjects into a social reality, thus providing them with a necessary and enjoyable sense of coherence that cannot easily be undermined by critical thinking (106, 119, 126; see also Barbara Biesecker 1998).

Despite these critical and unresolved definitional disputes, work in writing studies nonetheless uses *ideology* in remarkably stable ways to refer broadly to the dominant ideas underlying theories and practices. As Bruce McComiskey argued, even though notions of "false consciousness" do lurk within many post-Marxist understandings of *ideology*, the term still has considerable practical value for rhetoricians (McComiskey 2002, 172). Scholars use *ideology* in sub-fields such as **genre** studies, writing center studies, **literacy** studies, second language writing, and **technical communication** as a tool for revealing the dominant ideas undergirding a wide variety of rhetorical, linguistic, cultural, disciplinary, and pedagogical practices (e.g., ESL writing instruction, software documentation, legal discourse, composition pedagogy, workplace genres, etc.) without making the term's meaning the central concern of their work (see, for instance, Canagarajah 2010; Holborow 2006; Canagarajah

2010; Maher 2011; Paré 2002). Accepting the psychoanalytic uses of ideology would likely mean sacrificing some of this broad practical applicability, or at least reconceptualizing it.

It is important to note, however, that some recent scholarship in writing studies has both used ideology as an interpretive tool and made an explicit argument about its definition. Patricia Harkin's (2006) "Excellence is the Name of the (Ideological) Game" is a good case in point. Harkin reads the commonly-used Althusserian definition of ideology through a postmodern lens, drawing on Fredric Jameson's (1981) work in *The Political Unconscious* and Jean-François Lyotard's in *Just Gaming* (Lyotard and Thebaud 1985) to emphasize the "multiplicity of contradictory interpellations" that force academic subjects to measure their "excellence" in the language game of "grantsmanship" (Harkin 2006, 31, 36, 39). While the primary goal of Harkin's essay is to explain how the word *excellent* performs a specific ideological function within the university, it also keeps open questions of what *ideology* means and can mean, demonstrating that as long as we are willing to approach it from different theoretical perspectives, *ideology* can signify in productively different ways across writing studies.

References

Alcorn, Marshall, Jr. 1995. "Changing the Subject of Postmodernist Theory: Discourse, Ideology, and Therapy in the Classroom." *Rhetoric Review* 13 (2): 331–49. http://dx.doi.org/10.1080/07350199509359191.

Alcorn, Marshall, Jr. 2002. *Changing the Subject of English: Discourse Ideology, and Therapy in the Classroom.* Carbondale, IL: Southern Illinois University Press.

Althusser, Louis. 1994. "Ideology and Ideological State Apparatuses (Notes toward an Investigation)." In *Mapping Ideology*, ed. Slavoj Źiźek, 100–39. London: Verso.

Berlin, James. 1988. "Rhetoric and Ideology in the Writing Classroom." *College English* 50 (5): 477–94. http://dx.doi.org/10.2307/377477.

Berlin, James. 1992. "Poststructuralism, Cultural Studies, and the Composition Classroom: Postmodern Theory in Practice." *Rhetoric Review* 11 (1): 16–33. http://dx.doi.org/10.1080/07350199209388984.

Biesecker, Barbara. 1998. "Rhetorical Studies and the "New" Psychoanalysis: What's the Problem? Or, Framing the Problem of the Real." *Quarterly Journal of Speech* 84 (2): 222–40. http://dx.doi.org/10.1080/00335639809384215.

Bizzell, Pat. 1991. "Marxist Ideas in Composition Studies." In *Contending with Words*, ed. Patricia Harkin and John Schilb, 52–68. New York: Modern Language Association.

Canagarajah, Suresh. 2010. "Ideology and Theory in Second Language Writing: A Dialogical Treatment." In *Practicing Theory in Second Language Writing*, ed. Tony Silva and Paul K. Matsuda, 176–90. West Lafayette, IN: Parlor Press.

Clifford, John. 1991. "The Subject in Discourse." In *Contending with Words*, ed. Patricia Harkin and John Schilb, 38–51. New York: Modern Language Association.

Faigley, Lester. 1989. "The Study of Writing and the Study of Language." *Rhetoric Review* 7 (2): 240–56. http://dx.doi.org/10.1080/07350198909388859.

Harkin, Patricia. 2006. "Excellence is the Name of the (Ideological) Game." In *Identity Papers: Literacy and Power in Higher Education*, ed. Bronwyn Williams, 29–41. Logan: Utah State University Press.

Holborow, Marnie. 2006. "Ideology and Language: Interconnections between Neoliberalism and English." In *(Re-)Locating TESOL in an Age of Empire*, ed. Julian Edge, 84–103. Hampshire, UK: Palgrave Macmillan.

Holdstein, Deborah. 2008. "The Religious Ideology of Composition Studies." In *Judaic Perspectives in Rhetoric and Composition*, ed. Andrea Greenbaum and Deborah Holdstein, 13–22. Cresskill, NJ: Hampton Press.

Jameson, Fredric. 1981. *The Political Unconscious: Narrative as a Socially Symbolic Act*. New York: Cornell University Press.

Lyotard, Jean-Francios, and Jean-Loup Thebaud. 1985. *Just Gaming*. Trans. Wlad Godzich. Minneapolis: University of Minnesota Press.

Maher, Jennifer. 2011. "The Technical Communicator as Evangelist: Toward Critical and Rhetorical Literacies of Software Documentation." *Journal of Technical Communication* 41 (4): 367–401.

McComiskey, Bruce. 2002. "Ideology and Critique in Composition Studies." *JAC* 22 (1): 167–75.

Miller, Susan. 1997. "Technologies of Self-Formation." *JAC* 17 (3): 497–500.

Paré, Anthony. 2002. "Genre and Identity: Individuals, Institutions, and Ideology." In *The Rhetoric and Ideology of Genre*, ed. Richard Coe, Lorelei Lingard, and Tatiana Teslenko, 57–72. Cresskill, NJ: Hampton Press.

Rickert, Thomas. 2007. *Acts of Enjoyment: Rhetoric, Źiźek, and the Return of the Subject*. Pittsburgh, PA: University of Pittsburgh Press.

Sánchez, Raúl. 2001. "Composition's Ideology Apparatus: A Critique." *JAC* 21 (4): 741–59.

Źiźek, Slavoj. 1989. *The Sublime Object of Ideology*. London: Verso.

LITERACY

Julie Lindquist

In popular usage, the term *literacy* is most often associated with reading (understood as a process of decoding alphabetic text) and writing (understood as an act of inscribing alphabetic text). Among scholars, however, the term encompasses a much broader range of values, processes, and behaviors: "*literacy* is an abstract noun with no corresponding verb to tell us what range of actions might possibly be associated with it" (Lindquist and Seitz 2009, 7). **Research** on literacy thus occurs across the fields that take up writing studies, including history, psychology, sociology, anthropology, education, composition and rhetoric, and cultural studies, and the domain of inquiries associated with literacy is expansive and expanding. *Elements of Literacy*, for example, is organized into five "sites" of literacy research and practice: mind, culture, **class**, **work**, and **technology**. Cushman et al. (2001) likewise acknowledge this complexity, organizing their study into the following thematic sections: "Technologies for Literacy"; "Literacy, Knowledge, and Cognition"; "Histories of Literacy in the United States"; "Literacy Development"; "Culture and Community"; "Power, Privilege, and Discourse"; and "Mobilizing Literacy: Work and Social Change."

The interest in literacy has been directed less to language development and reading theory and more toward literacy (1) as cultural and social practices that are in some way related to reading and writing; (2) as a way to name relationships between forms of rhetorical activity and their educational implications, and (3) as a concept that reveals the terms and stakes of participation in the **discourse** of education. Just what acts and processes the terms *reading* and *writing* describe—and what it means to study these—has been a question of enduring interest in literacy studies. Earlier research on literacy by psychologists, historians, and anthropologists was largely motivated by the question of what literacy, once it is acquired by individuals and societies, makes happen (Goody 1986; Goody and Watt 1963; Ong 1982). These inquiries addressed contrasts between orality and literacy not only as modes of communication,

DOI: 10.7330/9780874219746.c020

but as ways of being. Theories of a "Great Divide" between orality and literacy spoke to the imagined effects of writing on culture and society and drew strong correlations between print culture and its cognitive and social "consequences"; Ong, for instance, goes so far as to speculate that "writing restructures thought" (Ong 1982).

Others have been more circumspect about the idea of global and predictable effects of written language, even given the obvious affordances of alphabetic literacy as a form that preserves communication in time and circulates widely. As literacy researchers have discovered the widely varying cultural uses, values, and contexts of reading and writing, a strong deterministic position has been more difficult to sustain. Scribner and Cole's (1981) famous study of writing among the Vai in Liberia concluded that behaviors earlier associated with alphabetic literacy per se were more likely to be products of schooling. Similarly, Shirley Brice Heath (1983), in her likewise famous study of oral and written practices in the Carolina Piedmont, found that acts of reading and writing were culturally situated and deeply interrelated practices, leading to a now common understanding that the effects of writing cannot be named or predicted without reference to contexts of use. Even Goody, whose early work had advocated a version of the "Great Divide" theory of literacy, eventually noted: "It is a gross ethnocentric error of Europe to attribute too much to the alphabet and too much to the West" (Goody 1987, 56, quoted in Nystrand 1996). In sum, literacy researchers, as David Bloome (1996) noted, have concluded that "the experiences of any one group of people should not constitute the evidential basis of claims and theories for others" (145).

The idea that *literacy* therefore names a highly **context**-dependent assemblage of social practices has inspired an array of studies seeking to learn how reading and writing are *used* in cultures and **communities**. As James Paul Gee puts it, "Because speech and writing so often go together and because both trade on contextual interactions for interpretation, it is often better to study *social practices* that include both writing and speech, as well as various values, ways of thinking, believing, acting, and interacting, and using various objects, tools, and technologies" (Gee 2006, 155). The "New Literacy Studies" thus describes an intellectual enterprise that covers a vast expanse of disciplinary and methodological territory, including ethnomethodology, the ethnography of speaking, cultural studies of science and technology, composition theory, narrative studies, and sociology.

Along with questions about what literacy means and how it is used, there has emerged another line of inquiry about what literacy *does* for its users and how it is enabled. Researchers have focused in particular on the economies of literacy—how literate practices accrue value and how they function as currency for their users. In her widely influential "Sponsors of Literacy," Deborah Brandt (1998) situates acts of literacy within social and economic structures and processes, describing literacy "sponsors" as "any agents, local or distant, concrete or abstract, who enable, support, teach, model, as well as recruit, regulate, suppress, or withhold literacy—and gain advantage by it in some way" (166). The idea of sponsorship foregrounds literacy as an unevenly distributed form of social capital that secures privileges and enables mobility. Observed Brandt: "literacy, like land, is a valued commodity in this economy, a key resource in gaining profit and edge . . . [and] this value helps to explain the lengths to which people will go to secure literacy for themselves and their children" (168).

Driven by the increasing pace of developments in communication technologies, the past two decades has seen a flurry of scholarship challenging the association of literacy with print culture and alphabetic text. In 1996, literacy scholars and researchers participating as members of the New London Group (1996) began discussing the "new communications environment" brought about by emerging digital/**networked** technologies, proposing that educators charged with literacy instruction "now must account for the burgeoning variety of text forms associated with information and multimedia technologies." Educational efforts directed to the formation of literate **citizens**, they argued, must now include communication in various modes, in "multiliteracies," including audio and visual literacies. The idea of "multiliteracies"—which include non-alphabetic, non-print, multimediated forms of meaning-making— has had an enormous impact on subsequent conversations about the meaning and conduct of literacy.

As composition studies sought to understand relationships between schooling and cultural practices, it also sought to consider what forms of literacy the project of education in composition itself should sponsor—to ask, that is, "whether the purpose of gaining power via literacy should be to *acquire* social power or to *critique* it," and whether the first responsibility of a writing teacher "should be to help students accumulate the things they need to gain entrance into cultures of power and access, or whether teachers should encourage these students to learn to exert some control over those cultures in the first place" (Lindquist and Seitz 2009, 126). These concerns led to the rise of "critical literacy" as an area of concern in the field, a development to which the philosophies of "critical" pedagogues such as Paulo Freire have been central.

Freire (1995) believed that a primary aim of schooling should be to engender political dissent and empowerment, and he saw literacy as a way to develop the "critical consciousness" necessary for freedom. In *Pedagogy of the Oppressed,* Freire described a "problem-posing" pedagogy that encourages students to become skeptical about the political implications of schooled literacy. Though Freire's work has attracted as many critics as devotees, his educational philosophy of literacy and power has been hugely influential to those seeking to understand the critical potential of writing instruction in education.

References

Bloome, David. 1996. "What Counts as Evidence in Researching Spoken and Written Discourses? Orality and Literacy: A Symposium in Honor of David Olson." *Research in the Teaching of English* 41 (2): 136–79.

Brandt, Deborah. 1998. "Sponsors of Literacy." *College Composition and Communication* 49 (2): 165–85. http://dx.doi.org/10.2307/358929.

Cushman, Ellen, Eugene Kintgen, Barry Kroll, and Mike Rose. 2001. *Perspectives on Literacy.* Boston: Bedford/St. Martin's Press.

Freire, Paulo. 1995. *Pedagogy of the Oppressed,* revised edition. New York: Continuum.

Gee, James P. 2006. "Oral Discourse in a World of Literacy. Orality and Literacy: A Symposium in Honor of David Olson." *Research in the Teaching of English* 41 (2): 136–79.

Goody, Jack. 1986. *The Logic of Writing and the Organisation of Society.* Cambridge: Cambridge University Press.

Goody, Jack. 1987. *The Interface between the Written and the Oral.* Cambridge: Cambridge University Press.

Goody, Jack, and Ian Watt. 1963. "The Consequences of Literacy." *Comparative Studies in Society and History* 5 (03): 304–45. http://dx.doi.org/10.1017/S0010417500001730.

Heath, Shirley Brice. 1983. *Ways with Words: Language, Life and Work in Communities and Classrooms.* Cambridge: Cambridge University Press.

Lindquist, Julie, and David Seitz. 2009. *Elements of Literacy.* Boston: Longman/Allyn and Bacon.

New London Group. 1996. "A Pedagogy of Multiliteracies: Designing Social Futures." *Harvard Educational Review* 66 (1): 60–92.

Nystrand, Martin. 1996. "Reponse to David Olson's 'Oral Discourse in World of Literacy.' A Symposium in Honor of David Olson." *Research in the Teaching of English* 41 (2): 136–79.

Ong, Walter J. 1982. *Orality and Literacy: The Technologizing of the Word.* London: Methuen. http://dx.doi.org/10.4324/9780203328064.

Scribner, Sylvia, and Michael Cole. 1981. *The Psychology of Literacy.* Cambridge, MA: Harvard University Press. http://dx.doi.org/10.4159/harvard.9780674433014.

LOCATION

Jennifer Clary-Lemon

Conversations in writing studies that employ the term *location* tend to explore the "sense of *where*" (Mauk 2003, 368, emphasis in original) that structures academic spaces, rhetorical situations, systems of writing, and material and physical sites in which discursive meaning is negotiated. Location often emphasizes the situatedness of **discourse** that spans diverse geographies. Its definition has, at differing times, involved the physical **body**, **contexts** of social life, discourses of the **public** sphere, **ecologies** of writing, classroom location, ecocomposition, service-learning, **contact zones**, and spatial mapping. The variety of uses of *location* reflect changing instantiations of the field played out on discursive terrain. *Location* is often read by metaphor and substitution, and it is often invoked in writing studies by the use of the terms *place, site, space*, and *local.*

The relevance of location to writing studies emerges "precisely because written texts so effectively erase the circumstances of their **production**" (Vandenberg, Hum, and Clary-Lemon 2006, 171). An interest in location has arisen out of the examination of site-based and material circumstances that guide rhetorical choices. In one of its first appearances in texts relevant to writing studies, the term *location* was imbued with similar connotations to that of the term *material*, following Adrienne Rich's suggestion in her widely cited essay, "Notes toward a Politics of Location": writers must move away from the process of abstraction and "begin with the material" (Rich 1985, 9). However, for Rich, location operates on analogous ground with the terms *identity* and *embodied situation*, as she encourages writers to "name the ground we're coming from" (13) in order to connect the world "out there" to an internal sense of self (Rich 1983, 533). Rich's grounding of location in the material, in feminist theory and scholarship, and in destabilizing politics encouraged **others** to continue to preface *location* with connotative terms.

One such construction, "a politics of location," became a commonplace reference in writing studies after the publication of Gesa E. Kirsch and Joy S. Ritchie's *College Composition and Communication* article

DOI: 10.7330/9780874219746.c021

"Beyond the Personal: Theorizing a Politics of Location in Composition Research." Kirsch and Ritchie (1995) argue that making new knowledge is wholly dependent on **personal** experience, as knowledge is connected to larger systems and embedded in **ideology** and culture. Central to their argument is a shift in use of *location* from noun to verb. For Kirsch and Ritchie, "it is not enough to claim the personal and locate ourselves in our scholarship and research"; rather, "composition researchers [must] theorize their locations by examining their experiences as **reflections** of ideology and culture" (8). Kirsch and Ritchie suggest in turn that composition researchers are both in the business of *locating* others' subjectivities, as well as *being located by* marginal positions (in this case, as women and as compositionists) (23). Here, *location* signifies beyond the realm of the individual to describe social and purposive rhetorical interaction.

It was this dynamic change in the use of *location* that led writing studies' scholars to define the term as a function of discourse. While much of the early **work** of location took as its starting point the body and the individual, "locating" oneself or others within writing studies research and scholarship came to signify a shift from conceiving "personal circumstance" to naming dynamic social interaction in which individuals move within, co-construct, and are constructed by, specific, local discursive and rhetorical circumstances. Writing studies scholars therefore increasingly found themselves engaged in the practice of locating the field and its circumstances—situating boundaries (for instance, between composition and creative writing; see Lardner 1999), establishing disciplinary paradigms or pedagogical practices (see McCracken 2008), or investing a concept or project with a sense of situatedness, as in "Locating the Feminism in Cyberfeminism" (Blair, Gajjala, and Tulley 2009; for other examples of this, see also Hull and Nelson 2005; Moon 2007; Rickert 2007). In this way, *location* has similarly functioned to impose structure, order, or weight on emergent situations in the field.

This is not to say that in the process of locating the field an emphasis on location-as-site has been ignored; instead, *location* now signifies dually or trebly to encompass the spatial and material/conceptual. This change may have been propelled in part by scholars who have examined composition as a distinctly North American project of place (see Muchiri et al. 1995), one imbued with site-specific arguments, guidelines, and rules about disciplinarity, naming, and situating the work and working conditions of teachers, researchers, and students (see Ede 2004; Mauk 2003). This use of *location* may also be influenced by the recognition of an economy of writing studies located physically, spatially, and geographically, ignorance of which, Nedra Reynolds (1998) argues, masks the material reality and power negotiations that must take place in any discursive situation, particularly those that engage the politics of **literacy** education. Reynolds argues that use of the term *location* often embraces a "spatial politics" (13), drawing our attention in focused ways to the use of spatial metaphors like *territory, place, boundary,* or *zone* (Reynolds 1998); to the mediation of built environments on discursive production (see Mahala and Swilky 2003); and to complex ecologies of writing and place that note relations of texts, power, individual **agency** and feeling, natural and urbanized landscapes, institutional complexities, economic constraints, and systemic flux.

In discussing the writing classroom, *location* is taken up as a descriptor in both writing-about-writing classrooms and contemporary rhetorical theory. Scholars who embrace place- or location-based pedagogy often ask students to engage a spatial imaginary beyond the classroom, to observe how events, texts, and discursive interventions are "necessarily tied to . . . spatial context—to the cultural, political, or economic fabric of . . . surrounding neighborhoods" (Jacobs, Adams, and Morris 2010, 116). Location-based pedagogy tends to frame writers as members of particular **communities**, environments, and publics, often with a strong element of social advocacy, whether this happens in a classroom in which students create discursive Google Maps (see Jacobs, Adams, and Morris 2010); or "read public discourse as an historical project" in the context of Chicago public school reform (Coogan 2006, 688); or use "deep maps" to connect with a specific place and interrogate their relationships with local infrastructure (see Brooke and McIntosh 2007); or create intertextual documents advocating for specific local changes (see Rivers and Weber 2011).

Cooper's 1986 piece, "The Ecology of Writing," was one of the first to theorize an ecological, systems-based theory of writing; since then, others have used *location* to denote a shift in focus from writing in the first-year classroom to writing beyond it—in/for/with/about specific discourse communities (Deans 2000). *Location,* on one hand, seems to function to separate our ways of knowing the "inside" from the "outside"; however, because location is taken up in areas as diverse as activity theory (see Bazerman and Russell 2003), service learning (see Coogan 2006; Deans 2007), ecocomposition (see Weisser and Dobrin 2001), and writing and **technology** (see Haynes 2007; Lindgren and Owens 2007), *location-as-system* seems to repurpose the notion of *location-as-place,* marking a rhetorical turn away from the politics of location qua individual subjectivity. *Location,* it seems, has come to mark a middle ground between language and **materiality** (see Fleckenstein 2010) without signifying a slide back into uncritical abstraction.

This attention to "the public" within theories of location has been as closely scrutinized as "the private." Margaret Syverson cautions that often conceptions of public rhetoric are "atomistic" in that they still assume a "focu[s] on individual writers, individual texts, isolated acts, processes, or artifacts" (Syverson 1999, 8) without "recognizing the agency of material and institutional forces" (Rivers and Weber 2011, 193). In such cases, *location* is caught up with earlier instantiations of its use to denote the individual and material, and its emerging use to signify ecological, systems-based models of public rhetorics.

Emerging definitions of *location* may be dissolving boundaries among audience, writer, exigence, constraints, and text (see Bitzer 1968) and adopting instead a model of rhetorical ecologies that "recontextualiz[e] rhetorics in their temporal, historical, and lived fluxes" (Edbauer 2005, 9). If so, *location* will come to mediate between individual bodies/written "wheres" and public/social/discursive spaces, and also come to invent publics in place by acknowledging that "the social field is not comprised of discrete *sites* but from events that are shifting and moving, grafted onto and connected with other events" (Edbauer 2005, 10)—events that are all discursive territories.

References

Bazerman, Charles, and David Russell, eds. 2003. *Writing Selves/Writing Societies: Research from Activity Perspectives.* Fort Collins, CO: WAC Clearinghouse.

Bitzer, Lloyd F. 1968. "The Rhetorical Situation." *Philosophy & Rhetoric* 1 (1): 1–14.

Blair, Kristine, Radhika Gajjala, and Christine Tulley. 2009. "The Webs We Weave: Locating the Feminism in Cyberfeminism." In *Webbing Cyberfeminist Practice: Communities, Pedagogies, and Social Action*, ed. Kristine Blair, Radhika Gajjala, and Christine Tulley, 1–22. Cresskill, NJ: Hampton.

Brooke, Robert, and Jason McIntosh. 2007. "Deep Maps: Teaching Rhetorical Engagement through Place-Conscious Education." In *The Locations of Composition*, ed. Christopher Keller and Christian Weisser, 131–150. Albany: SUNY P.

Coogan, David. 2006. "Service Learning and Social Change: The Case for Materialist Rhetoric." *College Composition and Communication* 57 (4): 667–93.

Cooper, Marilyn. 1986. "The Ecology of Writing." *College English* 48 (4): 364–75. http://dx.doi.org/10.2307/377264.

Deans, Thomas. 2000. *Writing Partnerships: Service Learning in Composition.* Urbana: NCTE.

Deans, Thomas. 2007. "Shifting Locations, Genres, and Motives: An Activity Theory Analysis of Service-Learning Writing Pedagogies." In *The Locations of Composition*, ed. Christopher Keller and Christian Weisser, 289–306. Albany: SUNY P.

Edbauer, Jenny. 2005. "Unframing Models of Public Distribution: From Rhetorical Situation to Rhetorical Ecologies." *Rhetoric Society Quarterly* 35 (4): 5–24. http://dx.doi.org/10.1080/02773940509391320.

Ede, Lisa. 2004. *Situating Composition: Composition Studies and the Politics of Location.* Carbondale: SIUP.

Fleckenstein, Kristie. 2010. "Bodysigns: A Biorhetoric for Change." *JAC: A Journal of Composition Theory* 21 (4): 761–90.

Haynes, Cindy. 2007. "In Visible Texts: Memory, MOOS, and Momentum: A Meditation." In *The Locations of Composition*, ed. Christopher Keller and Christian Weisser, 55–70. Albany: SUNY P.

Hull, Glynda A., and Mark Evan Nelson. 2005. "Locating the Semiotic Power of Multimodality." *Written Communication* 22 (2): 224–61. http://dx.doi.org/10.1177/0741088304274170.

Jacobs, Dale, Hollie Adams, and Janine Morris. 2010. "Writing New York: Using Google Maps as a Platform for Electronic Portfolios." *Composition Studies* 38 (2): 111–29.

Kirsch, Gesa E., and Joy S. Ritchie. 1995. "Beyond the Personal: Theorizing a Politics of Location in Composition Research." *College Composition and Communication* 46 (1): 7–29. http://dx.doi.org/10.2307/358867.

Lardner, Ted. 1999. "Locating the Boundaries of Composition and Creative Writing." *College Composition and Communication* 51 (1): 72–77.

Lindgren, Tim, and Derek Owens. 2007. "From Site to Screen, From Screen to Site: Merging Place-Based Pedagogy with Web-Based Technology." In *The Locations of Composition*, ed. Christopher Keller and Christian Weisser, 195–212. Albany: SUNY P.

Mahala, Daniel, and Jody Swilky. 2003. "Constructing Disciplinary Space: The Borders, Boundaries, and Zones of English." *JAC: A Journal of Composition Theory* 23 (4): 765–97.

Mauk, Jonathon. 2003. "Location, Location, Location: The 'Real' (E)states of Being, Writing, and Thinking in Composition." *College English* 65 (4): 368–88. http://dx.doi.org/10.2307/3594240.

Moon, Gretchen Flesher. 2007. "Locating Composition History." In *Local Histories: Reading the Archives of Composition*, ed. Patricia Donahue and Gretchen Flesher Moon, 1–13. Pittsburgh: University of Pittsburgh Press.

Muchiri, Mary N., Nshindi G. Mulamba, Greg Myers, and Deoscorous B. Ndoloi. 1995. "Importing Composition: Teaching and Researching Academic Writing beyond North America." *College Composition and Communication* 46 (2): 175–98. http://dx.doi.org/10.2307/358427.

McCracken, Moriah. 2008. "Locating Place in Writing Studies: An Investigation of Professional and Pedagogical Place-Based Effects." PhD diss., Texas Christian University, Fort Worth.

Reynolds, Nedra. 1998. "Composition's Imagined Geographies: The Politics of Space in the Frontier, City, and Cyberspace." *College Composition and Communication* 50 (1): 12–35. http://dx.doi.org/10.2307/358350.

Rich, Adrienne. 1983. "Blood, Bread, and Poetry: The Location of the Poet." *Massachusetts Review* 24 (3): 521–40.

Rich, Adrienne. 1985. "Notes toward a Politics of Location." In *Women, Feminist Identity, and Society in the 1980's: Selected Papers*, ed. Myriam Díaz-Diocaretz, and Iris M. Zavala, 7–22. Amsterdam: John Benjamins.

Rickert, Thomas. 2007. "Invention in the Wild: On Locating Kairos in Space-Time." In *The Locations of Composition*, ed. Christopher Keller and Christian Weisser, 71–90. Albany: SUNY P.

Rivers, Nathaniel A., and Ryan P. Weber. 2011. "Ecological, Pedagogical, Public Rhetoric." *College Composition and Communication* 63 (2): 187–217.

Syverson, Margaret. 1999. *The Wealth of Reality: An Ecology of Composition*. Carbondale: SIUP.

Vandenberg, Peter, Sue Hum, and Jennifer Clary-Lemon. 2006. *Relations, Locations, Positions: Composition Theory for Writing Teachers*. Urbana: NCTE.

Weisser, Christian R., and Sidney I. Dobrin, eds. 2001. *Ecocomposition: Theoretical and Pedagogical Approaches*. Albany: SUNY Press.

MATERIALITY

Anis Bawarshi

The term *materiality* has a wide range of meanings within the **discourses** of writing studies, often functioning as a modifier ("materialist") to **other** abstractions (as in, "materialist views of situation"). As reflected in its various significations within the field, materiality is used not only to account for the presence of matter and the material, but also to describe the operations of matter ("materialism"). As such, *materiality* is deployed both as a thing itself (an embodied presence), and as a thing that can act in the service of its own ends (as having **agency**). Materiality is used to signify that which surrounds us: the places we inhabit; the climate (political, geographical, ambient) that affects how we encounter one another, what we do, and how we do it; the tools that mediate our social activities and relations; and the institutions, resources, and socio-economic conditions that shape the means of textual **production**, distribution, and assessment. *Materiality* is also used to describe our bodies; our embodied experiences and expressions of emotion; our movements and gestures; the ways we negotiate space, objects, **technologies**, and time as we enact our daily routines and improvisations; and the embodied dispositions we carry with us that Pierre Bourdieu (1990) calls "habitus." These varied usages of the term are often deployed in contrast to terms like *imagined* and *socially constructed*, as in Nedra Reynolds' claim that, while "composition has invested heavily in imagined geographies" (Reynolds 2004, 7), it has ignored or taken for granted the materiality of spaces (27).

Over the past decade, as scholars have challenged writing studies to reconsider many of its key concepts (such as context, literacy, process, invention, the "social turn," *kairos*, the text, agency, cognition, and knowledge transfer), and the practices and relations these concepts make possible, we can observe how meanings attributed to *materiality* come into play with meanings attributed to or assumed in the use of these key concepts. For instance, scholars have accounted for **context** in multiple ways: from Lloyd Bitzer's (1968) definition of rhetorical situation in the 1960s to discourse communities (Bizzell 1982; Swales 1990),

DOI: 10.7330/9780874219746.c022

communities of practice (Lave and Wenger 1991), activity systems (Engeström 1999), and actor-networks (Latour 2005, Spinuzzi 2008) in the late-twentieth and twenty-first centuries. Bitzer (1968), by defining rhetorical situation as the precondition for rhetorical action, emphasized its material status: a rhetorical situation exists prior to rhetorical discourse and rhetors, and the exigence that characterizes it is likewise materialistic, defined as "an imperfection marked by urgency" (6). In this formulation, materiality refers to the ontological, physical nature of context, in comparison to what Reynolds has described as social constructionist notions of context as static and stable, with clearly defined social and discursive boundaries—insiders and outsiders (Reynolds 2004, 40). This meaning of *materiality* is implied in Peter Vandenberg and Jennifer Clary-Lemon's distinction when they describe rhetorical contexts as a "combination of the material, the social and the conceptual" (Vandenberg and Clary-Lemon 2007, 92).

Deployed in relation to context, *materiality* is used to argue that discourse **community** participation involves not only knowledge of discourse conventions but also access to certain technologies as well as embodied positions, movements, and relationalities in real time and space. In this formulation, *materiality* can be taken to acknowledge the **networks** that interact within and between systems of activity. As research in activity systems and, especially, actor-network theory demonstrates, "actor-networks are assemblages of humans and non-humans; any person, artifact, practice, or assemblage of these is considered a node in the network. . . . Links are made across and among these nodes in fairly unpredictable ways" (Spinuzzi 2008, 8). Here, the term *materiality* itself appears to have agency, as if it acts irrespective of the descriptive uses to which it is put. In this way, the term signifies the ways that "bodies occupy material situations that are in constant motion, interpret these flows through bodily knowledge and expression as much as language, and contribute to these assemblages by participating in their **public** gathering" (Hawk 2011, 77).

Another way that materiality signifies in the discourses of writing studies is as a term that modifies conceptions of situation. For example, Bleich (2001) has argued that rhetorical **genre** studies, with its focus on genres "as typified rhetorical actions based in recurrent situations" (Miller 1994, 31), has tended to privilege the socially defined nature of recurrence over the materiality of situation. In this formulation, *materiality* is again contrasted to *socially defined* in ways that allow the term to function as a modifier: a *materialist* approach to rhetorical genre study examines not only situated, typified cognition, but also how forms of cognition become "sedimented at a corporeal level where they are repeated as habits . . . lodged in bodily memory" (Coole and Frost 2010, 34) and taken up in improvised ways. In this context, *materiality* comes to represent arguments for a spatial turn in genre studies (Dryer 2010; Reiff 2011) and for ethnographic approaches to studying genre **performances** in the contexts of their use (Johns 1997; Reiff 2004).

By approaching writing processes not only as temporal performances, but also as performances that are embodied, emotioned, and localized within conditions of production, circulation, and consumption, scholars such as Sidney Dobrin and Nedra Reynolds inflect the meaning of *materiality* with discourses from geography, **ecology**, and economics. Jenny Edbauer's description of rhetoric as viral, as a weather system, as a "network of lived practical consciousness or structures of feelings" (Edbauer 2005, 1) and a "circulating ecology of effects, enactments, and events" (9) reflects such an investment in materiality as ecology. Geographical meanings of *materiality* operate in service-learning pedagogies that are grounded in locatedness and take into account "geographies of exclusion, the politics of space, [and] the construction of sociospatial differences" (Reynolds 2004, 133) that enable students to experience writing as "participation in lived space" (Feldman 2008, 9). More overt economic significations of *materiality* can be recognized in approaches that attend to (1) the technologies that shape access to and means of writing production; (2) the "networks for the distribution of writing" (Selfe 1999); (3) student subjectivities and social relations informed by race, **gender**, **class**, sexuality, generation; (3) class size and access to information (Horner 2000, xviii); and (4) students' varied discursive resources (Lu 2004).

Beyond spatial, economic, and ecological inflections, scholars have also brought affective and somatic perspectives to bear on meanings of *materiality*, as inferred in calls for an "embodied pedagogy" that acknowledges both the way discourses have material effects on the way we live (Fleckenstein 1999, 201) and how **literacy** has its basis in bodily movements and habits (Haas 1996, 228). Laura Micciche (2007) explores the role of emotion in writing, while rhetoricians have examined bodies in motion (Hawhee 2009), the affective impact of discourse on the **body** (Butler 1993), and material rhetorics (Biesecker and Lucaites 2009; Selzer and Crowley 1999). Likewise, acknowledging **research** itself as "a situated material-conceptual practice," Vandenberg and Clary-Lemon (2007) call for a graduate pedagogy of **location** that "promotes mutuality and connectedness, both to lived (rather than imagined) communities and to the material contexts that shape how, why, and for whom writing is valuable" (92).

We can observe the use of *materiality* as a modifier as well as an agent in the way it has been used to expand our understanding of concepts such as invention and *kairos*. Thomas Rickert has examined the emplacement of *kairos* as both opportunity time and opportunity space bound up in material context (Rickert 2007, 72). In this case, a materialist understanding of *kairos* locates invention not merely within the subjectivity of the writer or rhetor but also within agentive contexts that render individuals to act: "Thinking place kairotically, and *kairos* spatially, thereby moves us . . . to something like subjectivity as a condensation of probabilities realized in movement, materialized in space, and invented in place" (Rickert 2007, 85). Among these agentive uses of materiality, David Fleming (2008) has described how built space affects practices of political expression and debate. Cynthia Haynes, examining how digital spaces such as Multi-User Domain Object Oriented spaces (MOOs) call people into being (Haynes 2007, 63), also attends to the materiality of typography (see also Haas 1996; Trimbur 2002) and the ways that "writing in motion" within digital environments constitutes a new form of materiality.

Scholars have also brought economic meanings of *materiality* to bear on how we understand the "terms of work" in composition (Horner 2000). As Bruce Horner argues, the ways that meanings and relations of **work** in composition compete with each other have to do with distinctions between intellectual versus non-intellectual work, commodified/abstracted versus situated/alienated labor, all of which are based in a "failure to confront the materiality of *all* work in composition, including work deemed 'theoretical' or 'scholarly'" (xvii). Tony Scott has likewise focused on the "socio-material terms of labor" that shape pedagogical goals and practices (Scott 2009, 8).

More recently, research on writing development has begun to account for what can be called the materiality of knowledge transfer. Rebecca Nowacek (2011) and Elizabeth Wardle (2007), for instance, have described how transferability is a rhetorical act informed by material conditions and affordances, meditational means, affective investments, and embodied uptakes. In all these ways—as a modifier, as a thing itself, and as a thing that can act in the service of its own ends—materiality functions within the discourses of writing studies.

References

Biesecker, Barbara, and John Louis Lucaites. 2009. *Rhetoric, Materiality, and Politics.* New York: Peter Lang.

Bitzer, Lloyd F. 1968. "The Rhetorical Situation." *Philosophy & Rhetoric* 1 (1): 1–14.

Bizzell, Patricia. 1982. "Cognition, Convention, and Certainty: What We Need to Know about Writing." *Pre/Text* 3: 213–44.

Bleich, David. 2001. "The Materiality of Language and the Pedagogy of Exchange." *Pedagogy* 1 (1): 117–42. http://dx.doi.org/10.1215/15314200-1-1-117.

Bourdieu, Pierre. 1990. *The Logic of Practice.* Trans. Richard Nice. Stanford: Stanford UP.

Butler, Judith. 1993. *Bodies that Matter: On the Discursive Limits of "Sex."* New York: Routldege.

Coole, Diana, and Samantha Frost. 2010. *New Materialism: Ontology, Agency, and Politics.* Durham: Duke UP. http://dx.doi.org/10.1215/9780822392996.

Dryer, Dylan. 2010. "Taking Up Space: Genre Systems as Geographies of the Possible." *JAC* 28 (3–4): 503–34.

Edbauer, Jenny. 2005. "Unframing Models of Public Distribution: From Rhetorical Situation to Rhetorical Ecologies." *Rhetoric Society Quarterly* 35 (4): 5–24. http://dx.doi.org/10.1080/02773940509391320.

Engeström, Yrjo. 1999. "Activity Theory and Individual Social Transformation." In *Perspectives on Activity Theory,* ed. Y. Engeström, R. Miettinen, and R.-L. Punamaki, 19–38. Cambridge: Cambridge UP. http://dx.doi.org/10.1017/CBO9780511812774.003.

Feldman, Ann M. 2008. *Making Writing Matter: Composition in the Engaged University.* Albany: State U of New York P.

Fleckenstein, Kristie S. 1999. "Writing Bodies: Somatic Mind in Composition Studies." *College English* 61 (3): 281–306. http://dx.doi.org/10.2307/379070.

Fleming, David. 2008. *City of Rhetoric: Revitalizing the Public Sphere in Metropolitan America.* Albany: State U of New York P.

Haas, Christina. 1996. *Writing Technology: Studies on the Materiality of Literacy.* Mawhaw: Lawrence Erlbaum.

Hawhee, Debra. 2009. *Moving Bodies: Kenneth Burke at the Edges of Language.* Columbia: U of South Carolina P.

Hawk, Byron. 2011. "Reassembling Postprocess: Toward a Posthuman Theory of Public Rhetoric." In *Beyond Postprocess,* ed. Sidney I. Dobrin, J. A. Rice, and Michael Vestola. Logan: Utah State UP.

Haynes, Cynthia. 2007. "In Visible Texts: Memory, MOOs, and Momentum: A *Meditatio.*" In *The Locations of Composition,* ed. Christopher J. Keller and Christian R. Weisser, 55–70. Albany: State University of New York Press.

Horner, Bruce. 2000. *Terms of Work for Composition: A Materialist Critique.* Albany: State U of New York P.

Johns, Ann M. 1997. *Text, Role, and Context.* New York: Cambridge UP. http://dx.doi.org/10.1017/CBO9781139524650.

Latour, Bruno. 2005. *Reassembling the Social: An Introduction to Actor-Network Theory.* Oxford: Oxford UP.

Lave, Jean, and Etienne Wenger. 1991. *Situated Learning: Legitimate Peripheral Participation.* Cambridge: Cambridge UP. http://dx.doi.org/10.1017/CBO9780511815355.

Lu, Min-zhan. 2004. "An Essay on the Work of Composition: Composing English against the Order of Fast Capitalism." *College Composition and Communication* 56 (1): 16–50.

Micciche, Laura R. 2007. *Doing Emotion: Rhetoric, Writing, Teaching.* Portsmouth: Boynton Cook.

Miller, Carolyn. 1994. "Genre as Social Action." In *Genre and the New Rhetoric,* ed. Aviva Freedman and Peter Medway, 23–42. Bristol: Taylor and Francis.

Nowacek, Rebecca. 2011. *Agents of Integration: Understanding Transfer as a Rhetorical Act.* Carbondale: Southern Illinois UP.

Reiff, Mary Jo. 2004. "Mediating Materiality and Discursivity: Critical Ethnography as Meta-Generic Learning." In *Ethnography Unbound: From Theory Shock to Critical Praxis,* ed. Stephen G. Brown and Sidney I. Dobrin, 35–51. Albany: State U of New York P.

Reiff, Mary Jo. 2011. "The Spatial Turn in Rhetorical Genre Studies: Intersections of Metaphor and Materiality." *JAC* 31 (1–2): 207–24.

Reynolds, Nedra. 2004. *Geographies of Writing.* Carbondale: Southern Illinois University Press.

Rickert, Thomas. 2007. "Invention in the Wild: On Locating *Kairos* in Space-Time." In *The Locations of Composition*, ed. Christopher J. Keller and Christian R. Weisser, 71–89. Albany: State University of New York Press.

Scott, Tony. 2009. *Dangerous Writing: Understanding the Political Economy of Composition.* Logan: Utah State University Press.

Selfe, Cynthia L. 1999. "Technology and Literacy: A Story about the Perils of Not Paying Attention." *College Composition and Communication* 50 (3): 411–36. http://dx.doi.org /10.2307/358859.

Selzer, Jack, and Sharon Crowley. 1999. *Rhetorical Bodies.* Madison: University of Wisconsin Press.

Spinuzzi, Clay. 2008. *Network: Theorizing Knowledge in Telecommunications.* Cambridge: Cambridge University Press. http://dx.doi.org/10.1017/CBO9780511509605.

Swales, John. 1990. *Genre Analysis: English in Academic and Research Settings.* Cambridge: Cambridge University Press.

Trimbur, John. 2002. "Delivering the Message: Typography and the Materiality of Writing." In *Rhetoric and Composition as Intellectual Work*, ed. Gary A. Olson, 188–202. Carbondale: Southern Illinois University Press.

Vandenberg, Peter, and Jennifer Clary-Lemon. 2007. "Looking for Location Where it Can't Be Found." In *The Locations of Composition*, ed. Christopher J. Keller and Christian R. Weisser, 91–108. Albany: State University of New York Press.

Wardle, Elizabeth. 2007. "Understanding Transfer from FYC: Preliminary Results of a Longitudinal Study." *WPA: Writing Program Administration* 31 (1–2): 65–85.

MULTILINGUAL/ISM

Christine M. Tardy

In language studies, *multilingual/ism* refers to people who have some degree of competence in two or more languages or to settings in which two or more languages co-exist. Generally a distinction is not made between bilingualism and multilingualism, though *bilingual* typically refers specifically to the use of two languages by speakers, within policies or in settings. Use of the term *multilingual*, rooted in sociolinguistics, has increased since the early 1990s (Franceschini 2011). Today, the majority of people in the world are multilingual (Tucker 1999), and there is a growing recognition that most **English** users are multilinguals whose "mother tongue" is not English (Crystal 2003). Linguistic diversity has become more common worldwide as a result of both increased immigration patterns (Graddoll 2006) and globalization (Bloomaert, Collins, and Slembrouck 2005), and it is often thought to be characteristic of postmodernity.

Recognizing that Chomskyan linguistics assumed the ideal language speaker to be a native speaker, second language acquisition scholar Vivian J. Cook drew attention to the distinct language knowledge of multilinguals, proposing the notion of multicompetence, "the compound state of mind with two grammars" (Cook 1991, 112). Hall and her colleagues expand this concept beyond multilinguals, proposing that "*all* language knowledge is socially contingent and dynamic no matter how many language codes one has access to" (Hall, Cheng, and Carlson 2006, 229, emphasis in original). Approaches to language that assume such plurality and dynamism are also found in Braj Kachru's (1982) pioneering **work** on World Englishes, Brutt-Griffler and Samimy's (2001) interrogation of the native versus non-native speaker dichotomy, and Ofelia García's (2009) discussion of translanguaging, a common multilingual practice of switching among languages to complete activities that demonstrates languages to operate on a continuum rather than as discrete entities. These concepts have been used in contemporary writing studies to argue for a plurilingual understanding of language and language users (e.g., Canagarajah 2006; 2009).

DOI: 10.7330/9780874219746.c023

Within *College Composition and Communication,* the term *multilingual/ism* seems to have first surfaced in the 1990s, referring very broadly to "multilingual and multicultural" student populations (Lunsford 1990, 338; Harris and Silva 1993, 537) or to multilingual settings (Muchiri et al. 1995). More recently, writing scholars (and, to a lesser extent, teachers and institutions) have referred to "multilingual students" in seemingly more intentional ways. For instance, in "The Rhetorical Construction of Multilingual Students," Ruth Spack (1997) argues that labels themselves have meaning and rhetorically construct student identities, often in ways unintended by those assigning such labels; she points to the linguistic deficits highlighted by terms like *English as a Second Language* (ESL) or *Limited English Proficient* (LEP). Though Spack uses *multilingual students* in her article title, she never addresses the term directly. In his book *Critical Academic Writing and Multilingual Students,* A. Suresh Canagarajah (2002) similarly uses this phrase implicitly, but he does offer a description of the students with whom his book is concerned: those from former British colonial **contexts** learning English as a second language, and those from contexts in which English serves as an auxiliary or "foreign" language (often the users' second or third language). He directly contrasts these student populations with "L1 students," defined as "those who are 'traditionally native' in English, largely monolinguals, coming from the former colonizing communities that still claim ownership over the language" (Canagarajah 2006, 9).

Recent preference in writing studies for referring to students as multilingual (rather than, for example, "ESL") may be rooted in concerns regarding the discursive construction of these students that Spack (1997) highlights: "multilingual" foregrounds students' multiple linguistic resources (rather than a language deficit) and simultaneously calls attention to the monolingualism of most L1 students in the United States. Zawacki and Habib (2010), for example, explain their decision to use *multilingual* as a student label as a way "to recognize [these students'] fluency in multiple languages, dialects, and **discourses**, while not relegating any of their other languages as secondary or subordinate to American English" (58). Nevertheless, **identity** labels are a complex issue, particularly when applied to students, who usually have little say in the matter. Multiple studies have highlighted the extent to which students individually identify with labels such as ESL, English Language Learner (ELL), non-native English speaker (NNES), Generation 1.5, bilingual, or multilingual, generally finding their associations and affiliations to be highly variable (Chiang and Schmida 1999; Costino and Hyon 2007; Ortmeier-Hooper 2008). Such studies serve as reminders that, though labels provide a necessary shorthand, they tend to serve the purposes of stakeholders other than students.

Historically, terms such as *foreign students, international students,* and *ESL* have come in and out of fashion in the past century (Matsuda 2003), at least somewhat in relation to student demographics and prevailing cultural attitudes. As the population of multilingual students within the United States has diversified in recent years—including large numbers of international/visa-holding students, immigrant and refugee students, and students who defy these easier classifications—difficulties in labeling have increased, perhaps contributing to the popularity of *multilingual* as a broad and relatively inclusive term. In professional organizations in the United States and abroad, however, "second language writing/writers" still retains strong currency, as suggested by the title of the *Journal of Second Language Writing,* the annual Symposium on Second Language Writing, the CCCC Statement on Second Language Writing and Writers, and the TESOL Second Language Writing Interest Section. In their state-of-the-art synthesis of second language (L2) writing research, Leki, Cumming, and Silva (2008) chose to use *L2 writing* as a default label, acknowledging that all available labels "are inappropriate in some ways for the many varieties of writers that might be included here" (9) but that they see *L2 writer* as a more neutral term.

Some compositionists have argued that all students are multilingual in the sense that they have access to multiple language varieties, even within a single language (Horner et al. 2011, 311). This broad interpretation may be particularly useful for drawing attention to the fluid and multiple nature of language, but a potential danger of stretching the term in this manner is the loss of emphasis on differences between writers who can draw on multiple languages and those writers who can draw on language varieties within a single language. A rich **body** of **research** demonstrates the differences between these learner groups—including their texts (Silva 1993), the construction of their identities by institutions and instructors (Harklau 2000), and their social situations (Dong 1998)—so conflating them brings risks as well as benefits.

Scholars concerned specifically with US college composition have brought attention to the ways in which monolingual assumptions and ideologies pervade institutional, programmatic, and disciplinary discourses and practices (Canagarajah 2006; Horner 2006; Horner and Trimbur 2002; Matsuda 1999; Trimbur 2006). Horner has argued that, through a "tacit policy of monolingualism" (Horner 2006, 569), students are generally assumed to be monolingual English users writing for audiences of monolingual English users—a situation that Matsuda has labeled "the myth of linguistic homogeneity" (Matsuda 2003, 637) perpetuated by various practices and a "disciplinary division of labor" that has assigned language-related concerns to second language specialists rather than to compositionists (Matsuda 1999).

Scholarship identifying a contradiction between monolingual assumptions and the multilingual reality of the composition classroom has led to calls for action, including changes to placement practices and disciplinary training (Matsuda 2003), increased dialogue with modern language departments and possible establishment of bilingual sections of writing classes (Horner and Trimbur 2002), and the use of a range of languages within writing programs and even universities (Trimbur 2006). Horner et al. (2011) have also called for a new pedagogical paradigm, a "translingual approach" to writing pedagogy, which assumes multilingualism as the social and situational norm. They define such an approach as seeing "difference in language not as a barrier to overcome or as a problem to manage, but as a resource for producing meaning in writing, speaking, reading, and listening" (Horner et al. 2011, 303). A translingual pedagogy explicitly examines and critiques prevailing assumptions of monolingualism and views language as fluid and multiple.

The emergence of *multilingual/ism* as a critical term within US college composition studies may further demonstrate a growing interdisciplinary spirit within writing studies, in which aspects of writing—such as language—are no longer delegated to other fields of study.

References

Bloomaert, Jan, James Collins, and Stef Slembrouck. 2005. "Spaces of Multilingualism." *Language & Communication* 25 (3): 197–216. http://dx.doi.org/10.1016/j.langcom.2005.05.002.

Brutt-Griffler, Janina, and Keiko K. Samimy. 2001. "Transcending the Nativeness Paradigm." *World Englishes* 20 (1): 99–106. http://dx.doi.org/10.1111/1467-971X.00199.

Canagarajah, A. Suresh. 2002. *Critical Academic Writing and Multilingual Students.* Ann Arbor: University of Michigan Press.

Canagarajah, A. Suresh. 2006. "The Place of World Englishes in Composition: Pluralization Continued." *College Composition and Communication* 57 (4): 586–619.

Canagarajah, A. Suresh. 2009. "Multilingual Strategies of Negotiating English: From Conversation to Writing." *JAC* 29: 17–48.

Chiang, Yuet-Sim D., and Mary Schmida. 1999. "Language Identity and Language Ownership: Linguistic Conflicts of First-Year University Writing Students." In *Generation 1.5 Meets College Composition: Issues in the Teaching of Writing to U.S.-Educated learners of ESL,* ed. Linda Harklau, Kay M. Losey, and Meryl Siegel, 81–96. Mahwah, NJ: Lawrence Erlbaum Associates.

Cook, Vivian J. 1991. "The Poverty-of-Stimulus Argument and Multicompetence." *Second Language Research* 7 (2): 103–17. http://dx.doi.org/10.1177/026765839100700203.

Costino, Kimberly A., and Sunny Hyon. 2007. "'A Class for Students Like Me': Reconsidering Relationships among Identity Labels, Residency Status, and Students' Preferences for Mainstream or Multilingual Composition." *Journal of Second Language Writing* 16 (2): 63–81. http://dx.doi.org/10.1016/j.jslw.2007 .04.001.

Crystal, David. 2003. *English as a Global Language,* 2nd edition. Cambridge: Cambridge University Press. http://dx.doi.org/10.1017/CBO9780511486999.

Dong, Yu Ren. 1998. "Non-Native Graduate Students' Thesis/Dissertation Writing in Science: Self-Reports by Students and Their Advisors from Two US Institutions." *English for Specific Purposes* 17 (4): 369–90.

Franceschini, Rita. 2011. "Multilingualism and Multicompetence: A Conceptual View." *Modern Language Journal* 95 (3): 344–55. http://dx.doi.org/10.1111/j.1540-4781 .2011.01202.x.

García, Ofelia. 2009. *Bilingual Education in the 21st Century: A Global Perspective.* West Sussex, UK: Wiley-Blackwell.

Graddoll, David. 2006. *English Next: Why Global English May Mean the End of "English as a Foreign Language."* British Council.

Hall, Joan Kelly, An Cheng, and Matthew T. Carlson. 2006. "Reconceptualizing Multicompetence as a Theory of Language Knowledge." *Applied Linguistics* 27 (2): 220–40. http://dx.doi.org/10.1093/applin/aml013.

Harklau, Linda. 2000. "From the 'Good Kids' to the 'Worst': Representations of English Language Learners across Educational Settings." *TESOL Quarterly* 34 (1): 35–67. http://dx.doi.org/10.2307/3588096.

Harris, Muriel, and Tony Silva. 1993. "Tutoring ESL Students: Issues and Options." *College Composition and Communication* 44 (4): 525–37. http://dx.doi.org/10.2307 /358388.

Horner, Bruce. 2006. "Introduction: Cross-Language Relations in Composition." *College English* 68 (6): 569–74.

Horner, Bruce, and John Trimbur. 2002. "English Only and US College Composition." *College Composition and Communication* 53 (4): 594–630. http://dx.doi. org/10.2307/1512118.

Horner, Bruce, Min-Zhan Lu, Jacqueline Jones Royster, and John Trimbur. 2011. "Language Difference in Writing: Toward a Translingual Approach." *College English* 73 (3): 303–21.

Kachru, Braj. 1982. *The Other Tongue: English across Cultures.* Urbana: University of Illinois Press.

Leki, Ilona, Alister Cumming, and Tony Silva. 2008. *A Synthesis of Research on Second Language Writing in English.* New York: Routledge.

Lunsford, Andrea. 1990. "Reply by Andrea Lunsford." *College Composition and Communication* 41 (3): 337–38. http://dx.doi.org/10.2307/357663.

Matsuda, Paul Kei. 1999. "Composition Studies and ESL Writing: A Disciplinary Division of Labor." *College Composition and Communication* 50 (4): 699–721. http://dx.doi.org /10.2307/358488.

Matsuda, Paul Kei. 2003. "Second Language Writing in the Twentieth Century: A Situated Historical Perspective." In *Exploring the Dynamics of Second Language Writing,* ed. Barbara Kroll, 15–34. Cambridge: Cambridge University Press. http://dx.doi.org /10.1017/CBO9781139524810.004.

Muchiri, Mary N., Nshindi G. Mulamba, Greg Myers, and Deoscorous B. Ndoloi. 1995. "Importing Composition: Teaching and Researching Academic Writing beyond North America." *College Composition and Communication* 46 (2): 175–98. http://dx.doi.org /10.2307/358427.

Ortmeier-Hooper, Christina. 2008. "English May Be My Second Language, but I'm Not ESL." *College Composition and Communication* 59 (3): 389–419.

Silva, Tony. 1993. "Toward an Understanding of the Distinct Nature of L2 Writing: The ESL Research and Its Implications." *TESOL Quarterly* 27 (4): 657–77. http://dx.doi .org/10.2307/3587400.

Spack, Ruth. 1997. "The Rhetorical Construction of Multilingual Students." *TESOL Quarterly* 31 (4): 765–74. http://dx.doi.org/10.2307/3587759.

Trimbur, John. 2006. "Linguistic Memory and the Politics of US English." *College English* 68 (6): 575–88. http://dx.doi.org/10.2307/25472176.

Tucker, G. Richard. 1999. "A Global Perspective on Bilingualism and Bilingual Education." *CAL*. Center for Applied Linguistics (August). http://www.cal.org /resource-center/briefs-digests/digests. Accessed July 18, 2012.

Zawacki, Terry Myers, and Anna Sophia Habib. 2010. "'Will Our Stories Help Teachers Understand?': Multilingual Students Talk about Identity, Voice, and Expectations across Academic Communities." In *Reinventing Identities in Second Language Writing*, ed. Michelle Cox, Jay Jordan, Christina Ortmeier-Hooper, and Gwen Gray Schwartz, 54–74. Urbana, IL: National Council of Teachers of English.

NETWORK

Jason Swarts

In writing studies, the term *network* is commonly used in two ways: as a noun and as a verb. As a noun, "the network" is a place of interconnectedness and linked **computers** (Eyman 1996), but, more generally, a "network is a set of interconnected nodes" (Castells 2001b, 3). Scholars argue for seeing a network as a thing, an "environment" (Hawisher and Selfe 1991, 55) that might be a specific **location** comprised of conventional nodes like servers and user terminals, as in a campus computer network (Palmquist et al. 1995, 336). **Others** see networks as thing-like and place-like but comprised of nodes that are far more heterogeneous, made up of "different components accommodated by [an] open architecture" (Terranova 2004, 56) that enables the network to grow and the nodes to interrelate.

As a verb, *networking* is often equated with the democratized sharing of content, afforded by the links that interconnect nodes. *Networking* is shaped by an underlying "protocol" that "refers to all the technoscientific rules and standards that govern relationships within networks" (Galloway and Thacker 2007, 28). These protocols are rooted in "economic, political, and cultural issues" (Abbate 2000, 152) thought to influence how activities occur across a network. In this manner, networking is described as a rule-governed activity, taking place in a network that is shaped by its various protocols that constitute a "cultural **ecology**" (Hawisher et al. 2004, 644).

Underlying this action-oriented understanding of network and networking is an assumption that "the network" has become a cultural mindset, "an extension of life as it is, in all its dimensions, and with all its modalities" (Castells 2001b, 118). Networks in this sense are frames of action, created and made significant by our existence in a broader sociological context of "informationalism" or "a technological paradigm based on the augmentation of the human capacity of information processing and communication" (Castells 2004, 9). Networks and networking as a frame of action drives a "feedback loop" spurring the continued

DOI: 10.7330/9780874219746.c024

innovation, development, distribution, and integration of information generating, processing, and networking **technologies** into the world around us (Castells 1996, 1, 31). In this sense, the network is ubiquitous. It transcends the material boundaries of telecommunication infrastructure, fusing with our motivations and values and expectations. It is both place and frame of action.

In writing research, scholars emphasize the technological qualities of networks as affordances that enable writers and writing teachers to recast the normally-solitary act of composing "as a social, collaborative act, as an act of synthesizing and negotiating knowledge" (Eldred 1991, 49). Past **research** associated networking with a "new pedagogical dynamic" (Batson 1988, 32) that promoted a spirit of egalitarianism and democracy (Bump 1990, 54). Barker and Kemp articulate the perceived value of networking by noting that it facilitates "textual transaction between students . . . so managed by the network to encourage a sense of *group knowledge*" (Barker and Kemp 1990, 15, emphasis in original). Yet scholars have also found reasons to be critical of networks and the origins of their various technical components, as well as of networking and its subtly invasive protocols of action. Critics see networks as sites of "surveillance" (Hawisher and Selfe 1991, 63) built on infrastructures that are owned, influenced, and politicized by others (Selfe and Selfe 1994).

Those seeing value in the idea of *networks* and *networking* sometimes rely on the terms metaphorically to describe and theorize growth, disciplinary diversification, and **creativity**. Networks have been used to talk about our citation practices as "networks of interaction," showing how fields of writing, and **technical communication** in particular, "have diversified—[while] individually we specialize" (Smith 2000, 176). The terms have also been used to describe the setting and character of knowledge **work** (Johnson-Eilola 2005; Spinuzzi 2008; Winsor 2001) that takes place across disciplinary boundaries and that requires everyone to become "strong rhetors" who negotiate the connections between people and things (Spinuzzi 2008, 201).

Networks also emerge as settings in which new kinds of literate information gathering, processing, and composing practices emerge. These practices show up in research on the use of social networks in disaster communication, in which those affected by disaster "forage for information and then assemble that information in an ad hoc, but still coordinated, manner" (Potts 2009, 284). These practices take place online and also across multiple sources, constituting a "kind of literate activity" (284). They show up in research on risk communication to describe a "quality of **civic** spaces" (Simmons and Grabill 2007, 431) that "extends outside computer interfaces" (439), serving as both a means and **context** of action that serves a larger **public** good (see Callon, Lascoumes, and Barthe 2011). Fraiberg notes that networks fundamentally change our expectations of writing, both in terms of the kinds of interactions we have with others and the kinds of content we can share. It is a perspective that "demands increased attention to ways that **multilingual**-multimodal activities are knotted into lived experiences" (Fraiberg 2010, 112). Cast as a process of writing in itself, networking creates possibilities for remixing and generating other new forms of composing, meaning, and acting that "depend greatly on the principle of response—how writers engage with, produce, and continue writing because of how responses are exchanged in a given electronic space" (Rice 2009, 296). These practices are always concretely mediated by the spatial qualities of networks—for McNely (2009) and Mueller (2009), networking technologies create a vibrant "backchannel" in which we spend time productively engaged with people and information through social networking infrastructures, while our **bodies** inhabit another space entirely (McNely 2009, 297).

These various uses show how writing researchers have begun to understand the term *network*. While in one sense *network* refers to places of writing and work, scholars in the field are continually theorizing and describing ways in which networking alters our expectations about writing while continually expanding the scope of its effect. One concrete way in which this kind of outlook has been extended in recent years is seen in an increased attention to the construction of technologies for writing and collaboration, built upon infrastructures that assume "meditational relationships" between a variety of actors that may include humans and non-humans—such as texts and other interfaces (Read, DelaMerced, and Zachry 2012, 336) interacting in complex "ecologies" of **genres**, texts, interfaces, data points, and other people (Spinuzzi 2003, 68)—and that take on functional, technological form as "views" and content management interactions (Hart-Davidson 2005). Recent work on network continues to focus not only on understanding, in a qualitative sense, how networks influence the processes of writing and collaboration but is also increasingly turning toward questions about accommodation and how to build document infrastructures and writing environments that leverage the capabilities of networks.

References

Abbate, Janet. 2000. *Inventing the Internet*. Cambridge, MA: The MIT Press.

Barker, Thomas, and Fred Kemp. 1990. "Network Theory: A Postmodern Pedagogy for the Writing Classroom." In *Computers and Community: Teaching Composition in the Twenty-First Century*, ed. Carolyn Handa, 1–27. Portsmouth, NH: Boynton/Cook.

Batson, Trent. 1988. "The ENFI Project: A Networked Classroom Approach to Writing Instruction." *Academic Computing* 2 (5): 32–33.

Bump, Jerome. 1990. "Radical Changes in Class Discussion Using Networked Computers." *Computers and the Humanities* 24 (1/2): 49–65. http://dx.doi.org/10.1007/BF00115028.

Callon, Michel, Pierre Lascoumes, and Yannick Barthe. (2001) 2011. *Agir dans un monde incertain: Essai sur la democratie technique. Editions du Seuil. Translated by Graham Burchell as Acting in an Uncertain World: An Essay on Technical Democracy*, 2nd ed. Cambridge: The MIT Press.

Castells, Manuel. 1996. *The Rise of the Networked Society*, vol. 1. San Francisco: Wiley-Blackwell.

Castells, Manuel. 2001a. "Informationalism and the Network Society." In *The Hacker Ethic*, ed. Pekka Himanen, 155–78. New York: Random House.

Castells, Manuel. 2001b. *The Internet Galaxy: Reflections on the Internet, Business, and Society*. New York: Oxford University Press. http://dx.doi.org/10.1007/978-3-322-89613-1.

Castells, Manuel. 2004. "Informationalism, Networks, and the Network Society: A Theoretical Blueprint." In *The Network Society: A Cross-Cultural Perspective*, 3–45. Northampton, MA: Edward Elgar. http://dx.doi.org/10.4337/9781845421663.00010.

Eldred, Janet. 1991. "Pedagogy in the Computer-Networked Classroom." *Computers and Composition* 8 (2): 47–61. http://dx.doi.org/10.1016/8755-4615(91)80048-I.

Eyman, Doug. 1996. "Hypertext in the Computer-Facilitated Writing Class." *Kairos* 1 (2). http://english.ttu.edu/kairos/1.2/binder.html?features/eyman/index.html.

Fraiberg, S. 2010. "Composition 2.0: Toward a Multilingual and Multimodal Framework." *College Composition and Communication* 62 (1): 100–126.

Galloway, Alexander R., and Eugene Thacker. 2007. *The Exploit: A Theory of Networks*. Minneapolis: University of Minnesota Press.

Hart-Davidson, Bill. 2005. "Shaping Texts that Transform: Toward a Rhetoric of Objects, Relationships, and Views." In *Technical Communication and the World Wide Web*, ed. Carol Lipson and Michael Day, 27–42. Mahwah, NJ: Lawrence Erlbaum.

Hawisher, Gail E., and Cynthia L. Selfe. 1991. "The Rhetoric of Technology and the Electronic Writing Class." *College Composition and Communication* 42 (1): 55–65. http://dx.doi.org/10.2307/357539.

Hawisher, Gail E., Cynthia L. Selfe, Brittney Moraski, and Melissa Pearson. 2004. "Becoming Literate in the Information Age: Cultural Ecologies and the Literacies of Technology." *College Composition and Communication* 55 (4): 642–92. http://dx.doi.org/10.2307/4140666.

Johnson-Eilola, Johndan. 2005. *Datacloud: Toward a New Theory of Online Work*. Cresskill, NJ: Hampton Press.

McNely, Brian. 2009. "Backchannel Persistence and Collaborative Meaning-Making." In *Proceedings of the 27th ACM International Conference on Design of Communication*, 297–304.

Mueller, Derek. 2009. "Digital Underlife in the Networked Writing Classroom." *Computers and Composition* 26 (4): 240–50. http://dx.doi.org/10.1016/j.compcom.2009.08.001.

Palmquist, Mike, Dawn Rodrigues, Kate Kiefer, and Donald E. Zimmerman. 1995. "Network Support for Writing across the Curriculum: Developing an Online Writing Center." *Computers and Composition* 12 (3): 335–53. http://dx.doi.org/10.1016/S8755-4615(05)80073-8.

Potts, Liza. 2009. "Using Actor Network Theory to Trace and Improve Multimodal Communication Design." *Technical Communication Quarterly* 18 (3): 281–301. http://dx.doi.org/10.1080/10572250902941812.

Read, Sarah, Anna DelaMerced, and Mark Zachry. 2012. "Participatory Design in the Development of a Web-Based Technology for Visualizing Writing Activity as Knowledge Work." In *Proceedings of the 30th ACM International Conference on Design of Communication*, 333–40. SIGDOC '12. New York: ACM. http://dx.doi.org/10.1145/2379057.2379119.

Rice, Jeff. 2009. "Networked Exchanges, Identity, Writing." *Journal of Business and Technical Communication* 23 (3): 294–317. http://dx.doi.org/10.1177/1050651909333178.

Selfe, Cynthia L., and Richard J. Selfe. 1994. "The Politics of the Interface: Power and Its Exercise in Electronic Contact Zones." *College Composition and Communication* 45 (4): 480–504. http://dx.doi.org/10.2307/358761.

Simmons, Michelle, and Jeff Grabill. 2007. "Toward a Civic Rhetoric for Technologically and Scientifically Complex Places: Invention, Performance, and Participation." *College Composition and Communication* 58 (3): 419–48.

Smith, Elizabeth O. 2000. "Strength in the Technical Communication Journals and Diversity in the Serials Cited." *Journal of Business and Technical Communication* 14 (2): 131–84. http://dx.doi.org/10.1177/105065190001400201.

Spinuzzi, Clay. 2003. *Tracing Genres through Organizations: A Sociocultural Approach to Information Design.* vol. 1. Cambridge: The MIT Press.

Spinuzzi, Clay. 2008. *Network: Theorizing Knowledge Work in Telecommunications.* Cambridge: Cambridge University Press. http://dx.doi.org/10.1017/CBO9780511509605.

Terranova, Titziana. 2004. *Network Culture: Politics for the Information Age,* vol. 23. London: Pluto Press.

Winsor, Dorothy. 2001. "Learning to Do Knowledge Work in Systems of Distributed Cognition." *Journal of Business and Technical Communication* 15 (1): 5–28. http://dx.doi.org/10.1177/105065190101500101.

OTHER

Kathleen Kerr

G. W. F. Hegel (1994) helped to establish the epistemological founda-
tion for contemporary conceptions of *Other* (sometimes indicated in
lowercase) as an entity by positing the transformation of the subjective
"I" into an "inessential object" with a negative characterization, the non-
self (53). Philip Kain explains the notion of Hegel's "Absolute" (whole)
as individual consciousness that exists vis-à-vis cultural consciousness—
the Other (Kain 2005, 4). Similarly, Frederick Beiser suggests there
is a "subject-object **identity** because there is a single structure of self-
consciousness holding between self and other: the self knows itself in the
other as the other knows itself in the self" (Beiser 2005, 113).

Jacques Lacan identifies the Other as "the locus in which is constituted the I who speaks to him who hears" (Lacan 1977, 141). Stephen
Frosh suggests that Lacan would differentiate the "big Other of essential alienness" from the "little other of specular image" (Frosh 2002,
396), and Hans Dieter-Gondek, using quotations from *Ecrits*, outlines
five additional Lacanian articulations of *Other*: Other as the site where
"speech verifies itself in meeting the exchange of signifiers"; Other as
witness; Other as the "thesaurus of the signifier"; Other as "the **discourse**
of the Other"; and Other as "nothing else than the pure subject of modern game theory" (Dieter-Gondek 1998, 32). Like Lacan, Emmanuel
Lévinas distinguishes between *Other* and *other*, defining *Other* as the
"absolutely other" and describing "the relation" with the Other as discourse (Lévinas 1969, 39, 213). Mikhail Bakhtin articulates the depen-
dency between the self and the Other in the context of the dialogic,
stating, "the *I* hides in the other and in others," and "it wants to be only
an other for others, to enter completely into the world of others as an
other" (Bakhtin 1986, 147). Hence, one could interpret the Other in
dialogism as one of the "two distinct voices [present] in one utterance"
(Vice 1997, 45).

The concept of the Other is often defined in the context of self.
Judith Butler notes that the "notion of this Other *in* self, as it were,

DOI: 10.7330/9780874219746.c025

implies that the self/Other distinction is *not* primarily external . . . [that] the self is from the start radically implicated in the Other" (Butler 2002, 1497). Gayatri Spivak argues the possibility of the intellectual's complicity in the "persistent constitution of the Other as the Self's shadow" (Spivak 1994, 75), a possibility Donald Murray echoes when he suggests that, in writing, "the self speaks, the other self listens and responds. The self proposes, the other self considers. The self makes, the other self evaluates. The two selves collaborate" (Murray 1982, 140).

Jean-Paul Sartre calls the Other the "indispensable mediator between myself and me" and states, "I need the Other in order to realize fully all the structures of my being" (Sartre 1956, 198). However, Simone de Beauvoir presents woman as the Other, postulating: "He is the Subject; he is the Absolute. She is the Other" (Beauvoir 2009, 6). Roland Barthes introduces the Other as "sometimes—rarely—irreducible" and "a figure for emergencies: exoticism[,] . . . a pure object, a spectacle, a clown" (Barthes 1972, 152). Edward Said also points to this "exotic invention" of Otherness—the Orient—as "one of the deepest and most recurring images of the Other" (Said 1978, 1). Said views the Oriental/Other as a compliant construction resulting from the "Western style for dominating, restructuring, and having authority over the Orient" (3).

The "exotic" Other articulated by Barthes and Said also appears in the writing classroom. Janice Neuleib notes: "To teachers like me, the nonachieving student is 'other' almost in the same way that natives in distant cultures differ from investigators of those cultures" (Neuleib 1992, 231). Valerie Balester similarly argues that "there is an unfortunate bias in our profession to 'conflat[e] ethnicity, otherness, and basic writing'" (Balester 2000, 129), and Phillip Marzluf suggests that the "valorization of the 'authenticity' of students' voices . . . results in the proliferation of 'stereotyped binaries of "whiteness" and "otherness"'" (Marzluf 2006, 505). Timothy Barnett (2000) expands these conceptions of Otherness to their interconnectedness with discourses of **gender**, **class**, and religion, pointing out that "the discipline seems unable or unwilling to question 'whiteness' in all its complexity despite (because of?) the efforts of literary, creative writing, and composition teachers and scholars to bring to the foreground issues of race having to do with multiple 'Others'" (10).

Just as Said argues that in order to understand Orientalism it must be examined as a discourse (Said 1978, 3), Jean-François Staszak suggests "Otherness is due less to the difference of the Other than to the point of view and the discourse of the person who perceives the Other as such" (Staszak 2009, 1). He offers that "Otherness is the result of a discursive process by which a dominant in-group ('Us,' the Self) constructs one or many dominated out-groups ('Them,' Other) by stigmatizing a differ-ence—real or imagined—presented as a negation of identity and thus a motive for potential discrimination" (2). Staszak further argues that "dif-ference belongs to the realm of fact and otherness . . . to the realm of discourse, which makes sex a difference and gender otherness" (2). Joy Lei contends that the "dominant U.S. racial discourse . . . perpetuates the positioning of people of color as the Other, and the white European American culture as the mainstream and the norm" (Lei 2003, 158), just as meanings attributed to physical appearance and behaviors of the Other lead to "the **production** . . . of racialized, gendered Others" (160).

Yuet-Sim D. Chiang associates otherness with her **research** subjects, non-native **English** speakers, yet finds that because of her own, often similar, language experiences, "I had, very unexpectedly, become one of the 'others'—the very people I charted out to study" (Chiang 1998, 154). Chiang argues that, as a researcher, she was "at once both 'it' (the researcher) and 'other' (the researched)" (160). Ruth Spack like-wise acknowledges the otherness associated with students who are non-native English speakers, but she notes that non-English *languages* also constitute the other: "English is the norm against which the other, the different, is measured" (Spack 1997, 766). In her review of *Crossing Borderlands: Composition and Postcolonial Studies*, however, Taryn Okuma describes how writing studies scholars critically engage with difference "[r]ather than simply casting composition studies in the role of liter-ary or postcolonial studies' 'other'" (Okuma 2006, 189). Like Chiang, Deborah Mutnick views the students in her study as other, pointing out that "student and 'oppressed other' are often synonymous" and recog-nizing the potential for student writing to "giv[e] voice to people on the social margins" (Mutnick 2007, 629).

The social margins to which Mutnick refers relate to gender, race, ethnic, and class depictions of otherness, but *Other* has also been defined and described in the context of disease, aging, and **disability**. For exam-ple, Paula Treichler refers to media representations of the "contami-nated Other" in AIDS-related discourses (Treichler 1999, 139), and de Beauvoir notes both that "[a]mong primitive peoples, the aged man is truly the Other" (Beauvoir 1972, 85) and that "[w]ithin me it is the Other—that is to say the person I am for the outsider—who is old and that Other is myself" (284). Susan Wendell notes, however, that while able-bodied people consider the disabled to be the Other, the reverse is often true as well (Wendell 1997, 271). Judith Lorber broadly describes the Other as "that which lacks the valuable qualities the dominants exhibit" (Lorber 1994, 33), and Yiannis Gabriel similarly contends that the Other can be a racial, religious, sexual, gender, or national group for which "othering" implies the denial of "those defining characteristics of the 'Same': reason, dignity, love, pride, heroism, nobility, and ultimately any entitlement to human rights" (Gabriel 2008, 213). Like Gabriel, Frosh reflects on the humanity of the other, warning that "denying this humanity is the precondition and consequence of violence, an assault on the other that leaves the self bereft" (Frosh 2002, 393).

References

Bakhtin, Mikhail. 1986. *Speech Genres and Other Late Essays.* Trans. Vern W. McGee, ed. Caryl Emerson and Michael Holquist. Austin: University of Texas Press.

Balester, Valerie. 2000. "The Problem of Method: Striving to See with Multiple Perspectives." *College Composition and Communication* 52 (1): 129–32. http://dx.doi.org/10.2307/358547.

Barnett, Timothy. 2000. "Reading 'Whiteness' in English Studies." *College English* 63 (1): 9–37. http://dx.doi.org/10.2307/379029.

Barthes, Roland. 1972. *Mythologies.* Trans. Annette Lavers. New York: Hill and Wang.

Beauvoir, Simone de. (1970) 1972. *The Coming of Age.* Trans. Patrick O'Brian. New York: G. P. Putnam's Sons.

Beauvoir, Simone de. (1949) 2009. *The Second Sex.* Trans. Constance Borde and Sheila Malovany-Chevallier. New York, Canada: Alfred A. Knopp.

Beiser, Frederick. 2005. *Hegel.* New York: Routledge.

Butler, Judith. 2002. "Imitation and Gender Insubordination." In *Critical Theory Since Plato,* ed. Hazard Adams and Leroy Searle, 1490–99. Belmont, CA: Thomson Wadsworth.

Chiang, Yuet-Sim. 1998. "Insider/Outsider/Other?: Confronting the Centeredness of Race, Class, Color, and Ethnicity in Composition Research." In *Under Construction: Working at the Intersections of Composition Research, Theory, and Practices,* ed. Chris Anson, and Christine Farris, 150–66. Logan: Utah State University Press.

Frosh, Stephen. 2002. "The Other." *American Imago* 59 (4): 389–407. http://dx.doi.org/10.1353/aim.2002.0025.

Gabriel, Yiannis. 2008. *Organizing Words: A Critical Thesaurus for Social and Organization Studies.* Oxford: Oxford University Press.

Gondek, Hans-Dieter. 1998. "Cogito and *Séparation*: Lacan/Levinas." In *Levinas and Lacan: The Missed Encounter,* ed. Sarah Harasym, 22–55. Albany: State University of New York Press.

Hegel, Georg Wilhelm Friedrich. (1807) 1994. *Phenomenology of Spirit.* Trans. Howard P. Kainz. University Park: Pennsylvania State University Press.

Kain, Philip. 2005. *Hegel and the Other: A Study of the Phenomenology of the Spirit.* Albany: State University of New York Press.

Lacan, Jacques. 1977. *Ecrits: A Selection.* Trans. Alan Sheridan. London: Tavistock Publications.

Lei, Joy L. 2003. "(Un)Necessary Toughness?: Those 'Loud Black Girls' and Those 'Quiet Asian Boys.'" *Anthropology & Education Quarterly* 34 (2): 158–81. http://dx.doi.org/10.1525/aeq.2003.34.2.158.

Lévinas, Emmanuel. 1969. *Totality and Infinity: An Essay on Exteriority.* Trans. Alphonso Lingis. Pittsburgh: Duquesne University Press.

Lorber, Judith. 1994. *Paradoxes of Gender.* New Haven, London: Yale University Press.

Marzluf, Philip. 2006. "Diversity Writing: Natural Languages, Authentic Voices." *College Composition and Communication* 57 (3): 502–22.

Murray, Donald. 1982. "Teaching the Other Self: The Writer's First Reader." *College Composition and Communication* 33 (2): 140–47. http://dx.doi.org/10.2307/357621.

Mutnick, Deborah. 2007. "Inscribing the World: An Oral History Project in Brooklyn." *College Composition and Communication* 58 (4): 626–47.

Neuleib, Janice. 1992. "The Friendly Stranger: Twenty-Five Years as 'Other.'" *College Composition and Communication* 43 (2): 231–43. http://dx.doi.org/10.2307/357567.

Okuma, Taryn L. 2006. "Crossing Borderlands: Composition and Postcolonial Studies (review)," rev. ed., ed. Andrea Lunsford and Lahoucine Ouzgane. *College Literature* 33 (2): 188–91. https://muse.jhu.edu/login?auth=0&type=summary&url=/journals/college_literature/v033/33.2okuma.html.

Said, Edward W. 1978. *Orientalism.* New York: Vintage Books.

Sartre, Jean-Paul. 1956. *Being and Nothingness: A Phenomenological Essay on Ontology.* New York: Citadel Press.

Spack, Ruth. 1997. "The Rhetorical Construction of Multilingual Students." *TESOL Quarterly* 31 (4): 765–74. http://dx.doi.org/10.2307/3587759.

Spivak, Gayatri. 1994. "Can the Subaltern Speak?" In *Colonial Discourse and Post-Colonial Theory: A Reader,* ed. Patrick Williams and Laura Chrisman, 66–111. New York: Columbia University Press.

Staszak, Jean-Francois. 2009. "Other/Otherness." *International Encyclopedia of Human Geography,* ed. Rob Kitchin and Nigel Thrift. http://www.unige.ch/sciences-societe/geo/collaborateurs/publicationsJFS/OtherOtherness.pdf.

Treichler, Paula. 1999. *How to Have Theory in an Epidemic: Cultural Chronicles of Aids.* Durham, London: Duke University Press.

Vice, Sue. 1997. *Introducing Bakhtin.* Manchester, UK: Manchester University Press.

Wendell, Susan. 1997. "Toward a Feminist Theory of Disability." In *The Disability Studies Reader,* ed. Lennard J. Davis, 260–78. New York, London: Routledge.

PERFORMANCE

KT Torrey

In writing studies, performance is ancient and noveau, fundamental and restored, once absent but always present. "In its simplest terms," performance is "an action, a taking on of some act"; thus, "if writing is always an action," Ryan Claycomb (2008) argues, then "it is also a performance." For Candace Spigelman, "every writing is, to a great or lesser extent, a rhetorical *performance*" (Spigelman 2004, 49). Caroline Bergvall regards writing as "a textual performance" that takes place "on and through the space of the page" (Bergvall 1999, 112). For Stephen Greenblatt, composition is an action and "writing . . . a performance, like singing an aria or dancing a jig" (Greenblatt 2007, 40). Charles Bazerman, however, suggests that these definitions are too broad; for him, it is only the "meaningful text" that "is always a performance" (Bazerman 2003, 382).

For some, the term *performance* is the contemporary cousin of *delivery* in ancient rhetoric, that "two way process" between "the speaker or writer delivering the text and the audience delivering its response" (Skinner-Linnenberg 1997, 43). Indeed, Greek society cast "rhetoric as a "*bodily art* . . . learned, practiced, and performed by and with the **body** as well as the mind" (Hawhee 2002a, 144, emphasis in original). According to Jenn Fishman et al. (2005), though these connections were integral to rhetorical practice through the eighteenth century, "the growing hegemony of writing through the nineteenth century obscured the body and performance . . . [thus] shifting attention away from oral and embodied delivery to textual **production** of the printed page" (228). In this way, "writing broke away from oral performance" (Ong 1975, 12).

This break transformed the meaning of *performance* for rhetoric and served to define the term within early composition studies. "For most of the nineteenth and twentieth centuries," Shelley Manis writes, performance "has referred overwhelmingly to skill and assessment . . . rather than . . . a set of theorized and embodied practices" (Manis 2009, 141). For Claycomb, the "idea of performance as metric . . . is the notion of performance that our students are most likely to bring to the writing

DOI: 10.7330/9780874219746.c026

classroom." Composition studies itself helped to construct this under-standing by "convinc[ing] schools and colleges that testing writing means testing a practice or performance" (Elbow 1993, 15). Crafton (1996) points to the role of **technology** in this dynamic: "the word pro-cessor's insistence on the instrumental," he argues, has underscored "basic writers' perception of writing as an academic activity all about performance," one in which students "move through an alien medium that exists outside of and apart from themselves" (325). As a result, many students regard writing as a performance of competency rather than expression.

In the 1950s, a new and distinct definition of *performance* began to "seep . . . through disciplinary boundaries, around subjects, and into the public **discourse**," giving rise to the field of performance studies (Jon McKenzie, quoted in Love 2007, 14). Constructed in the border-lands among "theatre, sociology . . . anthropology, and linguistics," per-formance studies "takes the fluidity of self and the relationship between word and action as its central concepts" (Fishman et al. 2005, 227; Love 2007, 13). As a discipline, performance studies has "radically reinscribed, reinstalled, and redeployed" the notion of performance "in uncanny and powerful ways" (Jon McKenzie, quoted in Love 2007, 13). As a term, then, *performance* has become a means of understanding, a "pervasive . . . means of reading diverse cultural practices" (Allsopp 1999, 76–77).

In this way, performance studies offers writing studies new ways of thinking about writing as a performance of self, one of many "social per-formances" through which notions of **gender**, sexuality, and **identity** can be constructed (Butler 1988, 528). These are performances with which student writers are already familiar, for, as Fishman et al. observe, perfor-mance is "one of the many nonacademic knowledges that students pos-sess" when they enter the writing classroom (Fishman et al. 2005, 226). Indeed, outside of the classroom, students "are increasingly becoming aware of performance as a part of everyday activities" and of the ways in which "the audience, our fellow performers, the setting, the scene, the goal . . . influence . . . our performances of selves" (Jones 2010, 81; Love 2007, 16).

Given students' prior knowledge, Meredith Love contends that writ-ing instructors can ground writing for their students by making "a more explicit link between students' various [social] performances" and their **work** in composition (Love 2007, 17). As Fishman et al. suggest, such a practice builds upon the recognition that students routinely use these performance skills outside of the classroom to "help them negotiate unfamiliar territories" between high school and college, "especially the gaps . . . between theory and practice, abstract ideas and concrete examples" (Fishman et al. 2005, 233). Recognizing "writing as an activity—as an act always involving the body and performance"—makes concrete the connection between the performative skills the students already possess and those they can acquire through their writing (228).

One benefit of such an approach, Virginia Skinner-Linnenberg (1997) suggests, is that restaging the writing classroom as a performative space offers students access to a kind of critical reflectiveness about their work that instruction based upon the disembodiment of the nineteenth century does not. In such a model, the classroom becomes "a stage where students play with their identities, consider the artifice of **genres** and language, and make choices about their deliberate performances" (Love 2007, 27). Writing is staged as physical performance, one in which students work "by embodying its language and staging its structure" in front of an audience of their peers (Skinner-Linnenberg 1997, 56). Within such a classroom, the notion of a "whole theory of delivery"—abandoned almost two centuries ago—might be reestablished to explain how students "rejoin the noetic-thinking process with either physical gestures or speaking so that writing is more than simply moving a hand across paper" (56).

Performance can also be imagined as a disruptive force, one that subverts the notions of writing as a project of fixing a certain, stable meaning or identity into place. For Leigh Jones, teaching students to use "performance as a part of the writing process" helps them "to understand their ethos as provisional, in process, and in rehearsal, a continual 'trying on' and enacting" (Jones 2010, 82). In this way, students are "trained to understand and act as different characters in their writing," rather than shackled by the notion that writing must be a performance of some essential self (Love 2007, 21). Gere argues that "pedagogies of performance . . . [can] reinforce writing's liminal status between **materiality** and idea," disrupting the notion that writing is an act of permanently fixing ideas within space and time, and reinforcing its transient and contextual qualities (Gere 1994, 89). Performance thus emphasizes "not only that individual words shift meaning given their **context** within a sentence, but also that words shift meaning given their embodied context and their physical **location** in the world" (Fishman et al. 2005, 228).

A tangled, evolving keyword, *performance* "combines contradictory terms such as action/appearance, fiction/truth, and manages to find a reconciliatory medium for writing to go on" (Gurevitch 2000, 5). Performance is "both fun and deeply serious"; it is "[i]mmediate and face-to-face" (Fishman et al. 2005, 226). To a writer, performance offers a "discursive-material-bodily-temporal encounter, a force among forces" (Hawhee 2002b, 24). Yet, performance "is only a possibility that something might occur, a meeting, a real human engagement" between writer and reader (Bogart and Landau 2005, 144). Performance in writing "is not just about what you say . . . but about your desperate desire to say it, the quality and mystery of that desire; about your humanity" (Margolin 1997, 22). As a concept, an act, an opportunity, performance thus "propels us forward into a future perfect world, a world full of dangerous and fantastic possibilities" (Pollock 2007, 243).

References

Allsopp, Ric. 1999. "Performance Writing." *PAJ: A Journal of Performance and Art* 21 (1): 76–80. http://dx.doi.org/10.2307/3245984.

Bazerman, Charles. 2003. "Textual Performance: Where the Action at a Distance Is." *Journal of Advanced Composition* 23 (2): 379–96.

Bergvall, Caroline. 1999. "The Hungry Form (Greek Mix)." *PAJ: A Journal of Performance and Art* 21 (1): 112–16. http://dx.doi.org/10.2307/3245992.

Bogart, Anne, and Tina Landau. 2005. *The Viewpoints Book: A Practical Guide to Viewpoints and Composition.* New York: Theatre Communications Group.

Butler, Judith. 1988. "Performative Acts and Gender Constitution: An Essay in Phenomenology and Feminist Theory." *Theatre Journal* 40 (4): 519–31. http://dx.doi .org/10.2307/3207893.

Claycomb, Ryan. 2008. "Performing/Teaching/Writing: Performance Studies in the Classroom." *Enculturation* 6 (1). http://www.enculturation.net/6.1/claycomb.

Crafton, Robert. 1996. "Promises, Promises: Computer-Assisted Revision and Basic Writers." *Computers and Composition* 13 (3): 317–26. http://dx.doi.org/10.1016/S8755 -4615(96)90020-1.

Elbow, Peter. 1993. "The War between Reading and Writing: And How to End It." *Rhetoric Review* 12 (1): 5–24. http://dx.doi.org/10.1080/07350199309389024.

Fishman, Jenn, Andrea Lunsford, Beth McGregor, and Mark Otuteye. 2005. "Performing Writing, Performing Literacy." *College Composition and Communication* 57: 224–52.

Gere, Anne Ruggles. 1994. "Kitchen Tables and Rented Rooms: The Extracurriculum of Composition." *College Composition and Communication* 45 (1): 75–92. http://dx.doi.org /10.2307/358588.

Greenblatt, Stephen. 2007. "Writing as Performance." *Harvard Magazine* (Sept-Oct): 40–47.

Gurevitch, Zali. 2000. "The Serious Play of Writing." *Qualitative Inquiry* 6 (1): 3–7. http://dx.doi.org/10.1177/107780040000600101.

Hawhee, Debra. 2002a. "Bodily Pedagogies: Rhetoric, Athletics, and the Sophists' Three Rs." *College English* 65 (2): 142–62. http://dx.doi.org/10.2307/3250760.

Hawhee, Debra. 2002b. "Kairotic Encounters." In *Perspectives on Rhetorical Invention*, ed. Janet M. Atwill and Janice M. Lauer, 16–35. Knoxville: University of Tennessee Press.

Jones, Leigh A. 2010. "Podcasting and Performativity: Multimodal Invention in an Advanced Writing Class." *Composition Studies* 38 (2): 75–91.

Love, Meredith. 2007. "Composing through the Performative Screen: Translating Performance Studies into Writing Pedagogy." *Composition Studies* 35 (2): 11–30.

Manis, Shelley. 2009. "Writing as Performance: Using Performance Theory to Teach Writing in Theatre Classrooms." *Theatre Topics* 19 (2): 139–51. http://dx.doi.org /10.1353/tt.0.0072.

Margolin, Deb. 1997. "A Perfect Theatre for One: Teaching 'Performance Composition.'." *TDR* 41 (2): 68–81. http://dx.doi.org/10.2307/1146625.

Ong, Walter. 1975. "The Writer's Audience is Always a Fiction." *PMLA* 90 (1): 9–21. http://dx.doi.org/10.2307/461344.

Pollock, Della. 2007. "The Performative 'I.'" *Cultural Studies <=> Critical Methodologies* 7: 239–55.

Skinner-Linnenberg, Virginia. 1997. *Dramatizing Writing: Reincorporating Delivery in the Classroom.* Mahwah: Lawrence Erlbaum Associates, Inc.

Spigelman, Candice. 2004. *Personally Speaking: Experience as Evidence in Academic Discourse.* Carbondale: Southern Illinois University Press.

PERSONAL

Kathleen Kerr

Personal takes three grammatical forms—noun, adverb, and adjective—that seem ubiquitous in contemporary public discourse. We post personal ads, sell personal property, and shop for personal digital assistants, personal trainers, or personal care products. We protect the personal information on our personal computers lest hackers wreak havoc on our personal finances—an act we would take personally. Employers want to know personal histories to be reassured that employees will limit personal correspondence—in which it is acceptable to use personal pronouns—to personal time.

While the meaning of *personal* in these **public contexts** seems evident, the "myriad denotations of 'the personal' in academic discourse" (Hindman 2001b, 35) means that, as Anne Herrington puts it, "What is 'personal' or private is not self-evident" (Brandt et al. 2001, 47). Sue Campbell argues that the personal "is hard to locate or describe as a concept, value, or category" (Campbell 2002, 3), and Jane Tompkins contends the difficulty with defining *personal* is that "[w]hat is personal is completely a function of what is perceived as personal" (quoted in Freedman 2001, 200). Herrington expands that perspective, suggesting that "what is personal is at once socially, culturally and personally defined" (quoted in Brandt et al. 2001, 47). Gesa Kirsch likewise observes: "What counts as the personal is very much defined and delineated by current academic as well as Western cultural norms, norms that exclude as much as they include" (Brandt et al. 2001, 55). The challenge of defining *personal* extends to personal writing, which "has become so all-encompassing that it evades a single meaning or, even, one signifier" (Gere 2001, 204). Yet, as Freedman points out, "to speak of the personal 'always already' means to . . . recognize its rhetoricity" (Freedman 2001, 200).

Nonetheless, as Jane Hindman notes, "[a]ny academic even vaguely aware of current trends in scholarship has noted the preeminence of 'the personal' in the last few years" (Hindman 2001b, 34). Scholars

DOI: 10.7330/9780874219746.c027

associate "the personal" with a variety of concrete and abstract spaces. Susan Handelman, for example, uses the Hebrew word for face, *panim*, as the counterpart to personal, explaining, "The face is physically the distinctive mark of our individuality, the most 'personal' aspect of ourselves" (Handelman 2001, 129). Hindman too, invokes the notion of embodied writing, describing it as "personal, situated, and local" (Hindman 2001a, 106). In contrast, Campbell identifies "those areas of psychological life that might be thought of as most personal: emotions, feelings, memories, and expectations" (Campbell 2002, 2). In addition, *personal* is frequently defined by the oft-invoked feminist mantra that "the personal is political" (Hanisch 1969). Brenda Daly points out that practicing the personal as political means "challenging public hierarchies and practices with stories of their often painful consequences in the realm of so-called 'personal experience'" (Daly 2001, 79).

Personal is often defined in the context of *professional*, and Handelman reminds us that "[b]eing 'professional' is also commonly taken to mean being able to remove one's own 'personal' prejudices and emotions from the task at hand" (Handelman 2001, 122). Gesa Kirsch and Min-Zhan Lu ponder the "diverse ways individual members of the profession have negotiated the dichotomy of . . . personal versus professional in their day-to-day actions as well as their discursive practices" (Brandt et al. 2001, 42), and Kirsch points out "the tension between the professional and the personal that still permeates academic culture and institutions" (56). On the other hand, Kate Ronald and Hephzibah Roskelly argue that "The academic life is a personal life" (Ronald and Roskelly 2001, 253), and Pipes, Holstein, and Aguirre suggest that "there is often a reciprocal and causal relationship between elements within each of the two arenas [personal and professional]" (Pipes, Holstein, and Aguirre 2005, 327).

Contemplating the relationships between *personal* and *self*, Deborah Holdstein observes, "I suppose I could be personal—sort of, by not focusing entirely on myself but *meaning* myself" (Bleich and Holdstein 2001, 7). Hindman likewise challenges the idea that the personal is "inherently 'essentializing,'" a claim she says "centers in the belief that in narrating their life-experiences authors invariably construct a simplified, unified, and therefore fictive version of a complex 'essential self'" (Hindman 2001b, 36). On the other hand, Gere claims, "Our personal writing show[s] us to ourselves" (Gere 2001, 210), while Dan McAdams describes his story as "the personal myth—that I have tacitly, even unconsciously, composed over the course of my years" (McAdams 1991, 11). This "personal myth," he suggests, "delineates an **identity**, illuminating the values of an individual life. The personal myth is not a legend or a fairy tale, but a sacred story that embodies personal truth" (34). Jeffrey Gray similarly complicates the idea, noting that "the personal as deployed in much current academic writing is *not* personal— that is, not individual, not subjective in so far as subjects are distinct from other subjects, not interchangeable" (Gray 2001, 53). For Clement Webb, however, the personal is the "'subjective' element" whose "truth" meets "some purpose of human thought" (Webb 1904, 109)—an idea seconded by Janet Carey Eldred, who understands the personal as a means to "argue the 'case of one' under the vexed claim of 'universal truth'" (Eldred 2005, 5–6).

Personal is often defined in terms of *voice*: "For what else do we mean by the 'personal' than to . . . [give] voice to something?" (Handelman 2001, 129). Peter Elbow agrees, contending that "The voice formulation is a personal subjective projection" (Elbow 2000, 178), while Karen Paley Surman maintains that personal narrative "involves the use of a narratorial 'I' which seems to be the actual voice of the person who writes" (Surman 2001, 181). Handelman expands this intersection of *personal* and *voice* to include the members of one's audience: "One way a text is 'made personal,'" she says, "is by being embodied in the living voice, face, and being of the teacher in dialogue with the student, and the students with each other" (Handelman 2001, 131). Gere's conception of the personal, however, emphasizes not voice but **silence**: "Without incorporating its silent dimension, personal writing will . . . remain underdeveloped both conceptually and pedagogically" (Gere 2001, 204).

Furthermore, the personal has been portrayed as a rhetorical gambit, as a technique "used strategically and synechdochically" (Gray 2001, 53), and "as a frame to speculate on a broader topic" (Spigelman 2001, 65). Richard Miller suggests that "invoking the personal is inevitably a strategic move: it buys laughs or votes or credibility or the aura of authenticity or outsider status or tenure and promotion—or even, on rare occasions, a felt sense of genuine intimacy" (quoted in Brandt et al. 2001, 60). Freedman likewise notes that "the 'personal' is a multi-purpose route or ruse that invigorates academic learning, academic publishing, our various disciplines" (Freedman 2001, 199–200).

Jonathan Alexander points out that "In some ways, the personal has always been a vexed subject in composition" (Alexander 2008, 182), although Carol Steiner notes that problems relating to **technical communication** across disciplines are also "both cultural and personal" because professionals often "do not define themselves in terms of the personal possibilities the world grants them but in terms of the possibilities sanctioned by their discipline" (Steiner 1999, 384, 391). Indeed, since the advent of the Internet, some work in technical communication has sought to help students claim the personal in public and digital spaces (see Miles 1995, for instance), and recent work in global business communication likewise emphasizes that language "is a very personal thing" (Charles 2007, 274).

Finally, since "all writing is personal in the sense that both style and interest are features of social, political, and individual values and investments" (Spigelman 2001, 67), the personal can be understood as "a form of data collection," as "one way for students to begin to locate, and critically interrogate, their place in the world" (Schnee 2009, 43, 39). Thus, across writing studies, as Victor Villanueva puts it, "The personal cannot be ignored, even if it can be denied" (quoted in Brandt et al. 2001, 52).

References

Alexander, Jonathan. 2008. *Literacy, Sexuality, Pedagogy: Theory and Practice for Composition Studies.* Logan: Utah State University Press.
Bleich David, and Deborah H. Holdstein. 2001. "Introduction: Recognizing the Human in the Humanities." In *Personal Effects: The Social Character of Scholarly Writing*, ed. Deborah H. Holdstein and David Bleich, 1–24. Logan: Utah State University Press.
Brandt, Deborah, Ellen Cushman, Anne Ruggles Gere, Anne Herrington, Richard E. Miller, Victor Villanueva, Min-Zhan Lu, and Gesa Kirsch. 2001. "The Politics of the Personal: Storying Our Lives against the Grain. Symposium Collective." *College English* 64 (1): 41–62. http://dx.doi.org/10.2307/1350109.
Campbell, Sue. 2002. "Philosophy and the Protection of the Personal." *Resources for Feminist Research* 20 (1/2): 81–129.
Charles, Mirjaliisa. 2007. "Language Matters in Global Communication." *Journal of Business Communication* 44 (3): 260–82. http://dx.doi.org/10.1177/0021943607302477.
Daly, Brenda. 2001. "Radical Introspection in Scholarship and Teaching." In *Personal Effects: The Social Character of Scholarly Writing*, ed. Deborah H. Holdstein, and David Bleich, 79–92. Logan: Utah State University Press.
Elbow, Peter. 2000. *Everyone Can Write: Essays toward a Hopeful Theory of Writing and Teaching Writing.* New York: Oxford University Press.
Eldred, Janet Carey. 2005. *Sentimental Attachments: Essays, Creative Nonfiction, and Other Experiments in Composition.* Portsmouth, NH: Boynton/Cook.
Freedman, Diane P. 2001. "Life Work through Teaching and Scholarship." In *Personal Effects: The Social Character of Scholarly Writing*, ed. Deborah H. Holdstein, and David Bleich, 199–219. Logan: Utah State University Press.
Gere, Anne Ruggles. 2001. "Revealing Silence: Rethinking Personal Writing." *College Composition and Communication* 53 (2): 203–33. http://dx.doi.org/10.2307/359076.
Gray, Jeffrey. 2001. "In the Name of the Subject: Some Recent Versions of the Personal." In *Personal Effects: The Social Character of Scholarly Writing*, ed. Deborah H. Holdstein, and David Bleich, 51–76. Logan: Utah State University Press.
Handelman, Susan. 2001. "'Knowledge Has a Face': The Jewish, the Personal, and the Pedagogical." In *Personal Effects: The Social Character of Scholarly Writing*, ed. Deborah H. Holdstein, and David Bleich, 121–44. Logan: Utah State University Press.

Hanisch, Carol. 1969. "The Personal is Political." carolhanisch.org.

Hindman, Jane. 2001a. "Making Writing Matter: Using 'The Personal' to Recover[y] an Essential[ist] Tension in Academic Discourse." *College English* 64 (1): 88–108. http://dx.doi.org/10.2307/1350111.

Hindman, Jane. 2001b. "Introduction, Special Focus: Personal Writing." *College English* 64 (1): 34–40. http://dx.doi.org/10.2307/1350108.

McAdams, Dan P. 1991. *The Stories We Live By: Personal Myths and the Making of the Self.* New York: Wiliam Morrow and Company, Inc.

Miles, Thomas. 1995. "Teaching Technical Writing through E-Mail: Making Hyperspace Personal." *Technical Communication* 42 (4): 658–60.

Pipes, Randolph B, Jaymee E. Holstein, and Maria G. Aguirre. 2005. "Examining the Personal-Professional Distinction: Ethics Codes and the Difficulty of Drawing a Boundary." *American Psychologist* 60 (4): 325–34. http://dx.doi.org/10.1037/0003-066X.60.4.325.

Ronald, Kate, and Hephzibah Roskelly. 2001. "Learning to Take It Personally." In *Personal Effects: The Social Character of Scholarly Writing*, ed. Deborah H. Holdstein, and David Bleich, 253–66. Logan: Utah State University Press.

Schnee, Emily. 2009. "Writing the Personal as Research." *Narrative Inquiry* 19 (1): 35–51. http://dx.doi.org/10.1075/ni.19.1.03sch.

Surman, Karen Paley. 2001. "The Social Construction of 'Expressivist' Pedagogy." In *Personal Effects: The Social Character of Scholarly Writing*, ed. Deborah H. Holdstein, and David Bleich, 178–98. Logan: Utah State University Press.

Spigelman, Candace. 2001. "Argument and Evidence in the Case of the Personal." *College English* 64 (1): 63–87. http://dx.doi.org/10.2307/1350110.

Steiner, Carol J. 1999. "Getting Personal: Individuality, Innovation, and Technical Communication." *Journal of Technical Writing and Communication* 29 (4): 383–99. http://dx.doi.org/10.2190/CMBB-E8K1-827T-F38K.

Webb, Clement. 1904. "The Personal Element in Philosophy." *Proceedings of the Aristotelian Society*, n.s. 5: 106–16.

PRODUCTION

Melanie Yergeau

Like the term *design*, *production* represents a tension between print-based and digital forms of composing. And, also like *design*, it calls into being questions about process and product. The interrelations and interchangeability of the terms present **other** challenges as well. Do we design products, or do we produce designs?

In *Multimodal Discourse*, Kress and Van Leeuwen (2001) contend that, though intricately connected, *design* and *production* are different entities. Whereas design signifies "uses of semiotic resources" (5), production means the organization and arrangement of those resources, often into a tangible product meant for public consumption (21). While the distinction between design and production might be permeable at best, new media scholars such as Hocks (2003) and Delagrange (2009) understand design to represent a recursive process, one that signifies both local and global assemblage—ranging in scale from writing curricula to document design to the entirety of writing studies as a discipline. Hocks, for instance, characterizes design as movement. Conversely, she uses production (as well as rhetorical criticism and invention) to signify a destination (644). Karl Stolley's (2008) "Lo-Fi Manifesto" defines production similarly—as a process and practice that leads to materials available for distribution, consumption, and/or preservation.

The term *production*, then, most often (though not exclusively) emerges in the discussion of already-produced texts. As Kress and Van Leeuwen note, "Semiosis begins at the level of production" (Kress and Van Leeuwen 2001, 79). Production, they argue, embodies something concrete, taking shape as the selection and arrangement of elements. But for all its connections to new media, production signals other histories as well—namely, the process movement, as well as materialist critiques of writing and political economies. With the former, we might look to previous decades in the field, when scholars denounced product-centered theories of writing. Robert Zoellner's 1969 article in *College English*, for example, provides one such early example. Dismantling what

DOI: 10.7330/9780874219746.c028

he terms an "instrumentalist" theory of writing, Zoellner (1983) suggests compositionists redirect their attention from "written (past tense)" texts to the processes and behaviors involved in producing those texts (123). Similarly, Donald Murray's (1976) "Teach Writing as a Process Not Product" asserts that product-centered pedagogies embody finality; yet, he too seems to distinguish between product and production, suggesting that production encompasses both a process and an end.

In some sense, then, *production* as a term appears to suggest process-toward-product, but not all scholars subscribe to the concrete resonance that Kress and Van Leeuwen's definition suggests. It is perhaps in Marxist analyses of production that this tension becomes most visible. Whether the **context** is process-oriented pedagogy, cultural studies, or new media production, *production* summons cultural ideals concerning distribution, labor, and social mobility. Production's ability to transcend "chronological narrative" and "theoretical camp" perhaps reflects what Jason Palmeri (2012) proposes—that the taxonomies used to order theories of writing render our own cultural biases (12–14). Production is a storied mode of arrangement, one haunted by theories of capitalism and commodification. Horner's (2000) materialist critique of writing or Anderson's (2003) exploration of prosumerism, for example, suggest some ways in which production intersects with privilege and purchasing power. Such discussions on privilege of necessity invoke social **class** and its intersections with race, **gender**, and **disability**. In her chair's address at CCCC in 2012, Malea Powell (2012) explored multiple dimensions of privilege and its role in the (re)production of colonizing narratives. Marginalization and academic modes of production have begun to draw more sustained scholarly attention within the past decade, but not nearly enough, as Powell and others lament. Recent examples include James Zebroski (2006), who has critiqued representations of writing as a "vehicle for class mobility" (515), as well as Tony Scott's (2009) **work** on the institutional structures that impede access for working-class students and other underrepresented groups.

Compositionists' explorations of production-as-capitalist enterprise, then, touch on everything from the process of writing and the training of teachers to contingent labor and economic access. Parascondola (2004) sees *production* to stand for a pervasive mode and work as a metaphor for corporatization. When we invoke *production*, he suggests, we call into question not only the production of writing on a page, but the production of "credentialed workers," the production of knowledge and services, and the production of people (students, teachers, **citizens**) who can be "managed in predictable and profitable ways" (217). If we revisit one of the beginning lines of this essay—Kress and Van Leeuwen's (2001) contention that semiosis begins at the level of production—we might intuit that *production* signifies an organizing metaphor for bodies, much like it does for alphabetic text or multimodal artifacts. Tony Scott's (2009) *Dangerous Writing* rekindles this sense of production, one conceptualized as a concrete arrangement of "teachers and students laboring" (18).

Embodiment and the capitalist hues of *production* assign alternative meanings within new media contexts. Cynthia Selfe (1999), for example, explores Harvey Graff's conception of the "literacy myth" within cultural narratives of **technology**. In this context, **literacy** becomes a type of capital, a tool used to promote "good citizenry" and upward social mobility. Similarly, Alex Reid (2003) affirms that *production* carries a long technological lineage, one beyond that of artifacts and tools for composing. Production, then, represents a double entendre of sorts. It signifies not only the use of technologies but the role that such use plays in cultural scripts surrounding labor and technological literacy.

New media theorists have troubled other aspects of production as well. The open-access movement is one apt example. Karl Stolley (2008), for instance, has long urged the **computers** and writing **community** to resist proprietary and device-dependent software, which can serve as barriers to broader access and create file formats that "are destined for . . . obsolescence." While academic publishing has channeled much of its open-access energy toward issues concerning scale and distribution, calls like Stolley's underscore the *means* of production—technologies and literacies—that equip citizen-rhetors to become designers of texts and technologies.

But as much as Stolley's call for open-access production opens avenues for broader participation, such a focus potentially limits the scope of—and access to—digitally born production. Bill Hart-Davidson (2012) has offered one such critique. In essence, Hart-Davidson gives teacher-scholars permission to set aside code and explore production software instead. Here, Hart-Davidson does not directly counter Stolley's work; he too acknowledges the affordances of code-level production, describing production software as a stepping stone toward developing technological literacies. James Porter's (2009) treatise on recovering digital delivery offers similar sentiments vis-à-vis production and access. In it, he exhorts techno-rhetoricians to "help" individuals (notably, those with disabilities) gain access to production technologies that typically exclude non-normative users. The conflict here, interestingly, rests on alphanumeric text. Stolley and other "code warriors" assert the inherent flexibility of code and the back-end—which, among other things, enables the participation of screen reader users or individuals who cannot afford commercial software. Others, however, suggest that a code-centric framework poses other barriers to access, including time, technological support, and mathematical ability.

Still, debates regarding access and software return to questions of arrangement and semiosis. While much of this essay has focused on human participation, production, especially digital production, can include non-human practices and designs, or what Alex Reid (2012) has described as object-oriented rhetoric. Indeed, Lev Manovich's (2001) very definition of *digital production* centers on automation—on the filters and binary code that lie behind any human arrangement of digital artifacts. At what point, we might ask, do we attribute authorship to ourselves or to the complex algorithms of our word processing software? And while automation undergirds numerous discussions of computer-mediated design, it has percolated through other facets of composition studies for decades. **Genre** theory, for example, has long been conceptualized through a reproduction-oriented metaphor in which genres replicate, evolve, and merge in(ter)dependent of human help (see Devitt, Bawarshi, and Reiff 2003).

In sum, *production* engages many aspects of writing studies. The term embodies tensions concerning access, consumption, and **agency**. Its use calls into question our very understandings of design and cultural infrastructures. Order, means, and meaning—these are some of the abstractions that production supposedly makes concrete.

References

Anderson, Daniel. 2003. "Prosumer Approaches to New Media Composition: Consumption and Production in Continuum." *Kairos: A Journal of Rhetoric, Technology, and Pedagogy* 8 (1). http://kairos.technorhetoric.net/8.1/binder2.html?coverweb/anderson/index.html.

Delagrange, Susan H. 2009. "When Revision Is Redesign: Key Questions for Digital Scholarship." *Kairos: A Journal of Rhetoric, Technology, and Pedagogy* 14 (1). http://kairos.technorhetoric.net/14.1/inventio/delagrange/.

Devitt, Amy J., Anis Bawarshi, and Mary Jo Reiff. 2003. "Materiality and Genre in the Study of Discourse Communities." *College English* 65 (5): 541–88. http://dx.doi.org/10.2307/3594252.

Hart-Davidson, Bill. 2012. "Code? Not So Much." In *Sweetland Digital Rhetoric Collaborative.* http://www.digitalrhetoriccollaborative.org/2012/10/17/code-not-so-much/.

Hocks, Mary. 2003. "Understanding Visual Rhetoric in Digital Writing Environments." *College Composition and Communication* 54 (4): 629–56. http://dx.doi.org/10.2307/3594188.

Horner, Bruce. 2000. *Terms of Work for Composition: A Materialist Critique of Writing.* Albany: SUNY Press.

Kress, Gunther, and Theo Van Leeuwen. 2001. *Multimodal Discourse: The Modes and Media of Contemporary Communication*. London: Arnold.

Manovich, Lev. 2001. *The Language of New Media*. Cambridge: MIT.

Murray, Donald. 1976. "Teach Writing as a Process Not Product." In *Rhetoric and Composition*, ed. Richard L. Graves, 79–82. Rochelle Park, NJ: Hayden.

Palmeri, Jason. 2012. *Remixing Composition: A History of Multimodal Writing Pedagogy*. Carbondale: Southern Illinois University Press.

Parascondola, Leo. 2004. "'Write-to-Earn': College Writing and Management Discourse." In *Tenured Bosses and Disposable Teachers: Writing Instruction in the Managed University*, ed. Marc Bousquet, Tony Scott, and Leo Parscondola, 209–219. Carbondale: Southern Illinois University Press.

Porter, James E. 2009. "Recovering Delivery for Digital Rhetoric." *Computers and Composition* 26 (4): 207–24. http://dx.doi.org/10.1016/j.compcom.2009.09.004.

Powell, Malea. 2012. "2012 CCCC Chair's Address: Stories Take Place." *College Composition and Communication* 64 (2): 383–406.

Reid, Alex. 2003. "New Media's Long History and Global Future: The *Uniplanet* Project." *Kairos: A Journal of Rhetoric, Technology, and Pedagogy* 8 (1). http://kairos.technorhetoric.net/8.1/binder2.html?coverweb/reid/reid.swf.

Reid, Alex. 2012. "Composing Objects: Prospects for a Digital Rhetoric." *Enculturation*. http://www.enculturation.net/composing-objects.

Scott, Tony. 2009. *Dangerous Writing: Understanding the Political Economy of Composition*. Logan: Utah State University Press.

Selfe, Cynthia L. 1999. *Technology and Literacy in the Twenty-First Century*. Carbondale: Southern Illinois University Press.

Stolley, Karl. 2008. "The Lo-Fi Manifesto." *Kairos: A Journal of Rhetoric, Technology, and Pedagogy* 12 (3). http://kairos.technorhetoric.net/12.3/topoi/stolley/.

Zebroski, James T. 2006. "Social Class as Discourse: Mapping the Landscape of Class in Rhetoric and Composition." *JAC* 26 (3–4): 513–83.

Zoellner, Robert. (1969) 1983. "Talk-Write: A Behavioral Pedagogy for Composition." In *Theory and Practice in the Teaching of Composition: Processing, Distancing, and Modeling*, ed. Miles Myers and James Gray, 122–28. Urbana, IL: National Council of Teachers of English.

QUEER

Karen Kopelson

The term *queer* gathered force in activist and theoretical circles in the early 1990s, signifying both the reclamation of a reviled **identity** and a disruptive anti-identitarian current over and against established categorizations for gendered sexuality. In **other** words, while one can march in a gay pride parade wearing a t-shirt proclaiming oneself "queer," the use of "the term 'queer,'" as Teresa De Lauretis (1991) explained, "is intended to mark a certain critical distance from" the formulaic, "convenient" construction—"lesbian and gay"—and instead to "construct another discursive horizon, another way of thinking the sexual" (iv). Eve Kosofsky Sedgwick notes that "[t]he word 'queer' itself means *across*—it comes from the Indo-European root—*twerkw*, which also yields the German *quer* (transverse), Latin *torquere* (to twist), English *athwart*" (Sedgwick 1993, xii, emphasis in original). Thus, in its broadest (anti) formulations, *queer* is a "motive" or "movement" (xii), twisting and thwarting the entire "logic of the sexual order" (Warner 1993, xiii) and, more broadly still, "spin[ning] . . . outward along dimensions that can't be subsumed under **gender** and sexuality at all" to suggest the questioning of all identity-constituting **discourses** (Sedgwick 1993, 9).

As this brief history of the term's cultural–theoretical reappropriation in the 1990s illustrates, the "paradoxical reality" of *queer* is that it remains a "designation" (for a sexual minority) even as it connotes the rejection or disturbance of processes of designation (that exceed the sexual) (Duggan 1992, 13, 27). This paradox is evident in the ways *queer* circulates in writing studies: The term regularly serves to identify, categorize, and reflect minority status —for example, "queer faculty" may face unique pedagogical challenges or inhospitable working conditions (Fox 2007); "queer students" may face particular "dilemmas" in the writing **class** or have distinctive "**literacy** needs" (Wallace and Alexander 2009, 796)—yet it simultaneously **works** as a synonym for an "epistemological position" (Kopelson 2002, 25) that interrogates or "queries" (Alexander and Gibson 2004, 15) how and to what ends identities, both dominant

DOI: 10.7330/9780874219746.c029

and marginalized, are constructed, performed, and deployed. Harriet Malinowitz (1995) is often credited as one of the first writing studies scholars both to use *queer* in this latter sense and to reappropriate the term for the field more generally. In her chapter, "Queering the Brew," Malinowitz proposes a pedagogy that "would entail thinking about" the ways social "margins" and "centers" are produced and, in turn, productive of subject positions (251).

If Malinowitz's linkage of pedagogy to beer-making was atypical, her linkage of *queer* to pedagogy was prescient. Like many keywords, *queer* gathered force in writing studies through discussions of, and often as a modifier for, *pedagogy* (i.e., "queer pedagogy"), or, to similar effect, appended to *theory* ("queer theory") and attended by the question— sometimes implicit, but often explicit—of queer theory's applicability to or implications for the classroom (e.g., Alexander and Gibson 2004; Kopelson 2002; Monson and Rhodes 2004). When appended to "pedagogy," *queer* consistently signifies, as it did for Malinowitz, teaching that goes beyond the "mere 'inclusion'" of marginalized identities and perspectives in the writing class to complicate identity as such (Malinowitz 1995, 251). Yet, teacher-scholars in writing studies still mean different things when modifying **pedagogy** with *queer*. For some, "queer pedagogy" complicates identity via assignments or class activities that work to "explode stereotyped or stabilized notions of LGBT identity" (Barrios 2004, 356), or that encourage students to "[interrogate] naturalized narrations of sexuality, identity, and normalcy" (Alexander 2008, 102). For others, like Karen Kopelson, identity is complicated in queer pedagogies via teachers' **performances** of self that "strive to trouble sexual and other identity divisions . . . by exceeding what is thought and known about identity's 'evident' markers" (Kopelson 2002, 24; see also Kopelson 2003). In both conceptions of "queer pedagogy," however— whether *queer* represents a mode of inquiry for students or a performative, embodied mode of teachers' self-presentation—*queer* becomes synonymous with such terms as "exploding," "interrogating," and "troubling," and so the *queer* in "queer pedagogy" may be "thought of as a verb" (Britzman, quoted in Kopelson 2002, 25).

This mention of *queer*'s grammatical function is crucial to considering the layers of meaning surrounding the term. Mel Y. Chen has recently suggested that the "polyvalence" of the word *queer* is reflected and "instituted in part by [its] 'bleeding' . . . into diffuse parts of speech" (Chen 2012, 58). What happens when *queer* gets into grammatical position, then, causes it to diffuse further still. For example, following her assertion that *queer* be "thought of as a verb," and following Sedgwick's observation that *queer* "spins outward" beyond gender or sexuality, Kopelson notes that "any aspect of identity, or any *intersection* of aspects of identity, can be 'queered'"—that is, "troubled" or revealed to be in excess of itself (Kopelson 2002, 25). Spinning further still, so can spaces or even abstractions: Jan Cooper is interested in "queering **the contact zone**," for instance (Cooper 2004), and Brad Peters and Diana Swanson study "queering the conflicts" (Peters and Swanson 2004). Jonathan Alexander and William P. Banks observe that "various **technologies** disrupt traditional notions of writing and writing instruction, effectively queering spaces that were once dominated by pens, pencils, and loose-leaf paper" (Alexander and Banks 2004, 274–75). Catherine Fox also uses *queer* as both a verb and a synonym for interrogating or "troubling" when she insists that we must "'trouble' the heteronormative order of our departments and the ways in which we organize them around . . . family and kinship structures" (Fox 2007, 504).

"Bleeding" into its adjectival space, *queer* has modified many other of the field's keywords in addition to *pedagogy*, usually signaling—as it does when it modifies pedagogy—attention to processes of construction, constraint, and disruption. Barclay Barrios, among others, writes of the "queer classroom," which "enables all students to see . . . the ways in which . . . sexuality is created by and through cultural discourses, a realization that serves as a precondition for change in the larger political context" (Barrios 2004, 345). Wallace and Alexander offer "queer rhetorical **agency**," a formation which seeks to highlight and then subvert the ways in which "agency in our culture is heterosexualized" and thus prohibitive of "alternative narrations of life stories" (Wallace and Alexander 2009, 806). Jacqueline Rhodes proffers "queer text," or, alternatively, "queertext," which "dances in the openness of the margin between Signifier (Sr) and Signified (Sd)" to "subvert The Word" (Rhodes 2004, 388).

Queerness is another permutation of *queer* that circulates in writing studies, and it is in its nominal form that the "paradoxical reality" of *queer* again becomes especially evident. In some instances, *queerness* seems to refer to the state of being a queer individual: *queerness* is a minoritized sexual identity that a teacher/student may choose to "hide" or "disclose" and, in disclosing, "use . . . to challenge norms" (Alexander 2008, 35, 111, 178). In other instances, *queerness* is detached from the individual but remains a (minority) designation; it is an alternative state of being we can call attention to within institutional spaces to also challenge norms. Alexander and Banks write, "acknowledging queerness undermines the assumption of a family-centered heterosexuality and opens up a space for discussing those who live and craft their lives outside of the heteronormative paradigm," which, again, promotes the understanding that all sexuality is socially constituted (Alexander and Banks 2004, 274). In still other instances, *queerness* is more akin to a "state of disruption." Robert McRuer, for example, uses *queerness* as a synonym for the "de-composition and disorder" that "always haunt the composition classroom" fixated on the finished product (McRuer 2004, 55). He argues that the "critical project of resisting closure" promoted by process pedagogies reveals that queerness has long been a "subtext" of the field and is "desirable" (60). Alexander and Rhodes similarly define queerness as "the gesture of the unrepresentable" and illegible—"the insistence that not everything be *composed*" (Alexander and Rhodes 2011, 181, emphasis in original). Queerness thus "pushes hard at composition," and, rather than proving desirable, may finally prove incompatible with or—as they put it—"impossible" for "composition as it is [usually] currently configured and taught" (183, 179).

When *queerness* or *queer* is conceived as the inherently marginal, necessarily illegible, and "all together Other" (Alexander and Rhodes 2011, 181, 190), then indeed it "cannot become the basis for pedagogy," and perhaps "cannot be brought within the university as we know it," as Lynn Worsham once wrote of that other disruptive current, *écriture feminine* (Worsham 1991, 92). Yet, the polyvalence and paradoxes of *queer* suggest it may nevertheless remain a productively troubling term for writing studies.

References

Alexander, Jonathan. 2008. *Literacy, Sexuality, Pedagogy: Theory and Practice for Composition Studies.* Logan: Utah State University Press.

Alexander, Jonathan, and Jacqueline Rhodes. 2011. "Queer: An Impossible Subject for Composition." *JAC* 31 (1–2): 177–206.

Alexander, Jonathan, and Michelle Gibson. 2004. "Queer Composition(s): Queer Theory in the Writing Classroom." *JAC* 24 (1): 1–21.

Alexander, Jonathan, and William P. Banks. 2004. "Sexualities, Technologies, and the Teaching of Writing: A Critical Overview." *Computers and Composition* 21 (3): 273–93. http://dx.doi.org/10.1016/j.compcom.2004.05.005.

Barrios, Barclay. 2004. "Of Flags: Online Queer Identities, Writing Classrooms, and ActionHorizons." *Computers and Composition* 21 (3): 341–61. http://dx.doi.org/10.1016/j.compcom.2004.05.003.

Chen, Mel Y. 2012. *Animacies: Biopolitics, Racial Mattering, and Queer Affect.* Durham: Duke University Press. http://dx.doi.org/10.1215/9780822395447.

Cooper, Jan. 2004. "Queering the Contact Zone." *JAC* 24 (1): 23–45.

De Lauretis, Teresa. 1991. "Queer Theory: Lesbian and Gay Sexualities—An Introduction." *Differences: A Journal of Feminist Cultural Studies* 3 (2): iii–xviii.

Duggan, Lisa. 1992. "Making it Perfectly Queer." *Socialist Review* 22: 11–31.

Fox, Catherine. 2007. "From Transaction to Transformation: (En)Countering White Hetero-normativity in 'Safe Spaces.'" *College English* 69 (5): 496–511.

Kopelson, Karen. 2002. "Dis/Integrating the Gay/Queer Binary: 'Reconstructed Identity Politics' for a Performative Pedagogy." *College English* 65 (1): 17–35. http://dx.doi.org /10.2307/3250728.

Kopelson, Karen. 2003. "Rhetoric on the Edge of Cunning; Or, The Performance of Neutrality Reconsidered as Composition Pedagogy for Student Resistance." *College Composition and Communication* 55 (1): 115–46. http://dx.doi.org/10.2307/3594203.

Malinowitz, Harriet. 1995. *Textual Orientations: Lesbian and Gay Students and the Making of Discourse Communities.* Portsmouth: Boynton/Cook.

McRuer, Robert. 2004. "Composing Bodies; or, De-Composition: Queer Theory, Disability Studies, and Alternative Corporealities." *JAC* 24 (1): 47–78.

Monson, Connie, and Jacqueline Rhodes. 2004. "Risking Queer: Pedagogy, Performativity, and Desire in Writing Classrooms." *JAC* 24 (1): 79–91.

Peters, Brad, and Diana Swanson. 2004. "Queering the Conflicts: What LGBT Students Can Teach Us in the Classroom and Online." *Computers and Composition* 21 (3): 295–313. http://dx.doi.org/10.1016/j.compcom.2004.05.004.

Rhodes, Jacqueline. 2004. "Homo Origo: The Queertext Manifesto." *Computers and Composition* 21 (3): 385–88. http://dx.doi.org/10.1016/j.compcom.2004.05.001.

Sedgwick, Eve Kosofsky. 1993. *Tendencies.* Durham: Duke University Press.

Wallace, David L., and Jonathan Alexander. 2009. "Queer Rhetorical Agency: Questioning Narratives of Heteronormativity." *JAC* 29 (4): 793–819.

Warner, Michael, ed. 1993. "Introduction." In *Fear of a Queer Planet*, vi–xxxi. Minneapolis: University of Minnesota Press.

Worsham, Lynn. 1991. "Writing against Writing: The Predicament of *Ecriture Féminine* in Composition Studies." In *Contending With Words: Composition and Rhetoric in a Postmodern Age*, ed. Patricia Harkin and John Schilb, 82–104. New York: MLA.

REFLECTION

Kathleen Blake Yancey

The term *reflection* has informed writing studies almost from the beginning of the modern iteration of the field, drawing initially on Dewey's concept of experiential learning and Polanyi's (1969) felt sense, and later on Donald's Schon's (1987) account of reflective practice. In *How We Think,* Dewey defines reflective thinking as "the kind of thinking that consists in turning a subject over in the mind and giving it serious and consecutive consideration" (Dewey 1993, 3). Keyed to a learner's interest in solving a real problem, resolving an ambiguous situation, or addressing a dilemma (14), Deweyan reflective thinking relies on a dialogue among multiple perspectives: the believed and the known, with presuppositions and necessary conclusions. Emphasizing the finding of the problem as a key feature in reflection, Michael Polanyi (1969) points to its heuristic power and the thinking that develops through a dialogue between the felt and the known, the unarticulated and the explicit. Defining a "reflective practitioner," Schon (1987) observes that it is through reflecting on our own work that we theorize our own practices. Since epistemological operations of technical knowing are inappropriate for social organizations, Schon argues for "prototypical models of causal pattern that may guide inquiry in other organizational situations—prototypes that depend, for their validity, on modification and testing" in another situation, a generalization he refers to as "reflective transfer" (97).

In 1979, Sharon Pianko (1979) portrayed reflection as fundamental to success in writing, attributing to it "the essence of the difference between able and not so able writers." She defined it behaviorally, as "pauses and rescannings" stimulating "the growth of consciousness in students about the numerous mental and linguistic strategies" entailed in composing, and "the many lexical, syntactical, and organizational choices" made during composing (277–78). At about the same time, Sondra Perl (1980) pointed to two components of reflection, what she called projection and retrospection, "the alternating mental postures writers assume as they move through the act of composing" (389).

DOI: 10.7330/9780874219746.c030

Reflection has also been invoked as a pedagogical practice. Jeffrey Sommers' (1988) "Writer's Memo," for instance, requires students, in a student's words, to go "behind the paper" to describe "the composing process which produced the draft" (77). The memo's intent was twofold: to elucidate student composing activities in students' own descriptions in order to see what was otherwise invisible, and to provide a **context** for an instructor–student conversation about the draft. From its earliest instantiation, then, the pedagogical application of reflection was both individual and social. Dawn Swartzendruber-Putnam (2000) likewise imagines reflection as an intertextual phenomenon involving a Writer's Log: "a quick write that focuses on one week of writing"; a Draft Letter (much like a writer's memo): "longer writing that focuses on a single piece of work"; and a Portfolio Letter: "polished writing that discusses a body of work" (89). Most comprehensively, Kathleen Blake Yancey (1998) developed a Schonean-influenced, practice-based theory of reflection keyed to three related forms of reflective practice:

1. *reflection-in-action*, the process of reviewing, projecting, and revising, which takes place within a composing event

2. *constructive reflection*, the process of developing a cumulative, multi-selved, multi-voiced **identity**, which takes place between and among composing events

3. *reflection-in-presentation*, the process of articulating the relationships between and among the multiple variables of writing and the writer in a specific context for a specific audience. (200)

Reflection has also emerged as a keyword in discussions of **networked** classrooms and digital formats. For example, in studying MOO-based metacognition, Joel English (1992) observed that the environment of the MOO made available transcripts of discussions, which, unlike most classroom discussions, were recorded and thus available for reflection. Lennie Irvin (2004) likewise points to the ways that "networks greatly expand the ability to share texts" and to the opportunities they provide for students to see from multiple perspectives. At the same time, Yancey et al. (2013), note that, absent the benefit of the conventions of a **genre**, students' video reflections on their writing can become lengthy "talking head" exercises somewhat at odds with insightful reflection.

Reflection has been constructed as a major aspect of assessment, specifically in print and electronic portfolios—both defined as the result of three processes: collecting, selecting, and reflecting. While portfolios and their accompanying reflections are ubiquitous, the value of asking students to reflect is a point of tension in the field. Tony Scott (2005), for example, argues that in K–12 settings, reflection is a matter of coercion, with students being forced into telling external assessors what they want to hear. Julie Jung (2011), citing the work of O'Neill (2002), Mirtz (2002), and others, makes a parallel argument about faculty reflection: "when written and read within contexts of high-stakes assessment, all reflective writing is, in fact, rhetorical argument—discursive appeals targeted to external audiences for specific purposes" (629). While Ed White (2005) has suggested that the reflective text can function as a surrogate for the full portfolio in an assessment context, earlier research by Conway (1994) construes this cover letter as much more a **performance** piece for students, a mask through which to present the best possible student self (89).

Not surprisingly, reflection serves as a flashpoint in debates about the unified self—or the possibility of such a self. Scholars like Pat Belanoff (2001) contend that reflection "can enable the reconstituting—if only momentarily—of a unified self, which certainly enables one to act more effectively" (421), while others, including Conway (1994) and Emmons (2003), have objected that, in Jung's language, reflective writing tends "to legitimize liberal constructions of the writer as a single, unified self" (629). Thus, "reflective writing pedagogy, which aims to help student-writers assert authority as *writers*, ends up reinforcing some students' sense of themselves as 'only' *students*" (Jung 2011, 642, emphasis in original).

The many valences of *reflection* frequently situate it at the nexus of educational concerns. Scholars such as Weiser (1997) have worried about "schmootz," or students' tendency to tell us what they want to hear, but Metzger and Bryant (1993) discovered students also enacting schmootz: deliberately composing weaker texts so that they could improve them on a later draft and thus argue in their reflection that their writing had improved. Laurel Bower (2003) has also targeted the portfolio reflective assignment as problematic, noting its teacher audience, its brevity, and its end-of-the-term timing. Yancey and Morgan (1999), however, found that students could be differentiated into weaker and stronger students according to their composing knowledge as prompted by reflection. Likewise, Leaker and Ostman (2010) have demonstrated how nontraditional adult students earn college credit through documenting, contextualizing, and explaining their non-curricular learning in a reflective text.

Current interest in *reflection* constructs it as a key term in questions concerning the transfer of knowledge and practice. Scholars agree that reflection is necessary (Beaufort 2007; Downs and Wardle 2007), but even the most explicit theory of writing development, Anne Beaufort's, includes reflection without operationalizing it as term or practice. Most recently, Kara Taczak (2011) and Liane Robertson (2011) developed and researched a Teaching for Transfer (TFT) curriculum centering on writing as an object of study as well as practice; students are asked to learn about reflection as a mode of inquiry, and, through reflection, to create their own theory of writing. Their **research** demonstrates that, when compared to more conventional themed or expressivist curricula, the TFT curriculum provided much more support for the transfer of composing knowledge and practice.

Other noteworthy iterations of reflection in writing studies include Yameng Liu's (1995) argument that reflection's role in prompting self-doubt works toward a more ethical rhetoric, as well as Craig Hansen's (2004) use of reflection to help technical writing students in service learning contexts bring together theory and practice. In sum, *reflection* seems to be both a central yet productively open term: Dozier and Rutten (2005, 596) posit that reflection is "an essential attribute of effective literacy teaching," one needing better definitions and more sophisticated research.

References

Beaufort, Anne. 2007. *College Writing and Beyond: A New Framework for University Writing Instruction.* Logan: Utah State University Press.

Belanoff, Pat. 2001. "Silence: Reflection, Literacy, Learning, and Teaching." *College Composition and Communication* 52 (3): 399–428. http://dx.doi.org/10.2307/358625.

Bower, Laurel L. 2003. "Student Reflection and Critical Thinking: A Rhetorical Analysis of 88 Portfolio Cover Letters." *Journal of Basic Writing* 22 (2): 47–66.

Conway, Glenda. 1994. "Portfolio Cover Letters, Students' Self-Presentation, and Teachers' Ethics." In *New Directions in Portfolio Assessment: Reflective Practice, Critical Theory, and Large-Scale Scoring,* ed. Laurel Black, Donald Daiker, Jeffrey Sommers, and Gail Stygall, 83–92. Portsmouth, NH: Boynton/Cook.

Dewey, John. 1993. *How We Think,* 2nd ed. Boston: D. C. Heath.

Downs, Douglas, and Elizabeth Wardle. 2007. "Teaching about Writing, Righting Misconceptions: (Re)Envisioning 'First-Year Composition' as 'Introduction to Writing Studies.'" *College Composition and Communication* 58 (4): 552–84.

Dozier, Cheryl L., and Ilene Rutten. 2005. "Responsive Teaching Toward Responsive Teachers: Mediating Transfer through Intentionality, Enactment, and Articulation." *Journal of Literacy Research* 37 (4): 459–92. http://dx.doi.org/10.1207/s15548430 jlr3704_3.

Emmons, Kimberly. 2003. "Rethinking Genres of Reflection: Student Portfolio Cover Letters and the Narrative of Progress." *Composition Studies* 31 (1): 43–62.

English, Joel A. 1992. "MOO-based Metacognition: Incorporating Online and Offline Reflection into the Writing Process." *Kairos* 3 (1).

Hansen, Craig. 2004. "At the Nexus of Theory and Practice: Guided, Critical Reflection for Learning beyond the Classroom in Technical Communication." *In Innovative Approaches to Teaching Technical Communication,* ed. Tracy Bridgeford, Karla Saari Kitalong, and Dickie Selfe, 338–54. Logan: Utah State University Press.

Irvin, Lennie. 2004. *Reflection in the Electronic Writing Classroom.* Computers and Composition Online/Utah State University Press.

Jung, Julie. 2011. "Reflective Writing's Synecdochic Imperative: Process Descriptions Redescribed." *College English* 73 (6): 628–47.

Leaker, Cathy, and Heather Ostman. 2010. "Composing Knowledge: Writing, Rhetoric, and Reflection in Prior Learning Assessment." *College Composition and Communication* 61 (4): 691–717.

Liu, Yameng. 1995. "Rhetoric and Reflexivity." *Philosophy & Rhetoric* 28 (4): 333–49.

Metzger, Elizabeth, and Lizbeth Bryant. 1993. "Portfolio Assessment: Pedagogy, Power, and the Student." *Teaching English in the Two-Year College* 20 (4): 279–88.

Mirtz, Ruth M. 2002. "Teaching Statements and Teaching Selves." In *Composition, Pedagogy, and the Scholarship of Teaching*, ed. Deborah Minter and Amy Goodbum, 43–53. Portsmouth: Boynton/Cook.

O'Neill, Peggy. 2002. "Constructed Confessions: Creating a Teaching Self in the Job Search Portfolio." In *Composition, Pedagogy, and the Scholarship of Teaching*, ed. Deborah Minter and Amy Goodbum, 33–42. Portsmouth: Boynton/Cook.

Perl, Sondra. 1980. "Understanding Composing." *College Composition and Communication* 31 (4): 363–70. http://dx.doi.org/10.2307/356586.

Pianko, Sharon. 1979. "Reflection: A Critical Component of the Composing Process." *College Composition and Communication* 30 (3): 275–78. http://dx.doi.org/10.2307/356394.

Polanyi, Michael. 1969. *Knowing and Being.* Chicago: University of Chicago Press.

Robertson, Liane. 2011. "The Significance of Course Content in the Transfer of Writing Knowledge from First-Year Composition to Other Academic Writing Contexts." Dissertation, Florida State University.

Schon, Donald A. 1987. *Educating the Reflective Practitioner: Toward a New Design for Teaching and Learning in the Professions.* San Francisco: Jossey-Bass.

Scott, Tony. 2005. "Creating the Subject of Portfolios: Reflective Writing and the Conveyance of Institutional Prerogatives." *Written Communication* 22 (1): 3–35. http://dx.doi.org/10.1177/0741088304271831.

Sommers, Jeffrey. 1988. "Behind the Paper: Using the Student-Teacher Memo." *College Composition and Communication* 39 (1): 77–80. http://dx.doi.org/10.2307/357824.

Swartzendruber-Putnam, Dawn. 2000. "Written Reflection: Creating Better Thinkers, Better Writers." *English Journal* 90 (1): 88–93. http://dx.doi.org/10.2307/821737.

Taczak, Kara. 2011. "Connecting the Dots: Does Reflection Foster Transfer?" Dissertation, Florida State University.

Weiser, Irwin. 1997. "Revising Our Practices: How Portfolios Help Teachers Learn." In *Situating Portfolios*, ed. Kathleen Blake Yancey, and Irwin Weiser, 293–305. Logan: Utah State University Press.

White, Edward M. 2005. "The Scoring of Writing Portfolios: Phase 2." *College Composition and Communication* 56 (4): 581–600.

Yancey, Kathleen Blake. 1998. *Reflection in the Writing Classroom.* Logan: Utah State University Press.

Yancey, Kathleen Blake, Leigh Graziano, Jennifer O'Malley, and Rory Lee. 2013. "Reflection, ePortfolios, and WEPO: A Reflective Account of New Practices in a New Curriculum." In *Reflection and Metacognition in College Teaching: Across the Disciplines, across the Academy*, ed. Matthew Kaplan, Naomi Silver, Danielle LaVaque-Manty, and Deborah Meizlish, 175–202. Sterling, VA: Stylus.

Yancey, Kathleen Blake, and Meg Morgan. 1999. "Reflective Essays, Curriculum, and the Scholarship of Administration: Notes toward Administrative Scholarly Work." In *The Writing Program Administrator as Researcher*, ed. Shirley K. Rose and Irwin Weiser, 81–94. Westport, CT: Heinemann Boynton/Cook.

RESEARCH

Katrina M. Powell

In writing studies, the terms *research, scholarship,* and *inquiry* are often used interchangeably, evoking a sense of informed study around a topic from a particular theoretical stance. However, when most scholars use *research* as a term, they tend to mean empirical research as opposed to rhetorical research or inquiry. The distinctions are important yet debatable, as many scholars in the field see their research as doing both. As Janice Lauer and J. William Asher point out, "To investigate [empirical] questions, [researchers] use inductive processes instead of the deductive and analogical processes of rhetorical inquiry. Inductive processes take two forms: descriptive and experimental" (Lauer and Asher 1988, 6). Indeed, many researchers in writing studies use both rhetorical and empirical methods.

It is clear that research in writing studies is broad, varied, and contested. What counts includes a wide array of research types—participatory action, case study, ethnographic, community action, rhetorical, historiographic, meta-analysis, etc. Yet it is also clear that when some say *research* they are referring specifically to RAD research: that which is replicable, agreeable, and data-supported (Haswell 2005). For some, this is the only research that counts as "rigorous" or "systematic."

Lynn Worsham's (2011) essay, "Fast-Food Scholarship," laments that some recent scholarship in writing studies is not "substantive, rigorous, high-quality scholarship" that is "careful, methodical, fully developed intellectual **work**." Many would agree that Worsham's implicit definition of *research* is something for which to strive. Indeed, when Braddock, Lloyd-Jones, and Schoer (1963) published *Research in Written Communication*, they were tasked with summarizing the "most soundly based studies" in the field. In summarizing these studies, they "decided to use only research employing 'scientific methods,' like controlled experimentation and textual analysis" (1). Thus, from the early beginnings of the field, what counts as research has been contested and debated. The language of science sparked much debate and skepticism

DOI: 10.7330/9780874219746.c031

in the field, with a distinct suspicion of "objectivity," and since then writing scholars have worked to define what is meant by "rigorous" research.

While RAD has helped rhetoric and composition earn a place as a legitimate field, some scholars have remained wary of RAD data, presuming that "scientific" methods are rooted in positivism. As Charney (1996) and Haswell (2005) show, however, this mistrust seems to stem from a lack of understanding of the ways that the sciences have also questioned their data collection methods and methodologies. Despite Haswell's concern for the damage that the "war" metaphor underlying these exchanges can cause within the discipline, the conflict has been productive, as many writing studies researchers have been compelled to examine their methods more critically. Johanek (2000), Kirsch and Sullivan (1992), Lauer and Asher (1988), and MacNealy (1998) all see the value of multiple ways of conducting scholarship. While some have argued that some forms of research are better than others, many—like Kirsch and Sullivan—have recognized the vitality of a field that critically examines all research practices. Their collection therefore contributes "to a self-questioning stance" and questions the field's "methodological pluralism" (2, 10).

Many research methods courses in graduate programs are designed to help graduate students become "good consumer[s] of research" (MacNealy 1998, x). That is, they focus on the ways that research is designed, conducted, and written as well as how conclusions and interpretations follow from the theories driving the **design**. As MacNealy points out, "empirical research refers to research that carefully describes and/or measures observable phenomena in a systematic way planned in advance of the observation" (6). However, it is important to note that "rhetorical inquiry" is often also quite systematic and planned, just differently—usually in different contexts and with different "texts." As many teachers of methods courses point out, in reading scholarship in the field, whether it is teacher research, a longitudinal ethnographic study, or a meta-analysis, it is important for the reader to discern what the writer means by *research* and whether the research methods and methodologies are suited to the research questions asked. This requires a deep understanding of the epistemological stance of the writer, which can sometimes be determined through an explication of the assumptions he or she makes about composing and composers.

In 2008, Charles Bazerman compiled the colossal *Handbook of Research on Writing*. As he says in the preface, "The last 30 years have produced a wide interdisciplinary inquiry into how people write, how we learn to write, under what conditions and for what purposes we write, what resources and **technologies** we use to write, how our current forms and practices of writing emerged within social history, and what impacts writing has had on society and the individual" (Bazerman 2007, xi). What Bazerman's volume (and others like it) illustrates is the vast range of research questions that have been investigated since the early 1960s.

More recent developments in writing studies, however, further complicate the meanings of *research*, even beyond the difficulties raised by such a vast range of research questions and investigators' divergent epistemological and methodological approaches. For example, some scholars have constructed *research* as a range of ethical problems, such as whether and how to train novice researchers (including graduate and undergraduate students) as they go into the field for the first time. As ethnographic and field research continues to be valued in writing studies, it presents complex ethical issues for researchers to consider as they interpret various acts of composing, whether in writing classrooms, workplaces, or communities (Barton 2008; Mortensen and Kirsch 1996; Newkirk 1992; Powell and Takayoshi 2003). Relationships with participants, participants' contribution to research design, researcher positionality, and representations of individuals and their **community** spaces are ongoing ethical issues for researchers as they engage in unique research questions and sites. In like manner, as McKee and DeVoss (2007) suggest, source material located on digital spaces has presented new challenges for researchers as they cite the research and consider ethical issues about "**public**" (see civic/public) writing. The immediacy of fieldwork, the active and ongoing nature of research (not merely a reporting of what happened), and the ethical responsibilities to the communities we research are crucial issues addressed by Blythe (2007), Cushman (1998), and Moss (1992).

Of late, as writing studies has expanded the range of scholarly work in the field, *research* has also meant an effort to return to and reflect on seminal texts in order to appreciate their lasting contributions and reconfigure them to address an ever-increasing range of emergent questions. Simultaneously, the field's growing studies based on feminist and **queer** understandings of knowledges and practices reflect a broader commitment to inclusivity while also questioning how knowledge is produced and understood. Finally, recent collections about archival work and historiographic efforts—like Susan Jarratt's (2009) award-winning essay—move beyond discovery/recovery work and challenge what it means to "archive" material. Emerging scholars like K. J. Rawson (2012) challenge us to examine what either refuses to be archived (like non-permanent ink or dismantled websites/blogs) or what "counts" to be archived in the dominant discourses of particular institutions. While it is clear that conflicts over what *research* is and what it means have been and continue to be a productive, driving force in writing studies, it is also clear that, no matter a scholar's particular approach to research, writing studies is pre-occupied with what makes for "good" research and the rhetorical nature of all research practices. As the field (re)defines and disagrees about what counts as research and what criteria by which to measure "rigorous" research, recent collections by Kirsch and Rohan (2008), Nickoson and Sheridan (2012), Powell and Takayoshi (2003), and Schell and Rawson (2010) point to the field's ongoing commitment to engage these issues.

References

Barton, Ellen. 2008. "Further Contributions from the Ethical Turn in Composition/Rhetoric: Analyzing Ethics in Interaction." *College Composition and Communication* 59 (4): 596–632.

Bazerman, Charles, ed. 2007. *Handbook of Research on Writing: History, Society, School, Individual, Text.* New York: Routledge.

Blythe, Stuart. 2007. "Coding Digital Texts and Multimedia." In *Digital Writing Research: Technologies, Methodologies, and Ethical Issues,* ed. Heidi A. McKee and Danielle DeVoss, 203–28. New York: Hampton Press.

Braddock, Richard, Richard Lloyd-Jones, and Lowell Schoer. 1963. *Research in Written Communication.* Champaign, IL: National Council of Teachers of English.

Charney, Davida. 1996. "Empiricism is Not a Four-Letter Word." *College Composition and Communication* 47 (4): 567–93. http://dx.doi.org/10.2307/358602.

Cushman, Ellen. 1998. *The Struggle and the Tools: Oral and Literate Strategies in an Inner City Community.* Albany: SUNY Press.

Haswell, Rich. 2005. "NCTE/CCCC's Recent War on Scholarship." *Written Communication* 22 (2): 198–223. http://dx.doi.org/10.1177/0741088305275367.

Jarratt, Susan. 2009. "Classics and Counterpublics in Nineteenth-Century Historically Black Colleges." *College English* 72 (2): 134–59.

Johanek, Cindy. 2000. *Composing Research: A Contextualist Paradigm for Rhetoric and Composition.* Logan: Utah State University Press.

Kirsch, Gesa E., and Liz Rohan, eds. 2008. *Beyond the Archives: Research as a Lived Process.* Carbondale: Southern Illinois University Press.

Kirsch, Gesa E., and Patricia Sullivan, eds. 1992. *Methods and Methodology in Composition Research.* Carbondale: University of Southern Illinois Press.

Lauer, Janice M., and J. William Asher. 1988. *Composition Research: Empirical Designs.* New York: Oxford University Press.

MacNealy, Mary Sue. 1998. *Strategies for Empirical Research in Writing.* Boston: Longman.

McKee, Heidi, and Danielle DeVoss, eds. 2007. *Digital Writing Research: Technologies, Methodologies, and Ethical Issues.* Cresskill, NJ: Hampton Press.

Mortensen, Peter, and Gesa Kirsch. 1996. *Ethics and Representation in Qualitative Studies of Literacy.* New York: National Council of Teachers of English.

Moss, Beverly. 1992. "Ethnography and Composition: Studying Language at Home." In *Methods and Methodology in Composition Research,* ed. Gesa E. Kirsch and Patricia Sullivan, 153–71. Carbondale: University of Southern Illinois Press.

Newkirk, Thomas. 1992. "The Narrative Roots of the Case Study." In *Methods and Methodology in Composition Research,* ed. Gesa E. Kirsch and Patricia Sullivan, 130–52. Carbondale: University of Southern Illinois Press.

Nickoson, Lee, and Mary P. Sheridan, eds. 2012. *Writing Studies Research in Practice: Methods And Methodologies.* Carbondale: Southern Illinois University Press.

Powell, Katrina M., and Pamela Takayoshi. 2003. "Accepting Roles Created for Us: The Ethics of Reciprocity." *College Composition and Communication* 54 (3): 394–422. http://dx.doi.org/10.2307/3594171.

Rawson, K. J. 2012. "Archive This! Queering the Archives." In *Practicing Research in Writing Studies: Reflexive and Ethically Responsible Methodology*, ed. Katrina M. Powell and Pamela Takayoshi, 233–46. New York: Hampton Press, Inc.

Schell, Eileen, and K. J. Rawson, eds. 2010. *Rhetorica in Motion: Feminist Rhetorical Methods and Methodologies.* Pittsburgh: University of Pittsburgh Press.

Worsham, Lynn. 2011. "Fast-Food Scholarship." *The Chronicle for Higher Education.* http://chronicle.com/article/Fast-Food-Scholarship/130049/.

SILENCE

KT Torrey

Omnipresent yet elusive, an emptiness that deafens, *silence* in writing studies means many, often contradictory, things. On the one hand, silence is an absence, one in which we are "confronted by the original beginning of all things" (Picard, quoted in Metzger 1973, 248). Silence is a void, a space in which "there is no subject, no form, no language" (Murray 1989, 20). Yet it is also a presence, "an intense stimulus, an aesthetic intoxication, perhaps, as Beckett might say, 'a bodily need'" (Metzger 1973, 247). Silence is thus associated with "denial, conceal-ment, [and] evasion," but also with "ecstasy, bliss, communion" (Teleky 2001, 207). More pragmatically, Anne Ruggles Gere argues that "we can conceive of [silence] as a part of speech, located on a continuum that puts one in dialogue with the **other**" (Gere 2001, 206), and Cheryl Glenn observes that silence "is a rhetorical art that can be as powerful as the spoken or written word" (Glenn 2004, 9).

From its first formal practice in Athens, rhetoric has considered "who may speak, who may listen or who will agree to listen, and what can be said," questions that point to the tight-knit relation between speech and silence, between "language and power" (Glenn 1997, 1–2). Thus, as Gere notes, "[w]e are accustomed to thinking about the negative aspects of silence, to focusing on its limiting or disabling properties" (Gere 2001, 206). Indeed, as scholars have noted since the early 1990s, writing studies' own history is replete with the absence of women's voices within the rhetorical canon. Indeed, Glenn argues that "no intellectual endeavor . . . has so consciously rendered women invisible and silent" (Glenn 1997, 2).

In the classroom, writing studies engages not with its own silences but with those of its students, who, as Alerby and Elídóttir observe, "can elect to be silent, but in some situations silence is imposed, as one can-not find words to respond" (Alerby and Elídóttir 2003, 42). Many in writing studies have embraced the notion that "[t]hose who are denied speech cannot make their experience known and thus cannot influence

DOI: 10.7330/9780874219746.c032

the course of their lives or of history," and that a crucial role of the writing teacher is to fashion a pedagogical space in which otherwise-silent student voices can be heard (Gal 1989, 1). Such teaching clearly seeks to counter "the 'silencing' of marginalized groups such as the poor and women and other minority groups" by ideological constructs within the dominant **discourses** that are replicated by educational institutions (Belanoff 2001, 401).

As Heather Bruce observes, one such "orchestration of silence" hinges upon **gender**, on "the blotting out, erasure, and devaluing of women's political, textual, literary, and historic past" (Bruce 2003, 171). Indeed, Rebecca Belvins Faery (1987) notes that "women have written hauntingly and repeatedly" about the connection between silence and power-lessness, about environments in which women as a group are excluded by virtue of the absence of their voices (204). For Belanoff, the push for government institutions, including schools, to become "**English**-only" spaces shapes another kind of silence: "if you don't speak English, you will not be heard" (Belanoff 2001, 402). Allison Berg et al. highlight the writing teacher's responsibility for "breaking the silence surrounding the issue of sexual preference" in order to avoid "replicat[ing] a societal and instructional silence that is destructive to ourselves and our students" (Berg et al. 1989, 29). Likewise, Paul Heilker and Melanie Yergeau urge scholars and teachers in writing studies to engage our collective "silence about neurotypicality" so we may better understand and respond to autistic students in our classrooms (Heilker and Yergeau 2011, 486). Ultimately, as Kennan Ferguson argues, these connections between **identity** and expression "have become increasingly connected to a lingual politics," and, "the existence of silence has in turn been increasingly seen as the subjugation of these identities and activities" (Ferguson 2011, 115).

However, there is also what Krista Ratcliffe calls "the silence of the classroom, of students not knowing whether and/or how to speak" (Ratcliffe 1999, 211). As Gere observes, "[t]hose new to the academy and inexperienced as writers can fall into an inarticulate silence because they feel that their life experiences have not given them access to narratives that will please their teacher readers" (Gere 2001, 207). Moreover, a student's silence online might be what Diane Penrod calls "a sign of mistrust of the online writing situation or . . . inexperience with **technology**," as well as a signal of their discomfort with the traditional university environment (Penrod 2005, 10–11).

In addition, Candice Spiegelman foregrounds silence as a form of protest, as some students "passively resist" what they read as "the radical efforts of their writing teachers" to empower them via discussions of race, **class**, and gender—indeed, "their silence reflects . . . their ability to 'play along' with classroom authority" (Spiegelman 1998, 50). In this way, silence becomes a rhetorical act, a "means of protest," one that signals the students' displeasure with being asked to critique the very system to which, Spiegelman argues, they are attempting to gain access via their enrollment in college (54). In like manner, in sociolinguistic and creative writing, for instance, silence is understood as a "strategic defense against the powerful," one that is "essential not only to the writing process but to the process of building an identity as a writer" (Gal 1989, 1; Teleky 2001, 207). As Kennan Ferguson notes, then, "silence can serve as resistance to any institution that requires verbal participation" (Ferguson 2011, 119).

Indeed, while "the Western tendency to see some forms of silence as weak, passive, and subordinate" has proven difficult to shake, writing studies has acknowledged the productive nature of silence, particularly within Native Indian cultures who valued "meaningful silence" both as an everyday rhetorical practice and as a discursive strategy in their encounters with white men (Desser 2006, 316; Murphy 1970, 360). In this way, silence was used "as a rhetorical art of empowered action," as Glenn describes it some forty years later (Glenn 2004, 156). She argues, "the form of silence (the delivery) is always the same, but the function of specific acts, states, phenomena of silence—that is, its interpretation by and effect upon other people—varies according to the social-rhetorical context in which it occurs" (9). "[S]ilence takes many forms and serves many functions," Glenn notes, "particularly as those functions vary from culture to culture," and it can be used to signify agreement, disagreement, boredom, indecision, uncertainty over someone else's meaning, impoliteness, over-politeness, anger, communion, thoughtfulness, a lack of information, a lack of urgency, fearfulness, empathy, and/or a lack of attention (15–16).

The rhetorical nature of silence becomes even more complicated in classrooms that include ESL or ELL students. Jay Jordan argues that, in American classrooms, "speech ('class participation') is often so highly valued that it is difficult to think about silence except as a failure to engage academically" (Jordan 2011, 286), and he portrays second-language users as a source of "misunderstandings, snap judgments, and consternation on the part of native-speaking peers and instructors" (284). Indeed, research surrounding language acquisition has underscored the importance of what is sometimes called "the silent period," an initial stage of acquisition in which "the learner absorbs the sounds and rhythms of the new language . . . and generally communicates non-verbally" (Diaz-Rico 2004, 38). As Ferguson notes, then, any "search for *the* politics of silence, for the determinative classification of the power dynamics inherent within silence, is . . . doomed to fail" (Ferguson 2011, 126, emphasis in original).

In contemporary writing studies, there is a renewed emphasis upon the productive possibility of silence. Indeed, for Angelo Caranfa, "to create or to write is to make oneself the voice of silence as the very heart and soul of learning or of knowing" (Caranfa 2006, 98). Writing is a way of summoning "the presence of invisible ancestors whose voices, though quiet now, permeate the stillness, quicken the ancient wisdom silence holds" (Wideman 2001, 643). Ultimately, the "multiple, fragmentary, and overlapping dynamics of silence can be iterated, investigated, and explored, but they cannot be fixed nor predetermined" (Ferguson 2011, 126). Silence in writing studies, then, is understood to be a "quiet[,] unexpected and terrifying but productive, essential nothingness" (Murray 1983, 156).

References

Alerby, Eva, and Jorunn Elídóttir. 2003. "The Sounds of Silence: Some Remarks on the Value of Silence in the Process of Reflection in Relation to Teaching and Learning." *Reflective Practice* 4 (1): 41–51. http://dx.doi.org/10.1080/1462394032000053503.

Belanoff, Pat. 2001. "Silence: Reflection, Literacy, Learning, and Teaching." *College Composition and Communication* 52 (3): 399–428. http://dx.doi.org/10.2307/358625.

Berg, Alison, Jean Kowaleski, Caroline Le Guin, Ellen Weinauer, and Eric A. Wolfe. 1989. "Breaking the Silence: Sexual Preference in the Composition Classroom." *Feminist Teacher* 4 (2–3): 29–32.

Bruce, Heather. 2003. *Literacies, Lies, & Silences: Girls' Writing Lives in the Classroom.* New York: Peter Lang.

Caranfa, Angelo. 2006. "Voices of Silence in Pedagogy: Art, Writing, and Self-Encounter." *Journal of Philosophy of Education* 40 (1): 85–103. http://dx.doi.org/10.1111/j.1467-9752.2006.00499.x.

Desser, Daphne. 2006. "On Silence and Listening: 'Bewilderment, Confrontation, Refusal, and Dream.'" *JAC* 26 (1–2): 311–26.

Diaz-Rico, Lynne T. 2004. *Teaching English Learners: Strategies and Methods.* Boston: Pearson.

Faery, Rebecca Belvins. 1987. "Women and Writing across the Curriculum." In *Teaching Writing: Pedagogy, Gender, and Equity,* ed. Cynthia Caywood and Gillian Overing, 201–12. Albany: SUNY.

Ferguson, Kennan. 2011. "Silence: A Politics." In *Silence and Listening as Rhetorical Arts,* ed. Cheryl Glenn and Krista Ratcliffe, 113–29. Carbondale: Southern Illinois University Press.

Gal, Susan. 1989. "Between Speech and Silence: The Problematics of Research on Language and Gender." *IPrA Papers in Pragmatics* 3 (1): 1–38.

Gere, Anne Ruggles. 2001. "Revealing Silence: Rethinking Personal Writing." *College Composition and Communication* 53 (2): 203–23. http://dx.doi.org/10.2307/359076.

Glenn, Cheryl. 1997. *Rhetoric Retold: Regendering the Tradition from Antiquity through the Renaissance.* Carbondale: Southern Illinois University Press.

Glenn, Cheryl. 2004. *Unspoken: A Rhetoric of Silence.* Carbondale: Southern Illinois University Press.

Heilker, Paul, and Melanie Yergeau. 2011. "Autism and Rhetoric." *College English* 73 (5): 485–97.

Jordan, Jay. 2011. "Revaluing Silence and Listening with Second-Language English Users." In *Silence and Listening as Rhetorical Arts*, ed. Cheryl Glenn and Krista Ratcliffe, 278–92. Carbondale: Southern Illinois University Press.

Metzger, Deena. 1973. "Silence as Experience." *College Composition and Communication* 24 (3): 247–50. http://dx.doi.org/10.2307/356847.

Murphy, Majorie N. 1970. "Silence, the Word, and Indian Rhetoric." *College Composition and Communication* 21 (5): 356–63. http://dx.doi.org/10.2307/356085.

Murray, Donald M. 1983. "First Silence, Then Paper." In *Forum: Essays on Theory and Practice in the Teaching of Writing*, ed. Patricia Stock, 227–233. Upper Montclair: Boynton/Cook.

Murray, Donald M. 1989. *Expecting the Unexpected.* Portsmouth, NH: Heinemann.

Penrod, Diane. 2005. *Composition Convergence; The Impact of New Media on Writing Assessment.* Mahwah, NJ: Lawrence Erlbaum Associates.

Ratcliffe, Krista. 1999. "Rhetorical Listening: A Trope for Interpretive Invention and a 'Code of Cross-Cultural Conduct.'" *College Composition and Communication* 51 (2): 195–224. http://dx.doi.org/10.2307/359039.

Spiegelman, Candace. 1998. "Taboo Topics and the Rhetoric of Silence: Discussing *Lives on the Boundary* in a Basic Writing Class." *Journal of Basic Writing* 17 (1): 42–55.

Teleky, Richard. 2001. "'Entering the Silence': Voice, Ethnicity, and the Pedagogy of Creative Writing." *Melus* 26 (1): 205–19. http://dx.doi.org/10.2307/3185503.

Wideman, John Edgar. 2001. "In Praise of Silence." *Callaloo* 24 (2): 641–43. http://dx.doi.org/10.1353/cal.2001.0109.

TECHNICAL COMMUNICATION

Carolyn Rude

Technical communication can signify a practice in a variety of nonacademic and academic workplaces—a career field, a research area, and an academic field of study—all with instances in the United States and globally. The term is an update of *technical writing*, dominant into the 1970s, when some specialists began to argue that *writing* was too limiting a marker for a practice that includes visual and oral (and now digital and video) communication as well as related practices such as **research**, collaboration, management, usability studies, indexing, graphic **design**, and instructional design. The Society for Technical Communication (STC) adopted its name in 1971, replacing Society of Technical Writers and Publishers (Malone 2011, 286). The Association of Teachers of Technical Writing retains its name from 1973, but named its journal *Technical Communication Quarterly* in 1992. *Technical* reflects the engineering roots and settings in which this writing frequently occurs, although IBM has called its technical writers "information developers" since the 1980s. Some academic programs name their curricula "professional writing/communication" to escape the constraints of *technical*, but **others** resist the confusion of appearing to embrace journalism and creative nonfiction, which have related but different purposes and audiences. Nonetheless, the US Bureau of Labor Statistics (2012) recognizes "technical writing" as a profession, and in this context *writing* can be understood more broadly than as alphabetic text.

The various terms related to *technical communication* all acknowledge that texts—print, digital, verbal, visual, and/or multimedia—are ubiquitous for the purposes of learning and understanding, completing tasks, solving problems, organizing groups, making decisions, establishing positions, negotiating, and articulating the values of **communities**. As Charles Bazerman (1999) illustrates, writing is crucial to **technology**'s material realization and success; writing is a mediating artifact in all human activity. The development of texts requires inquiry, analysis, and presentation according to standards that include principles of effective

DOI: 10.7330/9780874219746.c033

communication, ethics, and the possibility of global audiences as well as audiences with special needs. Practitioners include engineers, managers, government analysts, and researchers (who communicate as part of job responsibilities), and career technical communicators (who develop various kinds of texts to inform, instruct, or support decision-making and other actions). Academics have explored connections to a variety of social issues, including the environment and health, which also depend on texts for information sharing, argument, and the shaping of values.

The **genres** of technical communication include instructions (print, online, video), proposals, reports, product and process descriptions, correspondence, and white papers, among others. Texts are often highly visual, using illustrations and page design to enhance understanding and use, and increasingly multimodal, with practitioners developing digital genres such as videos, wikis, blogs, and websites.

As Robert Connors (1982) has reported, people have communicated about transactions and tools since the Sumerians developed cuneiform writing to facilitate manufacturing and agricultural transactions. However, its rise as a subject of academic study in the United States parallels the creation of land-grant universities and departments of engineering after the Civil War, when the Industrial Revolution took hold. The exigence for technical writing service courses was the need to prepare engineers for their communication responsibilities. Career technical writers and editors were generally prepared in specific subject areas, such as engineering, agriculture, or science. Later, World War II expanded the need for technical instructions for new equipment used by the military.

The demand for career technical communicators increased in the 1980s with the development of desktop **computers** and the need to teach people how to use them. Academic programs were developed to meet the demand for technical communicators with knowledge of composing and the ability to explain complex technical information. The curriculum expanded beyond the service course to include such courses as editing, visual design, web writing, grant writing, ethics, intercultural communication, and project management. Dayton and Bernhardt (2004) describe curricula, goals, and emerging trends. Like the service course, **English** departments now offer most academic programs with an emphasis on writing and analytical thinking. Peeples and Hart-Davidson (2012) differentiate technical communication from composition by aligning the former with an undergraduate major, a professional orientation, and an emphasis on writing for and even with audiences rather than to them. Graduate programs, which prepare faculty to teach university courses and develop the field's research, link rhetoric, composition, and technical communication, recognizing common theoretical roots and an interest in the connections of writing, understanding, and deliberate action as well as in the ways in which human beings organize themselves, using texts to define their purposes and values.

Throughout the 1970s, technical writing instruction was dominated by an emphasis on style and correctness, and goals and standards of good writing included clarity, conciseness, objectivity, and accuracy. The dominant genre was the report. In spite of dramatic changes in practice, theory, and teaching, the sense of *technical communication* as a marker for this set of forms still lingers for some outside the field. In 1979, however, Carolyn Miller challenged the "windowpane theory of language" (Miller 1979, 612–13) indebted to logical positivism, and the emphasis on form and style at the expense of invention. She proposed instead a "consensualist perspective," recognizing that facts are human constructions (616). More recently, countering Miller's rhetorical approach, Patrick Moore (1996) makes a case for the humanity and ethics of unambiguous, instrumental **discourse**. And in his review of the controversy over the rhetorical-instrumental binary, Quinn Warnick (2008) finds the terms too polarizing for fruitful discussion of the common ground.

The pragmatic nature of technical communication—its interest in getting things done—raises questions about its intellectual substance. These questions partly mask political resistance to a new field claiming academic territory, but technical communication has been stronger in teaching and curriculum development than in articulating its research agenda and making it visible. Two major efforts to collect the research are the EServer Technical Communication Library, a portal of more than 20,000 **works**, and the STC's "Body of Knowledge" project (Coppola 2011). However, databases, while necessary for categorization and retrieval, do not necessarily point to what distinguishes the field's research from that of research in other communication fields. Johnson-Eilola and Selber (2004) collected influential articles from 1979 to 2002 that illustrate research areas and methods. And Carolyn Rude (2009) suggests a central research question linking studies in pedagogy, practice, social action, and disciplinarity: "How do texts and related communication practices mediate knowledge and action?" The sustainability of technical communication as an academic field depends on its ability to identify the locus of its research even as researchers find application in an increasing number of settings.

As a practice, technical communication has required rapid adaptation to new technologies—including means of **production**—and constant innovation. Content management systems now build texts dynamically from databases of information developed and codified by communicators.

Audiences are often international, and author teams often include global collaborators. Technical communicators who develop texts as self-contained documents linked to specific products may become the exception rather than the norm. Those who can imagine multiple uses for information for various audiences, who can design processes for making information available, and who can organize the people to create these information products will be the leaders in this field.

Texts in some form and the need to develop them will continue to be essential for the purposes of developing and sharing the knowledge required for human thought and transactions. Learning the complex activities of developing texts will require instruction. Practice and academic programs will evolve. But because of considerable changes in practice and the term's divergent meanings, *technical communication* may become most interesting as an artifact of history.

References

Bazerman, Charles. 1999. *The Languages of Edison's Light.* Cambridge: MIT Press.
Bureau of Labor Statistics. 2012. "Technical Writers." *Occupational Outlook Handbook.* http://www.bls.gov/ooh/Media-and-Communication/Technical-writers.htm.
Connors, Robert J. 1982. "The Rise of Technical Writing Instruction in America." *Journal of Technical Writing and Communication* 12: 329–51.
Coppola, Nancy W. 2011. "Professionalization of Technical Communication: Zeitgeist for Our Age: Introduction to This Special Issue (Part 1)." *Technical Communication* 58: 277–84.
Dayton, David, and Stephen A. Bernhardt. 2004. "Results of a Survey of ATTW Members 2003." *Technical Communication Quarterly* 13 (1): 13–43. http://dx.doi.org/10.1207/S15427625TCQ1301_5.
EServer Technical Communication Library. http://tc.eserver.org/.
Johnson-Eilola, Johndan, and Stuart Selber. 2004. *Central Works in Technical Communication.* New York: Oxford University Press.
Malone, Edward A. 2011. "The First Wave (1953–1961) of the Professionalization Movement in Technical Communication." *Technical Communication* 58: 285–306.
Miller, Carolyn R. 1979. "A Humanistic Rationale for Technical Writing." *College English* 40 (6): 610–17. http://dx.doi.org/10.2307/375964.
Moore, Patrick. 1996. "Instrumental Discourse is as Humanistic as Rhetoric." *Journal of Business and Technical Communication* 10 (1): 100–118. http://dx.doi.org/10.1177/1050651996010001005.
Peeples, Tim, and Bill Hart-Davidson. 2012. "Remapping Professional Writing: Articulating the State of the Art and Composition Studies." In *Exploring Composition Studies: Sites, Issues, and Perspectives*, ed. Kelly Ritter, and Paul Kei Matsuda, 52–67. Logan: Utah State University Press.
Rude, Carolyn D. 2009. "Mapping the Research Questions in Technical Communication." *Journal of Business and Technical Communication* 23 (2): 174–215. http://dx.doi.org/10.1177/1050651908329562.
Warnick, Quinn. 2008. "Toward a More Productive Discussion about Instrumental Discourse." *Orange Journal.* http://orange.eserver.org/issues/6-1/warnick.html.

TECHNOLOGY

Johndan Johnson-Eilola and Stuart A. Selber

In 1975, Ellen Nold published the first article on the role and function of **computers** in writing studies. Her argument was that teachers should involve themselves in the development of software programs so that computers could better serve the needs of students learning to write. In responding to drill and practice approaches that focused on memorization and recall, Nold encouraged teachers to **design** imaginative heuristics that "call forth **creativity**" (Nold 1975, 271–72). This early vision of digital technology in writing emphasized invention and teacher engagement, and it acknowledged that a technology can be interpreted and configured in multiple ways.

Even so, the status of writing as a technology has troubled and fascinated rhetoricians from the beginning. For example, Plato's Socrates—himself a text—famously subordinated text as an inferior offspring of speech (Plato 2006). He was, in short, suspicious of the fixity of writing, for written texts cannot respond to questions, preferring instead to develop and trade ideas with students through conversation and dialogue. And in her **work** on the printing press, Elizabeth Eisenstein (1980) traced the implications of technology's ability to stabilize and reproduce texts, showing how the transition from an oral to print culture augured significant social changes as the mass **production** of texts cataloged, systematized, and spread knowledge in new and different ways.

The notion that text itself is a *technology* advances a capacious view of this keyword, which can be found in a variety of approaches that have been appropriated by writing studies. Michel Foucault (1977), for example, enumerated the ways in which power is exercised in different forms of writing: medical records structure relationships among patients, ailments, physicians, treatments, and more (144); and one specific form of writing, the table ("a technique of power and a procedure of knowledge") distributes and orders everything from botanical gardens to the flow of wealth (148) to the design of websites. Foucault argued that

DOI: 10.7330/9780874219746.c034

large-scale structures (social and otherwise) are the product of a sustained process of applying a multitude of tiny forces, writing in particular. The computer, then, as a site for writing instruction and work, is the result of numerous interacting forces over time: hardware and labor costs, software philosophies and features, adoptions and implementations in **other** areas of education, uses in the home, practices of publishers, pedagogical perspectives, intellectual property laws, and many other developments, none of which on their own could effect change but in sum provoke a situation in which writing by hand or with a typewriter is considered to be anachronistic.

Stuart Hall pointed out, however, that the forces functioning within such structures are unevenly weighted and valued, that in particular contexts meaning can be constrained by ongoing, powerful associations with social significance for audiences (Grossberg 1986, 53). Consider, for example, the extent to which notions of technology and progress have been linked in the American public imagination (Segal 1994). In writing studies, the "lines of tendential force" (Grossberg 1986, 53) that constrain significations of *technology* involve disciplinary perspectives on the practice and pedagogy of **literacy**. That is, evolving approaches to writing, reading, and teaching have been instrumental to how the field has tended to define *technology*. Three frequent approaches characterize technology as a tool, as an artifact of culture, or as a medium for expression. Although seemingly discrete visions, they can reinforce and complement each other.

The first approach can be located in work on the integration of technology in the writing curriculum. Persistent advice for teachers in computer classrooms has been to remain focused on learning principles and foreground instructional goals. As the subtitle of an essay by Cynthia Selfe (1988) advised, "Forget Technology, Remember Literacy." In this formulation, technology does not really serve to shape or alter the possibilities for the project of composition. Rather, it is a neutral tool that can be used to support and extend pedagogical aims. James Kalmbach (1997) discussed an advantage of this perspective for new initiates in writing studies: "Viewing the computer as a tool has been a critical first step because writing teachers often [come] to the process of creating and administering computer-supported classrooms knowing little about computers but a lot about writing and the teaching of writing" (263). And Stuart Selber (2004) noted that "the level of **agency**" ascribed to users by the tool metaphor "can help inculcate in them a sense of control over technology as well as a sense of the professional responsibilities that might go along with using technological environments" (44).

There are drawbacks, of course, to the characterization of computers as tools, but it can encourage an attention to task objectives and **contexts** and to conventional pedagogical principles, including those associated with invention (Price 1997), collaboration (Warnock 2009), and online course design (Cook 2005).

The second approach is evident in projects on critical literacy. A central aim of critical literacy is to identify and show the ways in which power relations are exercised through **discourse** and discursive activities (Shor 1999), print, electronic, or otherwise. Langdon Winner (1986), a philosopher of technology who is often cited by scholars in computers and composition, argued that technologies have politics: computers, as artifacts of culture, instantiate the perspectives of designers and provide structures for writing and learning. Although these structures do not determine use, they can be taken for granted and accepted as an accurate description of how literacy works. In writing studies, this reality has been illustrated by work showing how software interfaces can be read as maps that value "monoculturalism, capitalism, and phallologic thinking" (Selfe and Selfe 1994, 486) and how grammar checkers can be at variance with sound pedagogical practices (McGee and Ericsson 2002). Such critical projects invite teachers to investigate the belief systems embodied in technology and imagine alternatives to technological systems if they are incompatible with the values of the profession.

The third approach relies on the rhetorical nature of writing as a technology. There are at least four attributes constituting this approach to writing as a technology: persuasion, deliberation, **reflection**, and social action (Selber 2004). Writing technologies, as we have already mentioned, attempt to persuade users to occupy specific positions. Using writing technologies, then, requires deliberation, choosing among multiple options in the absence of a single, correct answer. Furthermore, writing technologies, from the perspective of rhetoric, invite practitioners to reflect on their own approaches, moving back and forth between theory and practice in a complex, contingent, and constant dance constructed at the nexus of literacy and technology. Finally, rhetorical writing technologies enable social action and civic participation (Cooper and Holzman 1989), constructing technology as a medium for expression and users as producers of that medium.

There are, of course, numerous other ways to understand writing as a technology: for example, writing as an extension of the **body**, cyborg-like, enabling or enriching human activity; writing as a concrete instantiation of **personal** or professional experience; writing as a virus (it can touch everything and spread quickly, especially in digital spaces); writing as a weapon in class warfare; writing as a method or technique for quantifying the self; and writing as a structure or framework for invention. Writing is a machine that continually reinvents itself at the nexus of the myriad sociotechnical forces that constitute rhetorical contexts.

References

Cook, Kelli Cargile. 2005. "An Argument for Pedagogy-Driven Online Education." In *Online Education: Global Questions, Local Answers*, ed. Kelli Cargile Cook and Keith Grant-Davie, 49–66. Amityville, NY: Baywood Publishing Company.

Cooper, Marilyn, and Michael Holzman. 1989. *Writing as Social Action.* Portsmouth, NH: Heinemann.

Eisenstein, Elizabeth L. 1980. *The Printing Press as an Agent of Change.* Cambridge: Cambridge University Press. http://dx.doi.org/10.1017/CBO9781107049963.

Foucault, Michel. 1977. *Discipline & Punish: The Birth of the Prison.* New York: Vintage.

Grossberg, Lawrence. 1986. "On Postmodernism and Articulation: An Interview with Stuart Hall." *Journal of Communication Inquiry* 10 (2): 45–60. http://dx.doi.org/10.1177/019685998601000204.

Kalmbach, James. 1997. "Computer-Supported Classrooms and Curricular Change in Technical Communication Programs." In *Computers and Technical Communication: Pedagogical and Programmatic Perspectives*, ed. Stuart A. Selber, 261–74. Greenwich, CT: Ablex Publishing Corporation.

McGee, Tim, and Patricia Ericsson. 2002. "The Politics of the Program: MS Word as the Invisible Grammarian." *Computers and Composition* 19 (4): 453–70. http://dx.doi.org/10.1016/S8755-4615(02)00142-1.

Nold, Ellen W. 1975. "Fear and Trembling: The Humanist Approaches the Computer." *College Composition and Communication* 26 (3): 269–73. http://dx.doi.org/10.2307/356129.

Plato. 2006. *Phaedrus.* Trans. Benjamin Jowett. Fairford, England: Echo Press.

Price, Jonathan. 1997. "Electronic Outlining as a Tool for Making Writing Visible." *Computers and Composition* 14 (3): 409–27. http://dx.doi.org/10.1016/S8755-4615(97)90009-8.

Segal, Howard P. 1994. *Future Imperfect: The Mixed Blessings of Technology in America.* Amherst: University of Massachusetts Press.

Selber, Stuart A. 2004. *Multiliteracies for a Digital Age.* Carbondale: Southern Illinois University Press.

Selfe, Cynthia L. 1988. "The Humanization of Computers: Forget Technology, Remember Literacy." *English Journal* 77 (6): 69–71. http://dx.doi.org/10.2307/818623.

Selfe, Cynthia L., and Richard J. Selfe. 1994. "The Politics of the Interface: Power and Its Exercise in Electronic Contact Zones." *College Composition and Communication* 45 (4): 480–504. http://dx.doi.org/10.2307/358761.

Shor, Ira. 1999. "What Is Critical Literacy?" In *Critical Literacy in Action: Writing Words, Changing Worlds/A Tribute to the Teachings of Paulo Freire*, ed. Caroline Pari and Ira Shor, 1–30. Portsmouth, NH: Heinemann.

Warnock, Scott. 2009. *Teaching Writing Online: How and Why.* Urbana, IL: National Council of Teachers of English.

Winner, Langdon. 1986. *The Whale and the Reactor: A Search for Limits in an Age of High Technology.* Chicago: University of Chicago Press.

WORK

Dylan B. Dryer

Work is an exceptionally old word, as is its first documented association with the labor of writing ("On þære bec, þic worhte" *circa* 900 CE [Compact Oxford English Dictionary 1991, 2338]). Few **other** words have become such powerful organizing constructs for everyday life (Thompson 1967), or are as susceptible to changes produced and reflected by social and technological transformation (Takayoshi and Sullivan 2007), or are as vulnerable to specifically motivated interpretations (Gee, Hull, and Lankshear 1996). As Bruce Horner has already shown, its uses in composition studies are complex: its gerund (typically modifying *conditions*) is usually distinct from its noun, which tends to signify "published scholarship," and both those meanings are distinct from its predicate, which usually refers to teaching (Horner 2000, 1–29). Horner's discussion of the persistent idealization of these three meanings illustrates that arguments about work in composition are always partial views of what the field should be (or should resist becoming). *Work* is thus employed as much to retrench as to include.

While no amount of backing up will get the entire landscape of this problematically capacious word within the frame of this essay, it is still useful to recall that composition is also a "federation of knowledge structures" (Martin 2008, 807) initially forged in 1970s hotel conference rooms that "crackled . . . with the intensity of revival meetings" (North 1987, Preface). As composition emerged from (its memories of) those rooms, those bonds weakened under strains introduced, paradoxically, by composition's efforts to have its work recognized as legitimate by the departments in which it was housed (Bloom 2003; Mahala and Swilky 1997; 2003; Phelps 1995; Winterowd 1998). Hairston thus urged composition to end its exploitation by those who valued us only for our willingness to do the "work they don't want" and to resolve instead "to put our primary energy into the teaching of writing and into **research** that informs the teaching of writing" (Hairston 1985, 276, 281).

DOI: 10.7330/9780874219746.c035

It should be clear from Hairston's insistence on the primacy of teaching that there was already disagreement over what work in composition should be. But an attempt to reconsolidate the meaning of "our work" as "teaching writing" founders on disagreements concealed by the word itself: how writing should be taught, what sorts of writing should be taught, and how (or even whether) it should be assessed. Such disagreements are philosophical, but are also grounded in material conditions of practicability. In fact, since four-fifths of composition courses appear to be taught by "guest workers" (Columb 2010, 14) and administered by the so-called "boss compositionist" (Bousquet, Scott, and Parascondola 2004; Sledd 2001), the more relevant possessive pronoun is often *your* work (see Gere 2009). Alienation in these conditions is inevitable: some teachers will always find some elements of any mandatory curriculum objectionable (Welch 1993); some metrics for rehire are actively contradictory (Henry, Kahn, and Lynch-Biniek 2012, 2); and dominant assumptions about "your" **gender** (Grego and Thompson 1996, 65–68; Holbrook 1991; Miller 1991; Tuell 1993), "your" race (Behm and Miller 2012) or "your" job security (Crowley 1998; Fitts and Lalicker 2004; Schell and Stock 2000) persist.

Note that *work* is used to describe the vocational practice of teaching as well as the ubiquitous criterion for its everyday praxis: "what works." For instance, ERIC and comppile.org alone offer several hundred published arguments that particular techniques, exercises, courses, and programs "work." Certainly, as Fulkerson notes, "what 'works' is what we should be doing," although such overgeneralized statements about what "we" ought to do tend to flourish when not checked by specific, local outcomes and the means to measure them (Abrahamson 1976; Fulkerson 2011, 53). Volume 2.3 of *Freshman English News* is an interesting exception to this tendency; the title of each article (a case-study of a particular university) features the unusual stem "What's Working Well *For Us*" (*Freshman English News* 1974, 4–11, emphasis added).

Neither does the "work" of research have a stable referent, since composition cannot agree what research best "informs" the teaching of writing (or whether that is even the point of such work) (see Bishop 1999; Ching 2007; Dobrin 1995; 1997; Kopelson 2008; Sánchez 2005). Research "work," like the "work of teaching," is a site of contestation over what composition should value. On the one hand, at least three edited collections make a pointed effort to identify composition as "theoretical" or "intellectual work" (Clifford and Schilb 1994; Olson 2002; Slevin 2001), suggesting that in some quarters it continues to struggle against the perception that it is not. On the other hand, the fact that subsequent generations of compositionists were trained (and train their students) in departments of **English** exacerbates conflicts over the proper place of empirical inquiry. Perhaps most strikingly evident in the exchanges and counter-ripostes proliferating from Foster (1989) throughout the early 1990s (Arrington 1991; Berkenkotter 1989; Foster 1990; Reynolds 1990; Schilb 1990), the question of how to value empirical work in composition remains open (Barton 2000; Charney 1996; 1997) and, if anything, is expanding (Anson 2008; Gallagher 2010; Harris 2012; Haswell 2005).

As writing program administrators have sought to invest their work with similarly motivated adjectives (Council of Writing Program Administrators 2002; Horner 2007; Rose and Weiser 1999; 2002), and since dominant publishing conventions encourage a rhetorical construction of translocality for *any* research (Anson and Brown 1999, 145; Fox 2002), it is possible to see a trend irrespective of scale: "work" in and for (or about or on behalf of) *particular* FYC classes, teachers, or programs undermines the argument that work is tenably "academic" or constitutive of a discipline (Goggin 1997; North 2011; Petraglia 1995).

Its recent and extensive revisions notwithstanding, the "WPA Outcomes Statement for First-Year Composition" uses *writing* and *work* interchangeably to signify what students produce (Harrington et al. 2001; Dryer et al. 2014), so it is necessary to turn to those whose labor enables the field. Certainly composition students *do* work (classwork, groupwork, homework, fieldwork); sometimes they do work on the topic of work itself (Cahalan 1986; Gleason 2004; Shor 1977; 1980). Such usages can be set alongside an important cluster of meanings operating in **technical communication** around the term *workplace*—for example, attempts to structure classes as such, transfer of academic skills to, etc. (Dias et al. 1999; Dias and Paré 2000; Odell and Goswami 1985; Spilka 1993). But these usages must be distinguished from those that indict composition for doing a certain kind of work *on* or *to* students. The dispositive critique of non-credit basic writing courses frames them as "work" for negative exchange value, both in what students literally pay for the privilege of producing writing in conditions of no credit and in the work done *to* them by a course that tells them they are "basic writers" (Bartholomae 1993; Rodby 1996; Rodby and Fox 2000). Other lines of critique consider the work of composition curricula as inadvertently complicit with, for example, corporatism (Sledd 1988), fast capitalism (Gee, Hull, and Lankshear 1996; The New London Group 2000; see also Lu 2004), the military-industrial complex (Ohmann 1976), academic capitalism (Gunner 2012), social inequality (Bloom 1996; Brodkey 1994; Peckham 2010), "appropriate" subject position (Berlin 1996), or sequestering and intimidating postsecondary *arrivistes* more generally (Adams 1993; Shor 1997).

For these reasons, "working with students" seems the universally preferred coinage to "working on students," although few usages of "work with" achieve Slevin's provocative argument that any student is a full participant in the discipline "*[j]ust for showing up*[;]…the intellectual work of the discipline includes her work and our work with her" (Slevin 2001, 44–45, emphasis in original). Slevin's prepositions highlight composition's tendency to frame "work(ing) with" as something to be done against an obstacle (inertia, institutions) that makes that work hard and, by extension, scholarship that tries to make that difficulty manageable (see also Warnick 2010). Here, *work* tends to signify conceptualizing something not ordinarily thought of as within the purview of composition (wikis, photography, Twitter, etc.) or engaging someone assumed to be intransigent (editors, faculty in other disciplines, the "working class," English language learners, learning-disabled writers, etc.).

Schilb argues that the "actual interest" of most composition scholars is no longer "power" but "**agency**" (Schilb 2010; see also Daniel 2012; Nowacek 2011), a claim that illuminates an emergent meaning in the word *working*. While it still largely indicates a resigned acknowledgment of material conditions (a "working title" or a "working draft" is "for now" or "good enough"), another precipitant meaning can now be observed. Here, *working* refers to the deliberate negotiation of a condition to be "worked"—as one might be said to "work a crowd." Writers are increasingly characterized as working—for example, "rhetoric and composition" (Horner and Lu 2010); "English(es)" (Sohan 2009); "the game" (Ashley 2001); "boundaries" (Gorzelsky 2009); "consensus" (Maurer 2009); the "web" (McConaghy and Snyder 1999); constructions of "ability" (Price 2007), etc. That is, the student, teacher, writer, activist, or holder of an alternative sensibility is here making a policy, a convention, an institutional formation, or an **identity** position "work" for them.

References

Abrahamson, Richard F. 1976. "Do Not Give unto Others That Which Works in Your Own Classroom—A Modern English Tale." *Indiana English Journal* 10 (4): 26–8.

Adams, Peter Dow. 1993. "Basic Writing Reconsidered." *Journal of Basic Writing* 12 (1): 22–36.

Anson, Chris M. 2008. "The Intelligent Design of Writing Programs: Reliance on Belief or a Future of Evidence." *WPA: Writing Program Administration* 32 (1–2): 11–36.

Anson, Chris M., and Robert L. Brown, Jr. 1999. "Subject to Interpretation: The Role of Research in Writing Programs and Its Relationship to the Politics of Administration in Higher Education." In *The Writing Program Administrator as Researcher*, ed. Shirley K. Rose and Irwin Weiser, *Researcher*, 141–52. Portsmouth, NH: Boynton/Cook.

Arrington, Phillip. 1991. "The Agon over What 'Composition Research' Means." *Journal of Advanced Composition* 11 (2): 377–94.

Ashley, Hannah. 2001. "Playing the Game: Proficient Working-Class Student Writers' Second Voices." *Research in the Teaching of English* 35 (4): 493–524.

Bartholomae, David. 1993. "The Tidy House: Basic Writing in the American Curriculum." *Journal of Basic Writing* 12 (1): 4–21.

Barton, Ellen. 2000. "More Methodological Matters: Against Negative Argumentation." *College Composition and Communication* 51 (3): 399–416. http://dx.doi.org/10.2307/358742.

Behm, Nicholas, and Keith D. Miller. 2012. "Challenging the Frameworks of Color-Blind Racism: Why We Need a Fourth Wave of Writing Assessment Scholarship." In *Race and Writing Assessment*, ed. Asao Inoue, and Mya Poe, 127–138. New York: Peter Lang.

Berkenkotter, Carol. 1989. "The Legacy of Positivism in Empirical Composition Research." *Journal of Advanced Composition* 9 (1): 269–82.

Berlin, James A. 1996. *Rhetorics, Poetics, and Cultures: Refiguring College English Studies*. Urbana, IL: National Council of Teachers of English.

Bishop, Wendy. 1999. "Places to Stand: The Reflective Writer-Teacher-Writer in Composition." *College Composition and Communication* 51 (1): 9–31. http://dx.doi.org/10.2307/358957.

Bloom, Lynn Z. 1996. "Freshman Composition as a Middle-Class Enterprise." *College English* 58 (6): 654–75. http://dx.doi.org/10.2307/378392.

Bloom, Lynn Z. 2003. "Coming of Age in a Field that Had No Name." In *Teaching Composition/Teaching Literature: Crossing Great Divides*, ed. Michelle M. Tokarczyk and Irene Papoulis, 55–67. New York: Peter Lang.

Bousquet, Marc, Tony Scott, and Leo Parascondola, eds. 2004. *Tenured Bosses and Disposable Teachers: Writing Instruction in the Managed University*. Carbondale: Southern Illinois University Press.

Brodkey, Linda. 1994. "Writing on the Bias." *College English* 56 (5): 527–47. http://dx.doi.org/10.2307/378605.

Cahalan, James M. 1986. "Teaching Writing about Work: A Humanistic Pedagogy." *Journal of Teaching Writing* 5 (2): 343–50.

Charney, Davida. 1996. "Empiricism is not a Four-Letter Word." *College Composition and Communication* 47 (4): 567–93. http://dx.doi.org/10.2307/358602.

Charney, Davida. 1997. "Paradigm and Punish." *College Composition and Communication* 48 (4): 562–65. http://dx.doi.org/10.2307/358459.

Ching, Kory Lawson. 2007. "Theory and its Practice in Composition Studies." *JAC* 27 (3–4): 445–69.

Clifford, John, and John Schilb, eds. 1994. *Writing Theory and Critical Theory*. New York: MLA.

Columb, Gregory G. 2010. "Franchising the Future." *College Composition and Communication* 62 (1): 11–30.

Compact Oxford English Dictionary. 1991. 2nd ed. Oxford: Oxford University Press.

Council of Writing Program Administrators. 2002. "Appendix B: Evaluating the Intellectual Work of Writing Administration (1998)." In *The Writing Program Administrator's Resource: A Guide to Reflective Institutional Practice*, ed. Stuart C. Brown, Theresa Enos, and Catherine Chaput, 499–518. Mahwah, NJ: Erlbaum.

Crowley, Sharon. 1998. "Terms of Employment: Rhetoric Slaves and Lesser Men." In *Composition in the University: Historical and Polemical Essays*, 181–31. Pittsburgh: University of Pittsburgh Press.

Daniel, Beth. 2012. "Literacy, Rhetoric, Identity, and Agency." *College English* 74 (4): 366–74.

Dias, Patrick, and Anthony Paré, eds. 2000. *Transitions: Writing in Academic and Workplace Settings.* Cresskill, NJ: Hampton Press.

Dias, Patrick, Aviva Freedman, Peter Medway, and Anthony Paré. 1999. *Worlds Apart: Acting and Writing in Academic and Workplace Contexts.* Mahwah, NJ: Erlbaum.

Dobrin, Sidney I. 1995. "The Politics of Theory-Building and Anti-Intellectualism in Composition." *Composition Forum* 6: 90–99.

Dobrin, Sidney I. 1997. *Constructing Knowledges: The Politics of Theory-Building and Pedagogy in Composition.* Albany: State University of New York Press.

Dryer, Dylan B., Darsie Bowden, Beth Brunk-Chavez, Susanmarie Harrington, Bump Halbritter, and Kathleen Blake Yancey (for the WPA Outcomes Statement Revision Task Force). "Revising FYC Outcomes for a Multimodal, Digitally Composed World: The WPA Outcomes Statement for First-Year Composition (Version 3.0)." *WPA: Journal of the Council of Writing Program Administrators* 38 (1): 127–46.

Fitts, Karen, and William B. Lalicker. 2004. "Invisible Hands: A Manifesto to Resolve Institutional and Curricular Hierarchy in English Studies." *College English* 66 (4): 427–51. http://dx.doi.org/10.2307/4140710.

Foster, David. 1989. "What Are We Talking about When We Talk about Composition?" *Journal of Advanced Composition* 8 (1–2): 30–40.

Foster, David. 1990. "Hurling Epithets at the Devils You Know: A Response to Carol Berkenkotter." *Journal of Advanced Composition* 10 (1): 149–52.

Fox, Tom. 2002. "Working against the State: Composition's Intellectual Work for Change." In *Rhetoric and Composition as Intellectual Work,* ed. Gary A. Olson, 91–99. Carbondale: Southern Illinois University Press.

Freshman English News. 1974. 2 (3): 4–11.

Fulkerson, Richard. 2011. "The Epistemic Paradoxes of 'Lore': From *The Making of Knowledge in Composition* to the Present (Almost)." In *The Changing of Knowledge in Composition: Contemporary Perspectives,* ed. Lance Massey, and Richard C. Gebhardt, 47–62. Logan: Utah State University Press.

Gallagher, Chris W. 2010. "At the Precipice of Speech: English Studies, Science, and Policy (Ir)relevancy." *College English* 73 (1): 73–90.

Gee, James Paul, Glynda Hull, and Colin Lankshear. 1996. *The New Work Order: Behind the Language of the New Capitalism.* Boulder, CO: Westview Press.

Gere, Anne Ruggles. 2009. *Initial Report on Survey of CCCC Members.* University of Michigan Squire Office of Policy Research.

Gleason, Barbara. 2004. "Connected Literacies of Adult Writers: Work Ethnography in College Composition." In *Multiple Literacies for the 21st Century,* ed. Brian Huot, Beth Stroble, and Charles Bazerman, 39–56. Cresskill, NJ.

Goggin, Maureen Daly. 1997. "Composing a Discipline: The Role of Scholarly Journals in the Disciplinary Emergence of Rhetoric and Composition since 1950." *Rhetoric Review* 15 (2): 322–48. http://dx.doi.org/10.1080/07350199709359222.

Gorzelsky, Gwen. 2009. "Working Boundaries: From Student Resistance to Student Agency." *College Composition and Communication* 61 (1): 64–85.

Grego, Rhonda, and Nancy Thompson. 1996. "Repositioning Remediation: Renegotiating Composition's Work in the Academy." *College Composition and Communication* 47 (1): 62–84. http://dx.doi.org/10.2307/358274.

Gunner, Jeanne. 2012. "Disciplinary Purification: The Writing Program as Institutional Brand." *JAC* 32 (3–4): 615–44.

Hairston, Maxine. 1985. "Breaking our Bonds and Reaffirming our Connections." *College Composition and Communication* 36 (3): 272–82. http://dx.doi.org/10.2307/357971.

Harrington, Susanmarie, Rita Malencyzk, Irv Peckham, Keith Rhodes, and Kathleen Blake Yancey. 2001. "WPA Outcomes Statement for First-Year Composition." *College English* 63 (3): 321–25. http://dx.doi.org/10.2307/378996.

Harris, Joseph. 2012. "Using Student Texts in Composition Scholarship." *JAC* 32 (3–4): 667–94.

Haswell, Richard H. 2005. "NCTE/CCCC's Recent War on Scholarship." *Written Communication* 22 (2): 198–223. http://dx.doi.org/10.1177/0741088305275367.

Henry, Sharon, Seth Kahn, and Amy Lynch-Biniek. 2012. "Crossroads, not Cross Purposes: Contingency, Vulnerability, and Alliances in the Contemporary Writing Program." *Open Words: Access in English Studies* 6 (1): 1–5.

Holbrook, Sue Ellen. 1991. "Women's Work: The Feminizing of Composition." *Rhetoric Review* 9 (2): 201–29. http://dx.doi.org/10.1080/07350199109388929.

Horner, Bruce. 2000. *Terms of Work for Composition: A Materialist Critique.* Albany: State University of New York Press.

Horner, Bruce. 2007. "Redefining Work and Value for Writing Program Administration." *JAC* 27 (1–2): 163–84.

Horner, Bruce, and Min-Zhan Lu. 2010. "Working Rhetoric and Composition." *College English* 72 (5): 470–94.

Kopelson, Karen. 2008. "Back at the Bar of Utility: Theory and/as Practice in Composition Studies (Reprise)." *JAC* 28 (3–4): 587–608.

Lu, Min-Zhan. 2004. "An Essay on the Work of Composition: Composing English against the Order of Fast Capitalism." *College Composition and Communication* 56 (1): 16–50. http://dx.doi.org/10.2307/4140679.

Mahala, Daniel, and Jody Swilky. 1997. "Remapping the Geography of Service in English." *College English* 59 (6): 625–46. http://dx.doi.org/10.2307/378277.

Mahala, Daniel, and Jody Swilky. 2003. "Constructing Disciplinary Space: The Borders, Boundaries, and Zones of English." *JAC* 23 (4): 765–97.

Martin, J. R. 2008. "Incongruent and Proud: De-vilifying 'Nominalization.'" *Discourse & Society* 19 (6): 801–10. http://dx.doi.org/10.1177/0957926508095895.

Maurer, Elizabeth G. 2009. "'Working Consensus' and the Rhetorical Situation: The Homeless Blog's Negotiation of Public Meta-Genre." In *Genres in the Internet: Issues in the Theory of Genre*, ed. Janet Giltrow, and Dieter Stein, 113–42. Amsterdam: John Benjamins.

McConaghy, Cathryn, and Ilana Snyder. 1999. "Working the Web in Postcolonial Australia." In *Global literacies and the World-Wide Web*, ed. Gail Hawisher and Cynthia L. Selfe, 74–92. New York: Routledge.

Miller, Susan. 1991. "The Sad Women in the Basement: Images of Composition Teaching." In *Textual Carnivals*, 121–41. Carbondale: Southern Illinois University Press.

The New London Group. 2000. "A Pedagogy of Multiliteracies: Designing Social Futures." In *Multiliteracies: Literacy Learning and the Design of Social Futures*, ed. Bill Cope and Mary Kalantzis, 9–37. London: Routledge.

North, Stephen. 1987. *The Making of Knowledge in Composition: Portrait of an Emerging Field.* Portsmouth, NH: Boynton/Cook.

North, Stephen. 2011. "On the Place of Writing in Higher Education (and Why It Doesn't Include Composition)." In *The Changing of Knowledge in Composition: Contemporary Perspectives*, ed. Lance Massey, and Richard C. Gebhardt, 194–210. Logan: Utah State University Press.

Nowacek, Rebecca S. 2011. *Agents of Integration: Understanding Transfer as a Rhetorical Act.* Carbondale: Southern Illinois University Press.

Odell, Lee, and Dixie Goswami, eds. 1985. *Writing in Nonacademic Settings.* New York: Guilford.

Ohmann, Richard. 1976. *English in America: A Radical View of the Profession.* Hanover, NH: Wesleyan University Press.

Olson, Gary A., ed. 2002. *Rhetoric and Composition as Intellectual Work.* Carbondale: Southern Illinois University Press.

Peckham, Irvin. 2010. *Going North, Thinking West: The Intersections of Social Class, Critical Thinking, and Politicized Writing Instruction.* Logan: Utah State University Press.

Petraglia, Joseph, ed. 1995. *Reconceiving Writing, Rethinking Writing Instruction.* Mahwah, NJ: Lawrence Erlbaum.

Phelps, Louise Wetherbee. 1995. "Becoming a Warrior: Lessons of the Feminist Workplace." In *Feminine Principles and Women's Experience in American Composition and Rhetoric,* ed. Louise Wetherbee Phelps and Janet Emig, 289–339. Pittsburgh: University of Pittsburgh Press.

Price, Margaret. 2007. "Accessing Disability: A Nondisabled Student Works the Hyphen." *College Composition and Communication* 59 (1): 53–76.

Reynolds, John Frederick. 1990. "Motives, Metaphors, and Messages in Critical Receptions of Experimental Research: A Comment with Postscript." *Journal of Advanced Composition* 10 (1): 110–16.

Rodby, Judith. 1996. "What's It Worth and What's It For? Revisions to Basic Writing Revisited." *College Composition and Communication* 47 (1): 107–11. http://dx.doi.org/10.2307/358278.

Rodby, Judith, and Tom Fox. 2000. "Basic Work and Material Acts: The Ironies, Discrepancies, and Disjunctures of Basic Writing and Mainstreaming." *Journal of Basic Writing* 19 (1): 84–99.

Rose, Shirley K., and Irwin Weiser. 1999. *The Writing Program Administrator as Researcher.* Portsmouth, NH: Boynton/Cook.

Rose, Shirley K., and Irwin Weiser. 2002. *The Writing Program Administrator as Theorist.* Portsmouth: Boynton/Cook.

Sánchez, Raúl. 2005. *The Function of Theory in Composition Studies.* Albany, NY: State University of New York Press.

Schell, Eileen E. and Patricia L. Stock, eds. 2000. "Moving a Mountain: Transforming the Role of Contingent Faculty." In *Composition Studies And Higher Education,* 245–58. Urbana, IL: National Council of Teachers of English.

Schilb, John. 1990. "The Ideology of 'Epistemological Ecumenicalism': A Response to Carol Berkenkotter." *Journal of Advanced Composition* 10 (1): 153–56.

Schilb, John. 2010. "Turning Composition toward Sovereignty." *Present Tense: A Journal of Rhetoric in Society* 1.1. www.presenttensejournal.org/vol1/turning-composition-toward -sovereignty/.

Shor, Ira. 1977. "Reinventing Daily Life: Self-Study and the Theme of 'Work.'" *College English* 39 (4): 502–6. http://dx.doi.org/10.2307/375778.

Shor, Ira. 1980. "Monday Morning: Critical Literacy and the Theme of 'Work." In *Critical Teaching and Everyday Life,* 125–54. Boston: South End Press.

Shor, Ira. 1997. "Our Apartheid: Writing Instruction and Inequality." *Journal of Basic Writing* 16 (1): 91–104.

Sledd, James. 1988. "Product in Process: From Ambiguities of Standard English to Issues that Divide Us." *College English* 50 (2): 168–76. http://dx.doi.org/10.2307/377646.

Sledd, James. 2001. "On Buying In and Selling Out: A Note for Bosses Old and New." *College Composition and Communication* 53 (1): 146–49. http://dx.doi.org/10.2307 /359066.

Slevin, James F. 2001. *Introducing English: Essays in the Intellectual Work of Composition.* Pittsburgh: University of Pittsburgh Press.

Sohan, Vanessa Kraemer. 2009. "Working English(es) as Rhetoric(s) of Disruption." *JAC* 29 (1–2): 270–76.

Spilka, Rachel, ed. 1993. *Writing in the Workplace: New Research Perspectives.* Carbondale: Southern Illinois University Press.

Takayoshi Pamela, and Patricia Sullivan, eds. 2007. "Labor, Writing Technologies, and the Shaping of Composition." In *The Academy.* Cresskill, NJ: Hampton Press.

Thompson, E. P. 1967. "Time, Work-Discipline, and Industrial Capitalism." *Past & Present* 38 (1): 56–97. http://dx.doi.org/10.1093/past/38.1.56.

Tuell, Cynthia. 1993. "Composition Teaching as 'Women's Work': Daughters, Handmaids, Whores, and Mothers." In *Writing Ourselves into the Story*, ed. Sheryl I. Fontaine, and Susan Hunter, 123–39. Carbondale: Southern Illinois University Press.

Warnick, Chris. 2010. "Texts to Be Worked on and Worked With: Encouraging Students to See Their Writing as Theoretical." In *Teaching with Student Texts: Essays toward an Informed Practice*, ed. Joseph Harris, John D. Miles, and Charles Paine, 163–70. Logan: Utah State University Press.

Welch, Nancy. 1993. "Resisting the Faith: Conversion, Resistance, and the Training of Teachers." *College English* 55 (4): 387–401. http://dx.doi.org/10.2307/378649.

Winterowd, W. Ross. 1998. "Learning to Love Being a Second-Class Citizen." In *Teaching College English and English Education: Reflective Stories*, ed. Thomas H. McCracken and Richard L. Larson, with Judith Entes, 231–50. Urbana, IL: National Council of Teachers of English.

WRITING ACROSS THE CURRICULUM/ WRITING IN THE DISCIPLINES

Chris Thaiss

The terms *writing across the curriculum* and *writing in disciplines* have acquired considerable "staying power" over the roughly thirty-five years they have been used in US writing studies (Thaiss 2001, 312). This resilience reflects, in part, the basic recognition that student writing growth occurs *across* the subject areas of an institution—not only in "composition" courses—and that the writing that occurs in those various environments is worthy of scholarly **research** and pedagogical concern. Recent **work** on this idea at the national level includes the Common Core State Standards put forth by the National Governors Association Center for Best Practices, Council of Chief State School Officers (2010), in which writing expectations are explicitly defined for primary through secondary levels in all subject areas, and the *Framework for Success in Postsecondary Writing* (2011), co-authored by a task force of three leading US **literacy** organizations, which specifies among its objectives student writers' development of "habits of mind . . . that are both intellectual and practical and that will support students' success in a variety of fields and disciplines."

The term *writing across the curriculum* became popular in the 1970s (McLeod and Soven 2006). Nancy Martin and her colleagues, reporting on ten years' worth of work, coined the term for their 1976 book *Writing and Learning across the Curriculum, 11–16* (Martin et al. 1976), in which they described students and teachers using writing as a way to build student thinking and learning across different school environments in the United Kingdom. This **research** came to the US through the work of Janet Emig (1977); *writing across the curriculum* was quickly popularized by Emig and other early local leaders (see, e.g., Fulwiler 1987; Walvoord 1996) of the fledgling National Writing Project, which began in the early 1970s in the San Francisco Bay Area (Gray 2000) and spread rapidly across the United States, sparked by the federal matching of funding of new writing project sites.

DOI: 10.7330/9780874219746.c036

The acronym "WAC" quickly followed, and by 1981 the National (now International) Network of Writing across the Curriculum Programs was holding its first meeting at the Conference on College Composition and Communication (Thaiss 2006), held annually in the United States. The acronym has had much to do with the recognition of the concept itself, embodied in such entities as the publishing collective *The WAC Clearinghouse*, the *WAC Journal*, and "IWAC," the international biennial conferences that have been meeting since 1993.

The concept embodied in both term and acronym flourished in colleges and universities in the United States, mainly because of their already-established, required English composition programs and their broader concepts of general education. (See Graves and Graves 2012 for a contrast with, for example, Canadian tradition.) Hence, *writing across the curriculum* has long implied an organized effort within an institution to manage how writing is taught and learned. Not surprisingly, the term "WAC program" followed quickly in the 1970s; these programs were designed to carry out these concepts, often including elements such as "writing intensive requirements" (e.g., Townsend 2001) in courses offered throughout an institution. More broadly, a "WAC program" came to mean an institution's effort at building cross-curricular cultures of active concern for student writing (see Fulwiler and Young 1990; McLeod 1987; McLeod and Soven 1992; and McLeod et al. 2001).

In partial contrast, when not used synonymously with *writing across the curriculum*, *writing in disciplines* (or "WID") serves as a complementary but distinct term that emphasizes the ways in which **genres**, ways of thinking, and research methods and materials vary from one academic or professional **context** to another. Walvoord and McCarthy's (1990) *Thinking and Writing in College: A Naturalistic Study of Writing in Four Disciplines* was among the first scholarly books to present case studies in different disciplines, but as early as 1981 the textbook *Writing in the Arts and Sciences* (Maimon et al. 1981) emphasized the distinctions among diverse fields in the humanities, social sciences, and life sciences. Moreover, the many naturalistic or textual studies of writing carried out in specific academic or professional environments since the 1980s (e.g., Bazerman 1988; Blakeslee 1997; Henry 1994; Herrington 1985) stress the differences of these contexts.

It's important to note that outside the United States the term *WAC* has been infrequently used because university study has traditionally been seen as occurring primarily in separate disciplines, without cross-disciplinary requirements (Carlino 2012; Ganobcsik-Williams 2012). The idea of organizing teacher training in uses of writing across an institution is likewise rare outside the United States (Petelin 2002). In contrast, the term *writing in disciplines* has been used by scholars in many countries who study literacy environments in diverse subject areas, work spurred in large part by linguists researching the characteristics of genres in academic contexts (e.g., Halliday and Hasan 1989; J. Martin 1992) and by rhetoricians studying **discourse** differences within academic and professional contexts (e.g., Bawarshi and Reiff 2010; Beaufort 1999; Devitt 2004; Gustafsson and Boström 2012; Miller 1984; Thaiss and Zawacki 2006). Scholars in the United Kingdom have popularized the covalent term *academic literacies* to designate this same domain of study: the diverse environments in schools and universities in which students develop the tools of literacy (Deane and O'Neill 2011; Lea and Street 1998). Recent transnational collections such as Bazerman et al. (2010), Björk et al. (2003), and Thaiss et al. (2012) demonstrate how widespread the applications of *writing in disciplines* have become.

While some writers (e.g., Monroe 2003) have stressed the separateness of the terms *WAC* and *WID*, the relationship might best be understood as complementary, which is illustrated in the increasing use of the acronym "WAC/WID," either on program websites or in research programs such as the International WAC/WID Mapping Project (Thaiss and Porter 2010). This merging of acronyms may be seen as acknowledging the shared concepts as well as the distinctions. In any given context, the merger seems to say that, even though one term may be more comfortable to a particular reader, in this environment both are welcome.

For the faculty and administrators trying to begin or develop WAC/WID initiatives, however, the generality of the terms *WAC* and *WID* presents a quandary. WAC scholarship and teaching materials in collections, specific journals (e.g., *Across the Disciplines* and *The WAC Journal*), on program websites, and presented at conferences offer a wide array of organizational and pedagogic choices. The choices program leaders make among all these options strongly influence the success of WAC and WID in their particular academic communities. The success of WAC and WID as concepts, notwithstanding several typical "resistances" to WAC/WID on campuses, make program development and sustainability problematic. That WAC and WID programs work horizontally across departments rather than within the typical vertical reporting lines means that budgeting for these programs is rarely a priority (Russell 2002); moreover, faculty (and graduate student instructors) in disparate disciplines often see the teaching demands of assigning, responding to, and evaluating student writing as an unfamiliar, burdensome intrusion on their priorities for students. Hence, the program-building collections cited earlier—as well as Anson (2001), Bean and Weimer (2011), and others—all give plentiful and varied advice to programmers on how to respond to WAC/WID as a site of resistances and structural difficulties, representing it as an effort requiring repeated revisions and iterations in order to evolve toward an effective articulation within a given institution. Even then, WAC/WID leadership, which is itself subject to turnover (McLeod and Miraglia 1997; Thaiss and Porter 2010), can never take for granted that a successful status quo will last, but instead must focus on WAC/WID as a space of ongoing research, innovation, and adaptation (Fulwiler and Young 1990; Porter, forthcoming; Reitmeyer 2009).

References

Anson, C., ed. 2001. *The WAC Casebook: Scenes for Faculty Reflection and Program Development.* New York: Oxford University Press.

Bawarshi, A., and M. J. Reiff, eds. 2010. *Genre: An Introduction to History, Theory, Research, and Pedagogy.* Anderson, SC: Parlor Press.

Bazerman, C. 1988. *Shaping Written Knowledge: The Genre and Activity of the Experimental Article in Science.* Madison: University of Wisconsin Press.

Bazerman, C., R. Krut, K. Lunsford, S. McLeod, S. Null, P. Rogers, and A. Stansell, eds. 2010. *Traditions of Writing Research.* New York: Routledge.

Bean, J., and M. Weimer. 2011. *Engaging Ideas: The Professor's Guide to Integrating Writing, Critical Thinking, and Active Learning in the Classroom,* 2nd ed. San Francisco: Jossey Bass.

Beaufort, A. 1999. *Writing in the Real World: Making the Transition from School to Work.* New York: Teachers College Press.

Björk, L., G. Bräuer, L. Rienecker, and P. Stray Jörgensen, eds. 2003. *Teaching Academic Writing in European Higher Education.* Dordrecht: Kluwer Academic. http://dx.doi.org/10.1007/0-306-48195-2.

Blakeslee, A. 1997. "Activity, Context, Interaction, and Authority: Learning to Write Scientific Papers In Situ." *Journal of Business and Technical Communication* 11 (2): 125–69. http://dx.doi.org/10.1177/1050651997011002001.

Carlino, P. 2012. "Section Essay: Who Takes Care of Writing in Latin American and Spanish Universities?" In *Writing Programs Worldwide: Profiles of Academic Writing in Many Places,* ed. C. Thaiss, G. Bräuer, P. Carlino, L. Ganobcsik-Williams, and A. Sinha, 520–34. Greenville, SC: Parlor Press.

Deane, M., and P. O'Neill, eds. 2011. *Writing in the Disciplines.* London: Palgrave.

Devitt, A. 2004. *Writing Genres.* Carbondale: Southern Illinois University Press.

Emig, J. 1977. "Writing as a Mode of Learning." *College Composition and Communication* 28 (2): 122–28. http://dx.doi.org/10.2307/356095.

Framework for Success in Postsecondary Writing. 2011. *National Council of Teachers of English, National Writing Project.* Council of Writing Program Administrators.

Fulwiler, T. 1987. *The Journal Book.* Portsmouth, NH: Heinemann/Boynton/Cook.

Fulwiler, T., and A. Young. 1990. *Programs that Work: Writing across the Curriculum.* Portsmouth, NH: Heinemann/Boynton/Cook.

Ganobcsik-Williams, L. 2012. "Section Essay: Reflecting on What Can Be Gained from Comparing Models of Academic Writing Provision." In *Writing Programs Worldwide: Profiles of Academic Writing in Many Places,* ed. C. Thaiss, G. Bräuer, P. Carlino, L. Ganobcsik-Williams, and A. Sinha, 535–46. Greenville, SC: Parlor Press.

Graves, R., and H. Graves. 2012. "Writing Programs Worldwide: One Canadian Perspective." In *Writing Programs Worldwide: Profiles of Academic Writing in Many Places*, ed. C. Thaiss, G. Bräuer, P. Carlino, L. Ganobcsik-Williams, and A. Sinha, 121–32. Greenville, SC: Parlor Press.

Gray, J. 2000. *Teachers at the Center: A Memoir of the Early Years of the National Writing Project.* Berkeley, CA: National Writing Project.

Gustafsson, M., and T. Boström. 2012. "Multi-disciplinary, Multi-lingual Engineering Education Writing Development: A Writing Programme Perspective." In *Writing Programs Worldwide: Profiles of Academic Writing in Many Places*, ed. C. Thaiss, G. Bräuer, P. Carlino, L. Ganobcsik-Williams, and A. Sinha, 377–88. Greenville, SC: Parlor Press.

Halliday, M., and R. Hasan. 1989. *Language, Context, and Text: Aspects of Language in a Social Semiotic Perspective.* Oxford: Oxford University Press.

Henry, J. 1994. "A Narratological Analysis of WAC Authorship." *College English* 56 (7): 810–24. http://dx.doi.org/10.2307/378487.

Herrington, A. 1985. "Writing in Academic Settings: A Study of the Context for Writing in Two College Chemical Engineering Courses." *Research in the Teaching of English* 19: 331–61.

International WAC/WID Mapping Project. http://mappingproject.ucdavis.edu.

Lea, M., and B. Street. 1998. "Student Writing in Higher Education: An Academic Literacies Approach." *Studies in Higher Education* 23 (2): 157–72. http://dx.doi.org/10.1080/03075079812331380364.

Maimon, E., G. Belcher, G. Hearn, and B. Nodine. 1981. *Writing in the Arts and Sciences.* Boston: Little, Brown.

Martin, J. 1992. *English Text: System and Structure.* Amsterdam: Benjamins. http://dx.doi.org/10.1075/z.59.

Martin, N., P. D'Arcy, B. Newton, and R. Parker. 1976. *Writing and Learning across the Curriculum, 11–16.* London: Ward Lock.

McLeod, S., ed. 1987. *Strengthening Programs in Writing across the Curriculum.* San Francisco: Jossey Bass.

McLeod, S., and E. Miraglia. 1997. "Whither WAC? Interpreting the Stories/Histories of Mature WAC Programs." *WPA: Writing Program Administration* 20 (3): 46–65.

McLeod, S., E. Miraglia, M. Soven, and C. Thaiss, eds. 2001. *WAC for the New Millennium: Strategies for Continuing Writing-across-the-Curriculum Programs.* Urbana, IL: National Council of Teachers of English.

McLeod, S., and M. Soven, eds. 1992. *WAC: A Guide to Developing Programs.* Newbury Park, CA: Sage.

McLeod, S., and M. Soven, eds. 2006. *Composing a Community: A History of Writing across the Curriculum.* West Lafayette, IN: Parlor Press.

Miller, C. 1984. "Genre as Social Action." *Quarterly Journal of Speech* 70 (2): 151–67. http://dx.doi.org/10.1080/00335638409383686.

Monroe, J. 2003. "Writing and the Disciplines." Peer Review. http://www.aacu.org/peerreview/pr-fa03/pr-fa03feature1.cfm.

National Governors Association Center for Best Practices, Council of Chief State School Officers. 2010. *Common Core State Standards.* Washington, DC: National Governors Association Center for Best Practices, Council of Chief State School Officers.

Petelin, R. 2002. "Another Whack at WAC: Reprising WAC in Australia." *Language and Learning Across the Disciplines* 5 (3): 98–109.

Porter, T. Forthcoming. "WAC/WID Programs: A Qualitative Study of the Factors that Lead to Success and Sustainability." PhD diss., University of California, Davis.

Reitmeyer, M. 2009. "Programs that Work(ed): Revisiting the University of Michigan, the University of Chicago, and George Mason University Programs After 20 Years." Special Issue, Across the Disciplines 6. http://wac.colostate.edu/atd/technologies/reitmeyer.cfm.

Russell, D. R. 2002. *Writing in the Academic Disciplines: A Curricular History*, 2nd ed. Carbondale: Southern Illinois University Press.

Thaiss, C. 2001. "Theory in WAC: Where Have We Been, Where Are We Going?" In *WAC for the New Millennium: Strategies for Continuing Writing-across-the-Curriculum Programs*, ed. S. McLeod, E. Miraglia, M. Soven, and C. Thaiss, 299–326. Urbana, IL: National Council of Teachers of English.

Thaiss, C. 2006. "Still a Good Place to Be: More than 20 Years of the National Network of WAC Programs." In *Composing a Community: A History of Writing across the Curriculum*, ed. S. McLeod and M. Soven, 126–41. West Lafayette, IN: Parlor Press.

Thaiss, C., G. Bräuer, P. Carlino, L. Ganobcsik-Williams, and A. Sinha, eds. 2012. *Writing Programs Worldwide: Profiles of Academic Writing in Many Places*. Greenville, SC: Parlor Press.

Thaiss, C., and T. M. Zawacki. 2006. *Engaged Writers and Dynamic Disciplines: Research on the Academic Writing Life*. Portsmouth, NH: Boynton Cook Heinemann.

Thaiss, C., and T. Porter. 2010. "The State of WAC/WID in 2010: Methods and Results of the US Survey of the International WAC/WID Mapping Project." *College Composition and Communication* 61 (3): 534–70.

Townsend, M. 2001. "Writing-Intensive Courses and WAC." In *WAC for the New Millennium: Strategies for Continuing Writing-across-the-Curriculum Programs*, ed. S. McLeod, E. Miraglia, M. Soven, and C. Thaiss, 233–58. Urbana, IL: National Council of Teachers of English.

Walvoord, B. 1996. "The Future of WAC." *College English* 58 (1): 58–79. http://dx.doi.org /10.2307/378534.

Walvoord, B., and L. McCarthy. 1990. *Thinking and Writing in College: A Naturalistic Study of Writing in Four Disciplines*. Urbana, IL: National Council of Teachers of English.

ABOUT THE CONTRIBUTORS

STEVEN ACCARDI is an assistant professor of English at Pennsylvania State University, Hazleton, where he teaches courses in rhetorical theory, discourse analysis, and professional writing. His research interests include public rhetoric, rhetorical theory, community literacy, and the politics of undocumented immigration.

ANIS BAWARSHI is a professor of English and director of the Expository Writing Program at the University of Washington. He is currently the program profiles co-editor for *Composition Forum*. His publications include *Genre: An Introduction to History, Theory, Research, and Pedagogy* (with Mary Jo Reiff); *Genre and the Invention of the Writer: Reconsidering the Place of Invention in Composition*; *Scenes of Writing: Strategies for Composing with Genres* (with Amy Devitt and Mary Jo Reiff); *A Closer Look: A Writer's Reader* (with Sidney Dobrin); and recent articles and book chapters on genre, uptake, invention, and knowledge transfer in composition. Current projects include two co-edited books, one on ecologies of writing programs and another on public genre performances.

A. SURESH CANAGARAJAH is the Erle Sparks Professor at Pennsylvania State University. He teaches world Englishes, second language writing, and postcolonial studies in the departments of English and Applied Linguistics. He has taught previously at the University of Jaffna, Sri Lanka, and the City University of New York. His most recent publication is *Translingual Practice: Global Englishes and Cosmopolitan Relations* (Routledge, 2013). He was formerly the editor of *TESOL Quarterly* and president of the American Association of Applied Linguistics.

JENNIFER CLARY-LEMON is an associate professor in rhetoric, writing, and communications at the University of Winnipeg, and past editor of the journal *Composition Studies*. Her research interests include writing and location, disciplinarity, critical discourse studies, and research methodologies. Her recent publications may be found in *Discourse and Society*, *The American Review of Canadian Studies*, *Composition Forum*, *Oral History Forum d'histoire orale*, and *College Composition and Communication*.

AMY J. DEVITT is Chancellors Club and Frances L. Stieffel Teaching Professor of English at the University of Kansas. She received her PhD from the University of Michigan. Professor Devitt specializes in composition and English language studies, particularly in genre and standardization. Her books include *Standardizing Written English*, *Writing Genres*, and *Scenes of Writing*, the last coauthored with Anis Bawarshi and Mary Jo Reiff. Her articles have been published in *College Composition and Communication*, *College English*, and other journals and edited books. She has served over ten years as WPA at KU and regularly teaches courses in writing, composition studies, and genre.

DYLAN B. DRYER is an assistant professor of composition studies at the University of Maine. His work appears in *WPA*, *JAC*, the *Community Literacy Journal*, and *Written Communication*. In 2013, he received the Braddock Award for his *CCC* article "At a Mirror, Darkly: The Imagined Undergraduates of Ten Novice Teachers of Composition." Ongoing interests include the phenomenologies of genre uptake—particularly in institutional and civic locations—corpus linguistics, and the problem of construct validity in writing assessment.

Cynthia Fields is a PhD candidate in rhetoric and writing at Virginia Tech. Her research interests include epideictic rhetoric, space, public memory, and tourism. Her current research project examines Civil War tourist spaces as examples of epideictic rhetoric.

Johndan Johnson-Eilola works at Clarkson University in the Department of Communication and Media, where he teaches courses in typography and design, audio production, and information architecture. In addition to nearly fifty book chapters and journal articles, he has written, co-written, or co-edited books including *Datacloud*, *Writing New Media* (co-written with Anne Wysocki, Cindy Selfe, and Geoff Sirc), *Collected Works: Landmark Essays in Technical Communication*, and *Solving Problems in Technical Communication* (both co-edited with Stuart Selber). His work has won awards from NCTE, *Computers & Composition*, *Technical Communication Quarterly*, *Kairos*, and the National Council of Writing Program Administrators.

Kathleen Kerr is a PhD student in Virginia Tech's rhetoric and writing program. Her research interests include bureaucratic language and the Plain Writing Act of 2010, intercultural communication, and the rhetoric of human rights. Kathleen is a former foreign service officer who has served at US embassies in Saudi Arabia, Iraq, and Ukraine, as well as in Washington, DC. She was also a program analyst for the Department of Justice. Kathleen earned a BA in Russian studies at the University of Maryland, College Park, an MBA from Loyola University in Maryland, and an MA in English from the University of West Florida.

Karen Kopelson is an associate professor of English at the University of Louisville. She has published articles in such journals as *College English*, *College Composition and Communication*, *JAC*, *Postmodern Culture*, *Rhetoric Society Quarterly*, and *WPA*, and she is the recipient of both the Braddock Award (2004) and the Kinneavy Award (2005). She is co-editor, with Bruce Horner, of *Re-Working English in Rhetoric and Composition*.

Cynthia Lewiecki-Wilson, professor emerita of English, taught undergraduate and graduate courses in writing and rhetoric at Miami University and previously directed the first-year writing program and the English graduate program there. She is the author or co-editor of five books, including *Embodied Rhetorics: Disability in Language and Culture* with James C. Wilson (Southern Illinois UP), *Disability and the Teaching of Writing: A Critical Sourcebook* with Brenda Jo Brueggemann (Bedford/St. Martin's), and *Disability and Mothering: Liminal Spaces of Embodied Knowledge* with Jen Cellio (Syracuse UP).

Julie Lindquist is a professor of rhetoric and writing at MSU, where she teaches and directs the first-year writing program. She is author of *A Place to Stand: Politics and Persuasion in a Working Class Bar* (Oxford), and, with David Seitz, *Elements of Literacy* (Pearson). Her writings on rhetoric, class, literacy, and writing pedagogy have appeared in *College Composition and Communication*, *College English*, *JAC*, and *Pedagogy*. Her article, co-authored with Bump Halbritter, "Time, Lives, and Videotape: Operationalizing Discovery in Scenes of Literacy Sponsorship," was awarded the Richard Ohmann Award for Outstanding Article in *College English* for 2012.

Mark Garrett Longaker has taught writing in high schools and at universities in New Orleans, Philadelphia, and Austin. Now an associate professor of rhetoric and writing at the University of Texas, Austin, he is the author of *Rhetoric and the Republic: Politics, Civic Discourse, and Education in Early America* (University of Alabama Press, 2007) and the co-author, with Jeffrey Walker, of *Rhetorical Analysis: A Brief Guide for Writers* (Pearson, 2011).

Tim Mayers is the author of *(Re)Writing Craft: Composition, Creative Writing, and the Future of English Studies*, as well as of articles in *College Composition and Communication*, *College English*, and elsewhere. He is an associate professor of English at Millersville University of

Pennsylvania, where he teaches composition, creative writing, and the disciplinary histories of English studies.

STEVE PARKS is an associate professor of writing and rhetoric at Syracuse University,
where he also serves as director of graduate studies. His research focuses on literacy,
political activism, and community publishing. These interests have been the focus of his
two book-length publications, *Class Politics: The Movement for a Students Right To Their Own
Language* and *Gravyland: Writing beyond the Curriculum in the City of Brotherly Love*. He has also
founded two community presses, New City Community Press (newcitycommunitypress.
com) and Gifford Street Community Press, both of which focus on providing venues for
communities to gain rhetorical and political power.

KELLY PENDER is an associate professor of English at Virginia Tech, where she serves
as director of the PhD in rhetoric and writing and teaches courses in classical rhetoric,
critical theory, and professional writing. She is the author of the 2011 book, *Techne, from
Neoclassicism to Postmodernism: Understanding Writing as a Useful, Teachable Art*. Her other
work has appeared in journals such as *Rhetoric Society Quarterly* and *Rhetoric and Public
Affairs*.

PAUL PRIOR is a professor of English and director of the Center for Writing Studies at the
University of Illinois, Urbana-Champaign. Drawing on sociocultural theory and dialogic
semiotics, he has explored connections among writing, talk, enculturation, and activity. He
co-edited *Research in the Teaching of English* from 2008 to 2013 and is the author of *Writing/
Disciplinarity: A Sociohistoric Account of Literate Activity in the Academy* (1998). He is co-editor
with Charles Bazerman of *What Writing Does and How It Does It: An Introduction to Analyzing
Texts and Textual Practices* (2004) and with Julie Hengst of *Exploring Semiotic Remediation as
Discourse Practice* (2010).

KATRINA M. POWELL is an associate professor of English and director of women's and
gender studies at Virginia Tech. She is author of *The Anguish of Displacement* (UVA Press,
2007) and editor of '*Answer at Once': Letters of Mountain Families in Shenandoah National Park,
1934–1938* (UVA Press, 2009) and *Practicing Research in Writing Studies: Reflexive and Ethically
Responsible Research* (with Pamela Takayoshi, Hampton Press, 2012). Her work focuses on
displacement narratives, performative identities, and research methodologies and has
appeared in *College English, College Composition and Communication, Prose Studies, Biography,*
and *Women's Studies*.

CAROLYN RUDE served as a professor first at Texas Tech University and then at Virginia
Tech, and taught technical communication for thirty-two years. As a program director, she
developed curricula and led the development of degree programs, including an online
MA program in technical communication at Texas Tech and PhD programs at both universities. She is the author of *Technical Editing*, currently in its 5th edition, as well as of
articles and book chapters on technical communication. She is a fellow of the Association
of Teachers of Technical Writing (ATTW) and the Society for Technical Communication.
She previously served ATTW as its president.

STUART A. SELBER is an associate professor of English and director of Digital Education
for English at Penn State, where he serves as director of The Penn State Digital English
Studio. Selber is the author of *Multiliteracies for a Digital Age* (Southern Illinois University
Press, 2004) and editor or co-editor of *Central Works in Technical Communication* (Oxford
University Press, 2004), *Rhetorics and Technologies: New Directions in Writing and Communica-
tion* (University of South Carolina Press, 2010), and *Solving Problems in Technical Commu-
nication* (University of Chicago Press, 2013). Selber is a past president and fellow of the
Association of Teachers of Technical Writing.

CYNTHIA L. SELFE is Humanities Distinguished Professor in the English department at Ohio State University. She is co-founder of Computers and Composition Digital Press/ Utah State University Press (with Gail Hawisher) and the Digital Archive of Literacy Narratives (with H. Lewis Ulman). In 1996, Selfe was recognized as an EDUCOM Medal award winner for innovative computer use; in 2000, she won the Outstanding Technology Innovator award from the CCCC Committee on Computers (with Gail Hawisher); and in 2013, she, Gail Hawisher, and Patrick Berry were presented with the CCCC's Research Impact Award and the Knowledge Advancement Award for *Transnational Literate Lives in Digital Times.*

LORIN SHELLENBERGER is a PhD candidate in rhetoric and writing at Virginia Tech, where she has taught freshmen composition and is currently the editorial assistant for *the minnesota review.* Her research interests include rhetorics of the body, rhetorics of sport, feminist theory, Kenneth Burke theory, and classical rhetoric.

JASON SWARTS is an associate professor of English at NC State University, where he is also the director of the PhD program in communication, rhetoric, and digital media. He teaches courses on theory and research in technical communication, networks, and discourse analysis. His research focuses on genres of instructional communication, distributed work, and mobility.

CHRISTINE M. TARDY is an associate professor in the Department of English at the University of Arizona, where she also serves as associate director of the writing program. Her research interests include second language writing, genre theory and practice, academic writing, discourse analysis, and the policies and politics of English. Her work has been published in journals such as *Written Communication, College Composition and Communication, Research in the Teaching of English,* and *Discourse & Society,* as well as in several edited collections. She currently serves as co-editor of the *Journal of Second Language Writing.*

CHRIS THAISS is Clark Kerr Presidential Chair and professor at the UC Davis writing program. The first permanent director of the writing program (2006–2011), he currently chairs its PhD designated emphasis in writing, rhetoric, and composition studies and teaches undergraduate courses in scientific writing and writing in business. He directs the UC Davis Center for Excellence in Teaching and Learning. Coordinator of the International Network of Writing-Across-the-Curriculum Programs, his current research initiative (since 2006) is the International WAC/WID Mapping Project, which has produced the 2012 book *Writing Programs Worldwide: Profiles of Academic Writing in Many Places* (Parlor Press and WAC Clearinghouse).

KT TORREY is a doctoral candidate in rhetoric and writing at Virginia Tech. As a scholar, she wrestles with porn studies, sophistic rhetoric, and performance theory. Her current research combines these three approaches to explore women's negotiations of desire and pleasure in online discursive spaces. She also writes extensively (sometimes even academically) about metatextuality, fan fiction, and the American television show *Supernatural.*

CHRISTIAN R. WEISSER is an associate professor of English at Penn State Berks, where he coordinates both the professional writing program and the WAC program. Christian is the editor of *Composition Forum,* a peer-reviewed scholarly journal in rhetoric and composition. He is the author or editor of numerous publications, including *Moving beyond Academic Discourse, Natural Discourse* (with Sid Dobrin), and *The Locations of Composition* (with Christopher Keller). Christian's current research focuses on the ecology of writing, environmental rhetoric, and the discourse of sustainability.

KATHLEEN BLAKE YANCEY, Kellogg W. Hunt Professor of English and Distinguished Research Professor, teaches at Florida State University. She has served as president of

NCTE, chair of CCCC, and president of the Council of Writing Program Administrators. Editor of *College Composition and Communication,* she co-directs the Inter/National Coalition for Electronic Portfolio Research. Author/co-author of over ninety articles and chapters and author/co-editor of eleven scholarly books—including *Reflection in the Writing Classroom* and *Delivering College Composition: The Fifth Canon*—she has been recognized with the WPA Best Book Award and the Donald Murray Prize. Her co-authored *Writing across Contexts: Transfer, Composition, and Sites of Writing* will be released in 2014.

MELANIE YERGEAU is an assistant professor of English at the University of Michigan. She has published in *Disability Studies Quarterly, College English, Kairos,* and *Computers and Composition Online.* She is co-author of the *SAGE Reference Series on Disability: Arts and Humanities* and is an editor for Computers and Composition Digital Press, an imprint of Utah State University Press. Active in the neurodiversity movement, Melanie has served on the boards of the Autistic Self Advocacy Network and the Autism National Committee.

MORRIS YOUNG is professor of English at the University of Wisconsin, Madison, where he teaches courses on rhetoric, literacy, and Asian American literature and culture. His book, *Minor Re/Visions: Asian American Literacy Narratives as a Rhetoric of Citizenship* (Southern Illinois UP, 2004) received the 2004 W. Ross Winterowd Award and the 2006 Outstanding Book Award from the Conference on College Composition and Communication. With LuMing Mao, he co-edited *Representations: Doing Asian American Rhetoric* (Utah State University Press, 2008), which received an Honorable Mention for the 2009 Mina P. Shaughnessy Prize from the Modern Language Association of America.